KABBALAH CENTRE BOOKS

The Zohar *24 volumes by Rabbi Shimon bar Yoḥai, The cardinal work in the literature of Kabbalah. Original Aramaic text with Hebrew translation and commentary by Rabbi Yehuda Ashlag*

Miracles, Mysteries, and Prayer Volumes I and II, Rabbi P. Berg (also available in French, Spanish and Russian)
Kabbalah for the Layman Volumes I, Rabbi P. Berg (also available in Hebrew, Spanish, French, Russian, Italian, German, Persian, Chinese and Portuguese)
Kabbalah for the Layman Volumes II, III, Rabbi P. Berg (also available in Hebrew, Spanish, French and Italian)
Reincarnation: Wheels of a Soul Rabbi P. Berg (also available in Hebrew, Spanish, French, Italian, Russian and Persian)
Astrology: The Star Connection Rabbi P. Berg (also available in Hebrew, Spanish, French and Italian)
Time Zones: Creating Order from Chaos Rabbi P. Berg (also available in French, Spanish, Hebrew and Persian)
To The Power of One Rabbi P. Berg (also available in French, Spanish and Russian)
Power of the Aleph Bet Volumes I, II, Rabbi P. Berg (also available in Hebrew French and Spanish)
The Kabbalah Connection Rabbi P. Berg (also available in Spanish and Hebrew)
Gift of the Bible Rabbi Yehuda Ashlag, Foreword by Rabbi P. Berg (also available in French, Hebrew and Spanish)
Zohar: Parashat Pinḥas Volumes I, III, Translated, compiled and edited by Rabbi P. Berg (Vols. I and II are available in Spanish)
An Entrance to the Tree of Life Compiled and edited by Rabbi P. Berg (also available in Spanish)
Ten Luminous Emanations Rabbi Yehuda Ashlag, Volumes I, II, Compiled and edited by Rabbi P. Berg (also available in Hebrew, 7 Volume set)
An Entrance to The Zohar Compiled and edited by Rabbi P. Berg
General Principles of Kabbalah Rabbi M. Luzzatto (also available in Italian)
Light of Redemption by Rabbi Levi Krakovsky

SOON TO BE PUBLISHED

Ten Luminous Emanations Volume IV, Rabbi Yehuda Ashlag, compiled and edited by Rabbi P. Berg
Time Zones: Creating Order from Chaos Rabbi P. Berg, Russian Translation

BOOKS AND TAPES AVAILABLE
AT BOOKSELLERS AND KABBALAH CENTRES AROUND THE WORLD

The Zohar: Parashat Pinḥas

Volume II

KABBALAH

THE ZOHAR PARASHAT PINḤAS

WITH THE SULAM EXPLANATION AND COMMENTARY BY RABBI YEHUDA ASHLAG

VOLUME II

TRANSLATED AND EDITED BY

RABBI P. BERG

FIRST EDITION
1987
REVISED EDITION
June 1994

0-943688-53-1 (Soft Cover)

For further information:

RESEARCH CENTRE OF KABBALAH
83-84 115th Street, Richmond Hill
NEW YORK, 11418

— or —

P.O. BOX 14168
THE OLD CITY, JERUSALEM

NEW YORK (718) 805-9122
LOS ANGELES (310) 657-5404
FLORIDA (407) 347-7095
MEXICO CITY (525) 589-4464
TORONTO (416) 631-9395
PARIS (331) 43-56-01-38
TEL AVIV (03) 528-0570

PRINTED IN U.S.A.
1994

לנישואים מאושרים, אחדות משפחתית
אהבה, שלווה, בריאות, ילדים בריאים וחכמים
ושלמים מכל הבחינות גשמי ורוחני

למיכאל בן אברהם

ולמרים בת משה

ולשיגשוג ושפע כלכלי,
הצלחה בעסקים ללא גבולות,

פותח את ידך ומשביע לכל חי רצון
סאל וחתך

והברכה של המלאך דיקרנוסא **נגד**

חי

שזכות ספר הזוהר הזה
תביא רפואה שלמה לכל חולי עם ישראל
והעולם כולו
ותשמור עלינו בבריאות עד 190 שנים אמן

ולזכות את ההורים בכל הברכות הללו
לבריאות וחיים ארוכים

לאברהם בן משה

שושנה בת דוד

משה בן יהודה

אסתר בת אברהם

ABOUT THE CENTRES

KABBALAH is mystical Judaism. It is the deepest and most hidden meaning of the Torah, or Bible. Through the ultimate knowledge and mystical practices of Kabbalah, one can reach the highest spiritual levels attainable. Although many people rely on belief, faith, and dogmas in pursuing the meaning of life, the unknown, and the unseen, Kabbalists seek a spiritual connection with the Creator and the forces of the Creator, so that the strange becomes familiar, and faith becomes knowledge.

Throughout history, those who knew and practiced the Kabbalah were extremely careful in their dissemination of the knowledge for they knew the masses of mankind had not yet prepared for the ultimate truth of existence. Today Kabbalists know, through Kabbalistic knowledge, that it is not only proper but necessary to make available the Kabbalah to all who seek it.

The Research Centre of Kabbalah is an independent, non-profit institute founded in Israel in 1922. The Centre provides research, information, and assistance to those who seek the insights of Kabbalah. The Centre offers public lectures, classes, seminars, and excursions to mystical sites at branches in Israel in Jerusalem, Tel Aviv, Haifa, Beer Sheva, Ashdod, and Ashkelon, and in the United States in New York and Los Angeles. Branches have been opened in Mexico, Montreal, Toronto, Paris, Hong Kong and Taiwan. Thousands of people have benefited by the Centre's activities, and the Centre's publishing of Kabbalistic material continues to be the most comprehensive of its kind in the world including translations in English, Hebrew, Russian, German, Portuguese, French, Spanish, Farsi (Persian) and Chinese.

Kabbalah can provide one with the true meaning of their being and the knowledge necessary for their ultimate benefit. It can show one spirituality which is beyond belief. The Research Centre of Kabbalah will continue to make available the Kabbalah to all those who seek it.

About the Zohar

THE ZOHAR, the basic source of the Kabbalah, was written by Rabbi Shimon bar Yoḥai while hiding from the Romans in a cave in Pe'quin for 13 years. It was later brought to light by Rabbi Moses de Leon in Spain and further revealed through the Safed Kabbalists and the Lurianic system of Kabbalah.

The programs of the Research Centre of Kabbalah have been established to provide opportunities for learning, teaching, research, and demonstration of specialized knowledge drawn from the ageless wisdom of the Zohar and the Jewish sages. Long kept from the masses, today this knowledge should be shared by all who seek to understand the deeper meaning of our Jewish heritage, a more profound meaning of life. Modern science is only beginning to discover what our sages veiled in symbolism. This knowledge is of a very practical nature and can be applied daily for the betterment of our lives and of humankind.

Our courses and materials deal with the zoharic understanding of each weekly portion of the Torah. Every facet of Jewish life is covered and other dimensions, hitherto unknown, provide a deeper connection to a superior Reality. Three important beginning courses cover such aspects as: Time, Space and Motion, Reincarnation, Marriage, Divorce, Kabbalistic Meditation, Limitation of the five senses, Illusion-Reality, Four Phases, Male and Female, Death, Sleep, Dreams, Food: what is kosher and why, Circumcision, Redemption of the First Born, Shatnes, Shabbat...

Darkness cannot prevail in the presence of Light. A darkened room must respond even to the lighting of a candle. As we share this moment together we are beginning to witness, and indeed some of us are already participating in a people's revolution of enlightenment the darkened clouds of strife and conflict will make their presence felt only as long as the Eternal Light remains concealed.

The Zohar now remains a final, if not the only, solution to infusing the cosmos with the revealed Light of the Force. The Zohar is not a book about religion. Rather, the Zohar is concerned with the relationship between the unseen forces of the cosmos, the Force, and the impact on Man.

The Zohar promises that with the ushering in of the Age of Aquarius the cosmos will become readily accessible to human understanding. It states that in the days of the Messiah "there will no longer be the necessity for one to request of his neighbor, teach me wisdom." (Zohar III, p58a) "One day they will no longer teach every man his neighbor and every man his brother, saying Know the Lord. For they shall all know Me, from the youngest to the oldest of them." (Jeremiah 31:34).

We can and must regain control of our lives and environment. To achieve this objective the Zohar provides us with an opportunity to transcend the crushing weight of universal negativity.

The daily perusing of the Zohar, without any attempt at translation or "understanding" will fill our consciousness with the Light, improving our well-being and influencing all in our environment toward positive attitudes. Even the scanning of the Zohar by those unfamiliar with the Hebrew Aleph Beth will accomplish the same result.

The connection that we establish through scanning the Zohar is a connection and unity with the Light of the Lord. The letters, even if we do not consciously know Hebrew or Aramaic, are the channels through which the connection is made and could be likened to dialing the right telephone number, or typing in the right codes to run a computer program. The connection is established at the metaphysical level of our being and radiates into our physical plane of existence...but first there is the metaphysical "fixing". We have to consciously, through positive thoughts and actions, permit the immense power of the Zohar to radiate love, harmony and peace into our lives for us to share with all humanity and the universe.

As we enter the years ahead, the Zohar will continue to be a people's book, striking a sympathetic chord in the hearts and minds of those who long for peace, truth and relief from suffering. In the face of crises and catastrophe it has the ability to resolve agonizing human afflictions by restoring each individual's relationship with the Force.

About the Editor

RABBI P. BERG is Dean of the Research Centre of Kabbalah. Born in New York City, into a family descended from a long line of Rabbis, he is an ordained Orthodox Rabbi (from the renowned rabbinical seminary Torat VaDaat). While traveling to Israel in 1962, he met his Kabbalistic master, Rabbi Yehuda Zvi Brandwein, student of Rabbi Yehuda Ashlag Z"L and then Dean of the Research Centre of Kabbalah. During that period the Centre expanded substantially with the establishment of the United States branch in 1965 through which it currently disseminates and distributes its publications. Rabbi Berg did research at the Centre under the auspices of his beloved teacher Rabbi Brandwein Z"L, writing books on such topics as the origins of Kabbalah, creation, cosmic consciousness, energy, and the myths of the speed of light and the light barrier. Following the death of his master in 1969, Rabbi Berg assumed the position of Dean of the Centre, expanding its publication program through the translation of source material on the Kabbalah into English and other languages. Rabbi Berg moved with his devoted and dedicated wife, Karen, to Israel in 1971, where they opened the doors of the Centre to all seekers of self identity, establishing centres in all major cities throughout Israel, while at the same time lecturing at the City University of Tel Aviv. They returned to the United States in 1981 to further establish centres of learning in major cities all over the world. In addition to publishing scientific and popular articles, Rabbi Berg is the author, translator and/or editor of eighteen other books, including the Kabbalah for the Layman series, Wheels of a Soul, and Time Zones.

TABLE OF CONTENTS

THE FAITHFUL SHEPHERD

THE YUD THAT PINḤAS EARNED IS THE YUD OF SHADDAI

ISRAEL IS COMPOSED OF PARTS OF THE SHEKHINAH

LET US MAKE MAN IN OUR IMAGE AFTER OUR LIKENESS (GENESIS 1:26)

THE FAITHFUL SHEPHERD

AN OLIVE'S BULK AND AN EGG'S BULK

THE TWELVE ḤALLOT

TEN THINGS THAT MAN MUST OBSERVE AT THE SABBATH TABLE

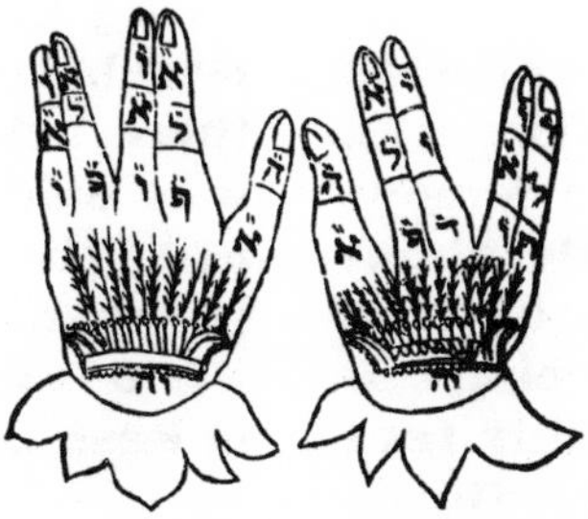

Parashat Pinḥas

"AND THEIR FEET WERE STRAIGHT FEET" (EZEKIEL 1:7)

316 **The fourth and fifth corrections are: "...from the appearance of his loins and upward, and from the appearance of his loins and downwards" (Ezekiel 1:27). About which it is said: "The thighs of the beings are equivalent to all of them" (above, *Beshallaḥ*, 269) and they are the *Sfirot* of *Netzaḥ* and *Hod*. For *Netzaḥ* and *Hod* are called loins, and `from the apparence of his loins and upward' is *Netzaḥ*, and `from the appearance of his loins and downward' is *Hod*. And Metatron is a sign in His hosts, for he has the form of a righteous one, which is *Yesod*, for righteous one, which is *Yesod* of *Zeir Anpin*, is a sign in His heavenly hosts, in *Atziluth*, while Metatron is a sign, in His earthly hosts, in *Briah*. Metatron [*mem tet tet resh vav* nun, 40 + 9 + 9 + 200 + 6 + 50 = 314] has the same numerical value as the `Almighty' [*Shaddai*: *shin dalet yud*, 300 + 4 + 10 = 314], about Whom it is said: "And the beings ran and returned as the appearance of a flash**

of lighting" (Ezekiel 1:14).

317 "And their feet were straight feet" (Ezekiel 1:7). For the feet of the demons are crooked, while about their feet, i.e. about the feet of the holy beings, it is said: "And their feet were straight feet." This is from the point of view of a living creature, which is Israel, and Israel includes three beings, about whom it is said: "The patriarchs are the Chariot" (cf. *Midrash -Genesis Rabba,* 47, 6 -quoted in the name of Resh Lakish).

Commentary:

For the secret of integrity (lit: straightness) is drawn from the central column, which is straight, not deviating to either right or left, but is straight in the center. This is not the case with the evil forces and the demons, for they deviate to the left side and are therefore crooked. On the text: "And their feet were straight feet" (Ezekiel 1:7). This is from the point of view of a living creature, which is Israel, i.e. from the side of the central column that is called Israel. Israel includes three beings, i.e. *Ḥesed*, *Gvurah*, and *Tiferet*, it being the central column. And this is not the case with the evil forces and the demons, for they have no desire in the central column, and so their feet are bent to the left, as the text says: "For the feet of the demons are all crooked."

318 "And the sole of their feet was like the sole of a calf's foot" (Ezekiel 1:7) because they are from the side of the beast that is called ox, which is the secret of the left column, and why they had a calf's foot. "And they sparkled like the color of burnished brass" (Ezekiel 1:7), i.e. from the side of the scurrying serpent that is in the sea and which ascends to it on the dry land, i.e. that ascends to fight with the serpent that is on the dry land. Serpent [*naḥash*] and brass [*neḥoshet*] are male and female, which are in the brightness (Ezekiel 1:13), and it is therefore

said: "And they sparkled like the color of burnished brass," i.e. from the side of the serpent who illuminates in them. "Ran" (Ezekiel 1:14), which is said about the beings, is from the side of *Nuriel* [*nun vav* resh yud aleph lamed, 50 + 6 + 200 + 10 + 1 + 30 = 297] which has the same numerical number as *"ratzo"* (ran) [*resh tzadi vav* and aleph, 200 + 90 + 6 + 1 = 297]. Similarly, "and returned," which is said about the beasts, is from the side of Almighty [*Shaddai*: *shin dalet yud*, 300 + 4 + 10 = 314], which has the same numerical value as 'and returned' [*vashov*: *vav* shin *vav* bet, 6 + 300 + 6 + 2 = 314]. And this is the numerical value of Metatron [*mem tet tet resh vav* nun, 40 + 9 + 9 + 200 + 6 + 50 = 314]. And this has already been explained above (*Vayetze*, 71 q.v.).

319 And whenever Israel heard the voice of Torah and prayer from the east, they would run to the east, and similarly to the west, and likewise to the south and to the north. Said the Holy One, blessed be He to the ministering angels: "Those who run to the ordained prayer, and who run to hear the lesson on the Sabbath, and run to do My will and who make repentance, they are to be received in the temple of this vision", i.e. in the temple of *Netzaḥ* and *Hod*. For by these signs, they run to the Torah and precepts and return in repentance, i.e. "ran and returned" (Ezekiel 1:14). They (Israel) are fellows with you (the ministering angels), for they run and return in Torah, just as the beasts who are running and returning, in the speech of *Halakha*, and they are recorded with you, them you shall bring into this temple.

320 And so it is that when the Jewish people pray, Michael flies round the world with one flap of his wings, and Gabriel with two, and when the speech emerges from Israel in *Halakha*, prayer, or any precept where the *Shekhinah* is, they run to her, to the *Shekhinah* and return with her, with the *Shekhinah*, on a mission from their master, to unite her (the *Shekhinah*) with

the Tetragrammaton. And in every place where the voice of Torah is heard, there the Holy One, blessed be He, is, and they run to that voice, and return with it on a mission from their master. And whenever there is a voice without the Tetragrammaton being there, or speech without 'The Lord' being there, Michael and Gabriel do not run and return there. And this is why "and their feet were straight feet" (Ezekiel 1:7),"for the ways of the Lord (the Tetragrammaton) are straight" (Hosea 14:9), this being the secret of the central column, where the way is straight (as above, 317). And if the Tetragrammaton is not there, the way is not straight.

321 Again: "And their feet were straight feet" (Ezekiel 1:7). The sages of the Mishnah said: "One who prays should arrange his feet during his prayer as do the ministering angels" (cf. *Talmud Bavli Berakhot* 10b), i.e. his feet should be straight "as the sole of a calf's foot" (Ezekiel 1:7), i.e. to be so recorded with them. And for this reason the sages taught: "When one prays, he should place his feet in proper position, as it says: "And their feet were straight feet." (Quoted in the name of R. Jose, son of R. Hanina, in the name of R. Eliezer b. Jacob, *Talmud Bavli, Berakhot 10b*.) And the Holy One, blessed be He, said to the ministering angels: Those who are thus noted in their prayer, that they place their feet as you do, for them, open the gates of the temple to enter this vision of *Netzaḥ* and *Hod*.

SIGHT, HEARING, SMELL AND SPEECH

322 The sixth correction is "I saw as it were the appearance of fire" (Ezekiel 1:27). This is the first time that he uses the words "I saw," for here the meaning is proper sight. Said the Holy One, blessed be He: Whoever enters in this vision, and during his prayer his heart is lifted up at the name of the Tetragrammaton and his eyes are cast down at the name of 'The Lord,' him shall you bring in to this temple, for he is like the angels about whom it is written: "As for their rims, they were high and they were dreadful" (Ezekiel 1:18). They were high, upwards at the Tetragrammaton, and they were dreadful, downwards, which is against the *Shekhinah*, which is the dread of the Tetragrammaton.

323 The Tetragrammaton rests on sight, hearing, smell and speech, for sight and hearing are yud hei, and smell and speech are *vav* hei. 'The Lord' rests on doing, feeling, using, and walking. This sight is that by light and by candle flame, about which it is said:"...and Torah is light" (Proverbs 6:23). Smell is the smell of the sacrifices, which are prayers. Speech is in Torah; speech is in prayer. And doing refers to precepts. Using also refers to precepts, as does feeling and walking. Where there is sight and hearing but no Torah and no precepts, neither do the Holy One, blessed be He, and His divine presence, rest there. For the Holy One, blessed be He, rests on sight, which is *Ḥokhmah*, and so does the *Shekhinah*, His divine presence, for it is Torah, and Torah is light, and His sight is the *Shekhinah*, for *Ḥokhmah* is not revealed other than in *Malkhut* (as above, 276). For the Tetragrammaton, which is *Zeir Anpin*, said: "I make Myself known to him in a vision" (Numbers 12:6), which is the *Shekhinah*, which is His vision.

324 The thought that is within the senses of sight, hearing, smell, and speech, is *Binah* [*bet yud nun hei*],whose letters can be re-arranged as *bet nun yud hei* (i.e. the son of *Yah*), because Israel, which is the secret of *Zeir Anpin*, who is called *ben* (son), arose in a thought, which is the secret of *Yah*. Inspiration is *Ḥokhmah*, a hint being sufficient for the wise man, i.e. inspiration is an embryonic thought. *Ḥokhmah* arose in a thought, which is *Binah*, since thought and inspiration are all one, for *Ḥokhmah* is known only through *Binah*, and *Binah* is in the heart. Thus thought is in the heart and inspiration is in the heart.

Commentary:

Ḥokhmah, which is on the right, is the secret of Father and Mother, for it is not known that *Ḥokhmah* is there, and there is nothing there except just *ḥasadim*. For *Ḥokhmah* on the right is only *Ḥesed* (see above, 206), and it is therefore understood as unknown. For in Father and Mother, the *yud* does not leave the air [*avir*: *aleph vav yud resh*]. (See above, *Bereshith Aleph*, 51). This is not the case with *Binah*, which is the secret of Israel, Grandfather and Understanding, in which the *yud* comes out of air [*avir*], and *Ḥokhmah* is revealed in it, in its left column. And this is the secret of heart (see above, 206), and it is therefore known and regarded that *Ḥokhmah* disappears from its own place and there is nothing but *Ḥesed*, but it is drawn down to *Binah*, and there it is known. And on the text: Inspiration is *Ḥokhmah*, a hint being sufficient for the wise man, for *Ḥokhmah* in its place is unformulated inspiration that is not yet revealed as a thought. *Ḥokhmah* arose in a thought, which is *Binah*, for *Ḥokhmah* is known in the place of *Binah*, and not in its own place. And on the text: Thus thought is in the heart and inspiration is in the heart; that is to say, even the inspiration is not in *Ḥokhmah*'s place, but in that of *Binah*, which is called heart. For there (in the heart) is right and left, *Ḥokhmah* and *Binah*, here *Ḥokhmah* is inspiration and *Binah* is thought.

325 Likewise, there is hearing in the Torah, for it is a precept that one should hear the reading of the scroll of the Torah. And likewise, in the nose there is a "sweet smell upon the Lord" (cf. Leviticus 6:14 etc). The *Shekhinah* is a sacrifice of the Tetragrammaton, His burnt offering, and prayer is as a sacrifice, for by means of the sacrifice or the prayer the *Shekhinah* ascends to the Tetragrammaton as a sweet smell unto Him, and is offered to Him in prayer. And, likewise,

about speech is written: "Is not My word like fire, says the Lord (the Tetragrammaton)?" (Jeremiah 23:29). The final *hei* of the Tetragrammaton, which is the *Shekhinah*, is His speech.

326 Just as the *Shekhinah* is His sight, His hearing, His sweet smell, His speech, in the head, so, in the hands, the *Shekhinah* is His performance of precepts, in the body His bowing, in the prayer His standing upright; and also in the prayer, it is His standing up, for receipt of the upper three *Sfirot* is called both standing upright and standing up, as above, for the *Shekhinah* stands before Him everywhere, and bows before Him and falls on her face at His feet to ask mercy from Him for her sons. She is His humility to Him and she is modest in His presence.

327 And she is not as the wicked bondwoman who is called Lillith, for this latter is insolent, having no humility and no modesty, and she is the mother of a mixed multitude. (See Exodus 12:38: "And a mixed multitude went up also with them.") For this reason, Solomon said: "A virtuous woman is a diadem to her husband; but she who does shamefully is as rottenness in his bones" (Proverbs 12:4). A virtuous woman refers to the *Shekhinah*, and she who does shamefully refers to the bondwoman Lillith, for the *Shekhinah* is Queen and her bondwoman is Lillith, who has no humility nor modesty before the Holy One, blessed be He. And her children are similar, being "a mixed multitude," and the Holy One, blessed be He, will in the future remove her and her children from the world, for they are bastards, born of the nine types of bastardy, as determined by the sages, not the law prescribed by the Torah itself, namely: the children of a) a wife raped; b) a wife hated; c) a wife ritually unclean (at the time of intercourse); d) a wife whose husband at the time of intercourse thought she was his other wife; e) a wife who was rebellious (at the time of intercourse); f) a wife drunk (at the time of intercourse); g) a wife divorced; h) a wife who is insolent; i) a wife who had relations with a number of men. (cf. *Talmud Bavli, Nedarim* 40b, and Rashi's, commentary there).

328 And likewise, the *Shekhinah* is the use of the Holy One, blessed be He, His unity with the righteous one, the life of the worlds, which is *Yesod*. And the *Shekhinah* who is called *Rivkah* [Rebeccah] came out to Him, to do His will. And so in sight, hearing, smell, speech, doing, body, use, walking and, indeed, in every part, it is a commandment to serve Him and to do His will.

329 And the children of the *Shekhinah*, namely Israel, are also of her form, for they are the sons of humility and modesty, all of them are as she is. And this is why the Holy One, blessed be He, commanded Moses: "You shall provide out of all the people able men, such as fear God, men of truth, hating unjust gain..." (Exodus 18:21, in the words of Jethro). 'Able men' are from the right side, which is Abraham, who is *Ḥesed* that becomes *Ḥokhmah*, and *Tiferet* ascend and become *Ḥokhmah, Binah*, and Da'at, as is known, for the sight of the Torah is there, as it is written: "At His right hand was a fiery law for them" (Deuteronomy 33:2). Such as fear God are from the side of Isaac, who is *Gvurah* that becomes *Binah*, for hearing is there, as the prophet Habakkuk said: "O Lord, I have heard the report of You, and I am afraid" (Habakkuk 3:2). 'Men of truth' are from the side of Jacob, who is *Tiferet* that becomes *Da'at*, for a sweet smell to the Tetragrammaton is there, in the nose. 'Hating unjust gain' is from the side of speech, which is *Malkhut*, the fourth column, which is the aspect of Adam who has joined together with the patriarchs, and is considered as *Malkhut* for them (as above *Vayeḥi*, 803). And *Malkhut* is called man, for the three beasts are lion, ox, and eagle, that are *Ḥesed*, *Gvurah*, and *Tiferet* in sight, hearing, and smell, as above, and the fourth column for them is "the face of a man" (see Ezekiel 1:10) in speech, i.e. Adam.

330 "And place such over them, to be rulers of thousands, rulers of hundreds, rulers of fifties, and rulers of tens." (Exodus 18:21). 'Rulers of thousands' [*alafim*], i.e. from the side of the letter *aleph* of 'The Lord' [*aleph dalet nun yud*]. 'Rulers of hundreds,' i.e. from the side of the letter *dalet* of 'The Lord,' which is the secret of the four (numerical value of the letter *dalet*) hundred years that Israel was enslaved in Egypt (see Genesis 15:13). 'Rulers of fifties,' i.e. the nun of 'The Lord,' the numerical value of *nun* being 50. 'Rulers of tens,' i.e. the *yud* of 'The Lord,' the numerical value of *yud* being ten.

331 Israel is recognized in these qualities to be the sons of the Holy One, blessed be He, and His *Shekhinah*; that is, that there should be amongst them able [*ḥaiyl*] men, as in the verse: "A virtuous [*ḥaiyl*] woman is a diadem to her husband" (Proverbs 12:4), for they are bestowed with *Ḥesed*, as against *Ḥesed* of *Zeir Anpin*. 'Such as fear God' parallels *Gvurah* of *Zeir Anpin*. 'Men of truth' parallels *Tiferet* of *Zeir Anpin*, and not men of falsehood, for the Children of "Israel shall not do iniquity, nor speak lies, neither shall a deceitful tongue be found in their mouth" (Zephaniah 3:13). 'Hating unjust gain' parallels *Malkhut*, as a man who rejoices in his portion (cf. *Mishnah, Pirke Avot*, 4, 1). And they (the Children of Israel) are not as a mixed multitude, the children of the wicked bondwoman, Lillith, who are as a serpent before whom is the whole land, as it is written: "And dust shall be the serpent's food" (Isaiah 65:25). With all this, he fears eating the dust until he is full, for he is afraid that there will not be enough for him. This is how it is with men of unjust gain, for even if they had all the money in the world, it would never be enough for them.

332 And this is why the sages of the Mishnah taught: "Not the expounding of the Law is the chief thing, but the doing of it" (*Mishnah, Pirke Avot*, 1, 17, in the name of Shimon ben Gamliel). For the Holy One, blessed be He, is concealed by the secrets of the Torah. In what, then, can he be known? In the precepts, for they are the *Shekhinah*, which is His form. Just as the Holy One, blessed be He, is humble, so is His *Shekhinah* humble. He is pious and she is pious. He is valiant, and she is valiant over all the nations of the world. He is truth and she is faith. He is a prophet and she is a prophetess. He is righteous and she is righteous. He is King and she is *Malkhut* (kingship). He is wise and she is *Ḥokhmah* (wisdom). He understands and she is His understanding. He is *Keter* (crown), and she is His diadem, "a diadem of *Tiferet* (beauty)" (see Isaiah 62:3, etc.). This is why the sages taught: "No disciple whose character [lit. inside —tr.] does not correspond to his exterior may enter the *Beit haMidrash*" [house of study] (cf. *Talmud Bavli, Berakhot* 28a, in the name of Rabban Gamliel). That is, the disciple will be as the form of the Holy One, blessed be He, who is his inside and the *Shekhinah* is his outside. He is the inside within and the *Shekhinah* is His exterior on the outside. And she that is on the outside has not changed from Him who is on the inside, that it should be known that she is His Atziluth, (nobility) and there is no separation there whatsoever, this being the secret of the verse: "...within and without you shall overlay it" (Exodus 25:11).

333 And since He, the Tetragrammaton is concealed from within, He is called only by His *Shekhinah*, 'The Lord.' And this is why the rabbis taught: "(Said the Holy One, blessed be He:) I am not written as I am read. In this world I am written with the Tetragrammaton but read as 'The Lord' [Explanatory note: Whenever the Tetragrammaton — *yud hei vav* and *hei* — appears in the Biblical text, or in the prayer-book, it is read as though 'The Lord' — *aleph dalet nun yud* — were written]. In the next world I am written with the Tetragrammaton and read with the Tetragrammaton" (*Talmud Bavli, Pesaḥim* 50a). And this is so that there will be mercy from all sides. And this is why the Holy One, blessed be

He, commanded the ministering angels: Whosever's character (lit. inside) does not correspond to his exterior, in all his parts, both internal and external, that person may not enter this temple. This is why Scripture says: "The Rock, His work is perfect" (Deuteronomy 32:4) and "You shall be perfect with the Lord your God" (Deuteronomy 18:13), i.e. his character inside exactly corresponds with his exterior.

RAINBOW, PHYLACTERIES, FRINGES, BLUE, WHITE AND RECITAL OF THE SHEMA YISRAEL

334 The seventh correction is as the vision of the rainbow that is visible in the clouds on a rainy day. The sages said: The Work of the Chariot is from "And I looked and, behold, a stormy wind..." (Ezekiel 1:4) until "As the appearance of the rainbow..." these are the work of the Chariot (ibid, v.28) (cf. *Talmud Bavli, Hagigah* 13a). And the sages further said: "When Rabbi Akiva was expounding the Work of the Chariot, fire came down from heaven and engulfed the trees, and the ministering angels assembled as though at a wedding feast. (cf. Talmud Bavli, Hagigah 14b, where a similar happening is related but not in connection with R. Akiva). For the Chariot is the secret of the unity of 'The Lord' and the Tetragrammaton, which are the secret of bride and groom. This is the reason for the Work of the Chariot (as described in Ezekiel, Chapter 1) to conclude with the verse starting "As the appearance of the rainbow..." (v. 28), for there is no unity and connection of the chariot of the Tetragrammaton [*yud hei vav* and *hei*] with "The Lord" other than by means of the righteous one, which is *Yesod,* also called rainbow, for in it is the upper chariot, which is the combination of 'The Lord' and the Tetragrammaton, namely: *yud aleph hei dalet vav* nun hei yud, complete.

335 The *Shekhinah* is the Work of Creation, and it has been taught: "The Work of Creation may not be expounded in the presence of only two people" (*Mishnah, Hagigah* 2, 1)

because the branches of the tree, which are the beings, are separated from above in the wings of the beings (312), with the Tetragrammaton to the right and 'The Lord' to the left, for *Zeir Anpin* is the secret of the *ḥasadim* on the right, and *Malkhut* is the secret of the left, without any unification between them, and it follows that the bridegroom is to the right while the bride is to the left. And when she (the bride) is brought to the wedding canopy (cf. *Terumah* 126) with a number of types of melody, Israel must awaken them from below to the unification with songs and praises and all sorts of melody in prayer, for, behold, they are approaching the wedding canopy, i.e. are coming into the unity (as was explained there).

336 And Israel must give the ring of betrothal from the bridegroom to the bride, with the knot of the hand phylactery, so that the *Shekhinah* should be bound to *Zeir Anpin,* and crown them with the head phylactery, which is the secret of bringing down to them the intelligence of the upper three *Sfirot,* which is glory [*pe'er*], as it is said: "Bind your headgear [*pe'er*] upon you" (Ezekiel 24:17). And the three loops of the strap upon the middle finger parallel the three holies, which are "Holy, Holy, Holy" "They proclaim you thrice holy" (cf. Isaiah 6:3 and *Sefardi Mussaf Amidah,* and see above, 298). And they have to be blessed with seven blessings (cf. the seven wedding blessings), which are the seven blessings of the recital of the *Shema Yisrael,* namely: two before and one after in the morning service, and two before and two after in the evening service. (cf. *Mishanah, Berakhot* 1, 4 and see the prayer-book for texts).

337 And the bride under the wedding canopy, i.e. in the unity of the recital of the *Shema Yisrael* which is called a wedding canopy (as above, *Terumah,* 126), is in the form of the wings of a precept, which, in the fringes, are gilded. That is to say that they are bound with blue, which is the secret of the illumination

of *Ḥokhmah,* which is drawn down from the left side of *Binah,* which is called gold. And thus the fringes are as though of gold in the blue. And the blue and the white that are in the fringes are the Throne of Judgment and the Throne of Mercy interwoven with each other, for blue is Judgment and white is Mercy. And there are number of knots and links surrounding the fringes with a number of pearls and precious stones, i.e. the lights of *Ḥokhmah* and *ḥasadim,* full of special characteristics surrounding it in the form of bells and pomegranates (as above, *Balak,* 435) of the apparel of the king and the queen, which are the four garments of white of *Zeir Anpin,* and the four garments of gold of *Malkhut,* which are from the side of the two names: The Tetragrammaton and 'The Lord.' As is His name, so is His throne, so is His wedding canopy, so is His apparel. His name is noted in All, for He is *Yesod,* who is called All when the bridegroom wishes to enter his palace to be there with his bride, in the 18 blessings of the prayer, where 18 hints at *Yesod,* which is "As the appearance of the rainbow" (Ezekiel 1:28), i.e. *Yesod,* as above.

THE WORK OF THE CHARIOT AND PRAYER

338 And regarding the *Shemoneh Esreh* prayer, they taught: "The Work of the Chariot may not be expounded before one person alone" (*Mishnah, Hagigah* 2,1), because he who expounds to a single person, is not that person with him during the exposition, and are they not two? And he does not have to let his voice be heard there in the prayer, but "only her lips moved, but her voice could not be heard" (1 Samuel 1:13). And in this lies the secret of the verse: "And the common man who draws near was to be put to death" (Numbers 3:38). And so it is with prayer: everyone should pray quietly in such a way that his prayer is not heard by his fellow, this being what they referred to when they said: "The Work of the Chariot may not be expounded before one person alone." It is just as

one who is expounding to his fellow and he wants to silence the speech to him, so that he (his fellow) should not hear; he does not have to do anything other than speak in silence, and then his fellow will not hear. All this is why the sages taught: "One who says the prayer so that it can be heard is of the small in faith" (*Talmud Bavli, Berakhot* 24b, and see Rashi there: Because he imagines that otherwise the Holy One, blessed be He, will not hear him).

339 And this is why the heavenly beings of fire speak as the branches of the tree, which are the ministering angels who assemble there at the wedding feast (as above, 334). And where is this to happen? At the unity of the recital of the *Shema Yisrael,* which is the secret of the wedding canopy (as above, *Terumah,* 126), for there it is said: "And I heard the sound of their wings" (Ezekiel 1:24), for the lower unity, *yud aleph hei dalet vav* nun hei yud, is not yet there and they are therefore speaking (as above 310). And there are 64 for each of the 4 wings. That is to say: The four beasts, each of which is composed of four, make 16 beasts. Each beast has four wings, making a total of 64 wings. But the wings are interwoven and there are four wings in each wing, thus 64 has to be multiplied by 4, making 256, and this is: "Sing with gladness for Jacob" (Jeremiah 31:6) [where the word for `sing' is *ranu*: *resh nun vav,* 200 + 50 + 6 = 256]. And when will this be? After he has wreaked vengeance on those who hate him and burnt their gods, as it is written: "When the wicked perish, there is joy" (Proverbs 11:10) [where the word for joy is *rinah*: *resh nun hei,* 200 + 50 + 5 = 255] which, inclusively, is the same as 256.

340 And the 64 is derived from eight times `then'; [*az*: *aleph zayin,* 1 + 7 = 8 and 8 x 8 = 64]. For az teaches about the eight letters of the unity, *yud aleph hei dalet vav* nun hei yud (as explained above, 260, and in *Tikunei haZohar, Tikkun* 38, page 78), and thus the 64 is derived from 8 times *az.*

And with the 64 on each of the four corners, the total is 256. And when he reaches *lev* [heart: *lamed bet*, 30 + 2 = 32], which is four times az [*aleph zayin*, 1 + 7 = 8], which is four times the letter *ḥet* (= 8), *yud* is joined with them on each side, making 'The Lord lives' [*ḥai* Tetragrammaton], i.e. that *Yesod* which is called life joins with the Tetragrammaton in the 18 [*ḥai*] blessings of the prayer, in which the Tetragrammaton appears 18 times, for a total of 72 letters (18 times four letters of each Tetragrammaton). At the moment the Tetragrammaton is joined with 'The Lord' by the Life of the Worlds, i.e. the combination *yud aleph hei dalet vav* nun hei yud is formed by *Yesod*, who is called Life of the Worlds. Immediately, the beasts of fire fall silent, for at the time of the unification they are quiet (as above, 314). What is written about them? "When they stood, they let down their wings" (Ezekiel 1:24), the meaning of which is: When Israel stands in prayer, this being the time of the unification, they let down their wings, that their presence should not be felt, until that time i.e. they fall silent.

341 And this is the meaning of "Only her lips moved, but her voice could not be heard" (1 Samuel 1:13), where 'lips' refer to the wings of the beings. For the electrum was previously beasts of fire who were speaking, while now they are silent. And this is why silent prayer was ordained, and thus the Work of the Chariot is without sound, for he speaks there to himself in a whisper. Three (daily) prayers were ordained [morning, afternoon, and evening — Tr.] and in each one the Tetragrammaton is enunciated 18 times, making 72 letters in each prayer, in the concluding sentences of each of the 18 blessings, and 3 x 72 makes 216 letters that are included in *Ḥesed;* and 3 x 72, with the 32 paths of *Ḥokhmah* comes to 250 less 2, i.e., adds up to 248, which is *Ḥesed*, and are included in the central column, which is *Ḥesed*.

342 From what is said about the sacrifices, prayer can be learned, and prayer is deduced from the sacrifices. Just as it is said above about prayer, "I heard the voice of their wings" (Ezekiel 1:24), so with regard to the *Kh'ruvim,* which are the secret of sacrifice, i.e. of the unification of the holy Name (Tetragrammaton) "The Lord' that is attained through the sacrifice — as it is said: "Then he heard the voice speaking to him" (Numbers 7:89). And so we deduce about prayer from the sacrifices. About the latter it is written: "the voice speaking...," which hints at both voice and speech, which are the Tetragrammaton and 'The Lord.' Similarly, about prayer it is said only: "I heard the voice of their wings," without speech being mentioned in this context. Nevertheless, speech is also included there. Just as with the ramp of the altar (cf. Numbers 28:4), on which sacrifices and burnt offerings ascend and descend, so in the prayer two angels ascend and two descend. And so it was at Mount Sinai, where Moses and Aaron ascended the mountain and descended, i.e. two went up and two came down. And all the precepts of the Torah are implied in this precept of prayer.

Commentary:

It is known that the central column corrects the columns, so that *Ḥokhmah* shines upwards from below (as above, *Bo*, page 60). Thus, the illumination of *Ḥesed* is termed descent, and the illumination of *Ḥokhmah* ascent. And on the text: Just as it is said "I heard the voice of their wings" (Ezekiel 1:24), so, with regard to the *Kh'ruvim*, "Then he heard the voice speaking to him" (Numbers 7:89): Voice is the secret of the illumination of *ḥasadim* of *Zeir Anpin*. Speech is the secret of the illumination of *Ḥokhmah*. And the one can be learned from the other. About prayer it is said: "And I heard the voice of their wings," and this can be understood to include speech also, just as in the case of the *Kh'ruvim*; i.e. in prayer are both the illumination of *ḥasadim* and the illumination of *Ḥokhmah*. And on the text: Just as with the ramp (they) ascend and descend: i.e. in it were the illumination of *Ḥokhmah*, which is the secret of ascend, and the illumination of *ḥasadim*, which is the secret of descend. Here also there are two types of illumination, by way of descent and by way of ascent, namely *Ḥokhmah* and *ḥasadim*, for all the precepts of the Torah are included in those two illuminations, for the 248 positive precepts are the secret of *ḥasadim* while the 365 negative precepts are the secret of the corrections of the illumination of *Ḥokhmah*.

343 Thus, when Rabbi Akiva started to discuss the Work of the Chariot, his mouth was Sinai and his voice was a ladder, on which angels ascended and descended. With every speech of his, the angel Metatron would ride on it. He rode to the *Shekhinah*, for included in him are the *Sfirot* of the central column, which is *Zeir Anpin*, which is *yud hei vav* hei. They are inside, while the *Shekhinah*, which is composed of ten *Sfirot*, is outside of him. And the Holy One, blessed be He, and His *Shekhinah* are *rekhev* [*resh kaf bet*: chariot] and *Merkavah* [*mem resh kaf bet hei*: chariot]. The central column is a chariot [*rekhev*] to ascend with for the Prime Cause, which is the Infinite One [*Ein Sof*], while his *Shekhinah* is a chariot [*rekhev*] for the central column. And the Prime Cause, which is the Infinite One, is the All-uniting and the All-arranging and the All-illuminating. His light passes through the soul and body and apparel, and He is unchanging, and without partnership, or account or picture or likeness of any chariot [*merkavah*] or vision or likeness that the mind can summon up. The upper and lower steps are *rekhev* and *merkavah* to him, but none ride on Him.

344 *Keshet* [*kuf shin tav*] stands for *teki'ah, shevarim, teru'ah* [the three calls on the *shofar*, the ram's horn and they are a sign for the patriarchs' chariot [*merkavah*].

Teki'ah is Abraham, *shevarim* Isaac, and *teru'ah* is Jacob, about whom it is said: "And the shouting [*teru'ah*] for the King is in him" (Numbers 23:21). And in it (the rainbow, *Keshet*) three colors are visible: white, red, and green. From the side of *Gvurah* it, *Yesod*, is called "The bows [*keshet*] of the mighty [*giborim*] are broken" (Samuel I, 2:4), and from the right side, which is *Ḥesed*, it is called "As the appearance of the bow that is in the cloud in the day of rain" (Ezekiel 1:28). When it appears on a rainy day, Mercy is visible, but when it appears when there is no rain, Judgment is visible. And when there is both rain and sun, this shows that Mercy and Judgment are both apparent. And this is the letter shin of *Shaddai* (the Almighty), that teaches about the three branches of the patriarchs, namely: The Tetragrammaton, Our God, the Tetragrammaton, these being the three names that parallel the three branches of the patriarchs, which are *Ḥesed*, *Gvurah*, and *Tiferet*, and these three names (the Tetragrammaton twice, our God, 4 + 6 + 4 = 14) contain 14 letters. And 14 is *dalet yud* (4 + 10 = 14), which, together with (above) spells shin *Shaddai* (Almighty). And *Shaddai* is *Yesod* of *Zeir Anpin*, and the apparel of *Shaddai* is Metatron [*mem tet tet resh vav* nun, 40 + 9 + 9 + 200 + 6 + 50 =314], which has the same numerical value as *Shaddai* [*shin dalet yud*, 300 + 4 + 10 = 314].

HE WHO SAYS "A PSALM OF PRAISE OF DAVID" EACH DAY

345 Rabbi Shimon said: Let he who has started continue! (This is the reaction of Rabbi Shimon to Rabbi Elazar's words, see above 237). Rabbi Elazar said: Whoever recites the psalm "Praise of David" (Psalm 145) three times daily is sure to inherit the world to come" (cf. *Talmud Bavli, Berakhot* 4b, where Rabbi Elazar quotes this in the name of Rabbi Abina). And we have already learned the reason, namely, that it contains the verse: "You open Your hand and satisfy every living thing with

favor" (Psalm 145:16), this being a prayer over food. If the reason has to do with provender and food for all the worlds, then he should say it twice (only, and not three times) each day, in the morning and the evening, for it is written: "When the Lord shall give you in the evening flesh to eat, and in the morning bread to the full" (Exodus 16:8). If a man eats only twice a day, why should he have to say "Praise of David" three times daily? The answer is that he says it twice for the food of mortal man, and for the whole world, and the additional once is to give force to that place where His hands are open.

346 These two foodstuffs of man (i.e. flesh and bread) differ from each other, for the one is for the rich and the other for the poor. And all three types of food are mentioned here in the psalm "Praise of David." "You give them their food in due season" (Psalm 145:15) refers to the food of the rich, for He gives them much food in due season. This is the first of the three. The second is "And satisfy every living thing with favor" (Psalms 145:16). This refers to the food of the poor, for they are satisfied not with much food but with favor. The third is the verse "You open Your hand" (ibid.), this being strength to that place, for when He opens His hands, favor and abundance for all emerge.

Commentary:

Hands: This is the secret of the two columns, the right and the left. And it is known that, before the central column united them, their illumination was most unclear, for the right column was without the upper three *Sfirot*, and the left column was with *Ḥokhmah* without *ḥasadim*, this being darkness, not light (as above, *Beresith Aleph*, page 47). And when the hands are closed, only a weak and limited illumination is drawn down from them, a situation that is corrected with the opening of the hands. And then it is the secret of food for the poor. And later, when the central column awakens the curtain of *Ḥirik* uniting it with the right (as above, *Lekh Lekha*, page 13), then the *Ḥokhmah* of the left unites with the *ḥasadim* of the right, and the light illuminates in all its perfection. And this refers to the opening of the hands after they were closed. And from then on the food for the rich is drawn down to the world. And we have here three matters:

a) The food of the poor, which is drawn down at the time when the hands are closed, and is corrected after the hands are opened.
b) The food of the rich, which is drawn down after the hands are opened.
c) The power of the central column, which opened the hands by the curtain of *Ḥirik* that is in it.

And on the text: "You give them their food in due season" (Psalms 145:15) this refers to the food of the rich, for they receive after the opening of the hands, which is in its due season. "And satisfy every living thing with favor" (Psalms 145:16) refers to the food of the poor, for they are satisfied with favor, that is, the unclear illumination from what they received prior to the opening of the hands; and now, with the opening of the hands, their sustenance is attired with ḥasadim, and so they are now only satisfied with favor, and not many provisions. And finally, on the text: "You open Your hand," this being strength to that place, for, when He opens His hands, favor and abundance for all emerge. This is the location of the curtain of *Ḥirik* in the central column, by which the hands were opened.

347 Again, I have learned that a man has to say "Praise of David" (Psalm 145) twice a day only for his daily food and sustenance. And these two times are mandatory for a person. And if he says it more than twice, this is not in fulfillment of an obligation, but in praise of the songs of praise of King

David. What is the reason? It is because it is not fitting that a man should ask for his sustenance until after the prayer, for the prayer itself is his Master's sustenance, and the King should eat first, and then his servants should eat afterwards.

I HAVE EATEN MY HONEYCOMB WITH MY HONEY; I HAVE DRUNK MY WINE WITH MY MILK

348 It is written: "I am come into my garden, my sister, my bride; I have gathered my myrrh with my spice; I have eaten my honeycomb with my honey; I have drunk my wine with my milk" (Song of Songs 5:1). The verse continues: "Eat, O friends. I have eaten my honeycomb" refers to that part of the prayer service that is said seated; i.e. from "Who forms light and creates darkness..." (immediately after the *Barekhu*) until the recital of the *Shema Yisrael*. "With my honey" refers to the recital of the *Shema Yisrael*. The explanation why "I have eaten my honeycomb" refers to that part of the prayer service that is said seated, is that it is the forest of Lebanon [the words for `honeycomb' and for `forest' appear identical] which is the world of *Beri'ah*, from `Who forms light and creates darkness,' including the wheels and the holy beings (cf. Ezekiel 1), all of which are called the forest of trees and the saplings in it. `With my honey' refers to the recital of the *Shema Yisrael*, which is the sweetest of all, like such nectar and sweetness.

349 `I have drunk my wine' is that part of the prayer service that is said standing, for it is the drawing down of the upper cellaret wine, which is the illumination of *Ḥokhmah* that is in *Binah*, and it is therefore said about it `I have drunk my wine.' And this is in the first three of the 18 blessings of the Amidah (or Shemoneh Esreh), paralleling *Ḥokhmah, Binah,* and *Da'at*. `With my milk' refers to the final three blessings of the Amidah, and they parallel *Netzaḥ, Hod,* and *Yesod*. And the illumination of *ḥasadim* is termed milk. And these are included in each other, i.e. the illumination of *Ḥokhmah*

and of *ḥasadim* are included in each other. To this point is the food of the King. And after the King has eaten, the friends on high may eat, i.e. the angels, as it says: "Eat, O friends" (Song of Songs 5:1). And the last part of the same verse, "Drink, yea, drink abundantly, O beloved," refers to the souls below.

350 And thus there is no obligation to offer praises for food until after the prayer, i.e. until after the King has eaten, as above. And what is the reason for the recital of "Praise of David" (Psalm 145) in the afternoon service before the *Amidah*? It is because the afternoon service parallels Isaac, which is Judgment. So before there is harsh judgment, i.e. before the prayer, while the King's countenance is still shining with *Ḥesed* (favor), let him say "Praise of David" in that order of foodstuffs in the three aspects (as above, 346), for after the prayer when Judgment prevails and hangs over the world is an inappropriate time for that. Rabbi Pinḥas came and kissed him.

NOW IT FELL UPON A DAY THAT THE SONS OF GOD CAME TO PRESENT THEMSELVES BEFORE THE LORD

351 Rabbi Yehuda said to Rabbi Shimon: Let my master say some beautiful things about *Rosh haShanah* (the New Year). Rabbi Shimon began by quoting: "It fell upon a day" (Kings II 4:18). Wherever it is written: 'It fell upon,' the meaning is anguish. And it fell upon days of anguish. Certainly "It fell upon a day" refers to a day on which there is anguish, and this is *Rosh haShanah,* a day on which harsh judgment is on the world. Similarly: "And it fell upon a day that Elisha passed to Shunem" (II Kings 4:8) was on *Rosh haShanah*. And wherever it is said "And it fell upon a day," the day referred to is *Rosh haShanah*. Consequently, "Now it fell upon a day that the sons of God came to present themselves before the Lord" refers to the day of *Rosh haShanah*.

352 *Rosh haShanah* always lasts for two days. What is the reason for this? It is so that Isaac,

who is the left column, which is the aspect of *Rosh haShanah,* should be composed of Judgment and Mercy, which are two days, and Isaac will not be just one. For were Isaac to be just one, without the inclusion of Mercy, he would destroy the world, and this is why it is written in Job twice: "Now it fell upon a day that the sons of God came to present themselves before the Lord" (Job 1:6 and 2:1).

353 "That the sons of God came" (Job 1:6). These are certainly the supreme court, the sons of God, who the sons of the King, i.e Israel, draw near before them. And they are the 70 officials who always surround the King, and they decree Judgment on the world. "To present themselves before the Lord" (ibid.). Should this verse be taken literally, i.e. to stand upon, or on the Lord? No, but when they stand to judge the world, the judgment of the first one is that of all. Who does not honor the holy Name and does not respect the Torah and His servants? So, too, who is not concerned about the honor of the holy Name, which is the *Shekhinah,* that it be not desecrated in the land, and who is not concerned over the honor of the Holy One, blessed be He, who is *Zeir Anpin*? Who, indeed, does not give honor to this Name? "And Satan came also amongst them" (ibid.). He came together with his Female, Lillith. And so it is here: "To present themselves before the Lord" (lit. `on the Lord') means that Satan, too, was concerned for the honor of this Name, that is to say, he came to incite about this.

RIGHTEOUS FOR WHOM THINGS GO BADLY AND WICKED FOR WHOM THINGS GO WELL

354 Here the first pillars of the world (the rabbinic sages) were divided. One said: Job was one of the pious of the nations of the world, and another said: Job was one of the pious of Israel, but was smitten in order to atone for the world (cf. *Talmud Bavli, Baba Batra* 15a & b, and cf. *Mishnah, Sotah* 5,5). One day Rav Hamnuna found Elijah (the prophet) and said to him: We have learned that there is a

righteous man in adversity and a wicked man who prospers. Rav Hamnuna said: A righteous man is one whose sins are few and who pays the price for them in this world, and thus is a righteous man in adversity. But if his sins are many and his good deeds few, then he receives his reward in this world, and thus is a wicked man who prospers. (cf. *Kiddushim* 3a). He said to him: The judgments of the Master of the World are profound, but when the Holy One, blessed be He, wants to make atonement for the sins of the generation, He smites their arm and through this action the generation is healed. It can be likened to a doctor who smites, i.e. lets blood, in the arm in order to save all the parts, as it is written: "But he was wounded because of our transgressions" (Isaiah 53:5). (cf., too, *Talmud Bavli, Berakhot* 7a.)

355 As we have learned, on that day of *Rosh haShanah* (New Year), 70 seats of justice arise to judge the world, some for the defense and some for the prosecution standing on high, those on the right for innocence and those on the left for guilt, to recall the sins of the world and the sins of each individual. A man has, therefore, to confess and specify his sins, each one just as it is, for whoever expounds his sins before the Holy One, blessed be He, judgment is passed on him by the Holy One, blessed be He, and by no other. And whoever is judged by the Holy One, blessed be He, it is for his good. This is why King David requested: "You be my judge, O God" (Psalms 43:1). You and no other. Similarly, Solomon said, "That He maintain the cause of His servant" (Kings I, 8:59). He and no other. But the heavenly court leaves him, i.e. does not pass sentence on him.

356 This is why the sins of every limb have to be expounded, and everything that he did in detail, as it is written: "I acknowledge my sin to You" (Psalms 32:5). And this same verse concludes: "And You forgave the iniquity of my sin, Selah." How do we know this? We know it from Moses, for it is written: "This people has sinned a great sin" (Exodus 32:31). And about Israel is written: "We have sinned because we have forsaken the Lord" (I Samuel 12:10). Should you suggest that the verse about Moses refers to an individual alone, while in public one does not have to specify one's sins, then the other verse "We have sinned because we have forsaken the Lord" comes to teach the opposite, for it is said in public. And should you agree that it is to be in public, but that it is not the representative (the prayer leader) who has to detail the sins out loud before everyone, the opposite is suggested, as it is written: "And Moses returned to the Lord and said: This people has sinned a great sin" (Exodus 32:31). And it is written in the continuation of the same verse: "And (they) have made them a god of gold." What is the reason? It is because the heavenly court leaves alone the person who expounds his own sins and does not find him guilty. Because a man may be considered as one of his own close relatives, and a relative is unacceptable as a witness. (See *Mishnah, Sanhedrin* 3,4). He is, therefore, not judged according to his own testimony.

357 Again, he does not let the prosecutor teach guilt and fault about him, because the person himself comes first (i.e. before the prosecutor) and tells all, leaving nothing (of his sins) for anyone else to mention. Then the Holy One, blessed be He, forgives him, as it is written: "But whoever confesses and forsakes (his transgressions) shall have mercy" (Proverbs 28:13).

358 the days of *Rosh haShanah*, the court prepares a throne for the King to judge the whole world. Israel comes in first to be judged before Him, so that Mercy will multiply, i.e before His anger is aroused at the sinners of the world (cf. *Talmud Bavli, Rosh haShanah* 8b). It is written "That He maintains the ...cause of His people Israel, as every day shall require" (I Kings 8:59). What is the meaning of "as every day shall

require?" The meaning is the two days of *Rosh haShanah*. And why are there two days? Because they are two courts joined together. There is the upper court which is stringent in its verdicts, and the lower court that is flexible, and both of them exist.

Commentary:

The secret of the blowing of the *Shofar* (ram's horn) is to awaken the judgments of the curtain of *ḥirik* of the central column in order to unite the two columns, the right and the left, in each other (see above, Emor, 193). And there are two actions in this curtain of *Ḥirik* vis-a-vis the left column. The first action is of the secret of the Lock, which is strict judgment. And the second action is of the secret of the Key, which is lenient judgment (as explained above, *Lekh Lekha* 13, and see there). And the lock is hidden in the upper three of each step, and the key is in the six ends of each step. Thus: the lock is called upper court, and the key is called lower court, and they always illuminate each other, for they need each other, for the key receives the power of judgment from the lock, and the lock receives the illumination of sweetness from the key. And on the text: "They are two courts joined together:" There is the upper court that is stringent in its verdicts, which is the secret of the lock that is hidden in the upper three *Sfirot*; and the lower court that is flexible, this being the secret of the key whose place is in the six ends. And both of them exist, for they illuminate each other, as above. And so: The first day of *Rosh haShanah* is the aspect of the upper three *Sfirot*, and the lock is in control there, which is harsh judgment, while the second day of *Rosh haShanah* is the aspect of the six ends, and there the key is in control.

359 And in this respect the Babylonians (i.e. the Jewish community of Babylonia) did not know the secret of the *shevarim* and *teru'ah* and

that both of them are required. The *teru'ah* is strict judgment. The three (notes) of the *shevarim* are lenient judgment, and it is like someone who groans from his heart, which is soft. They (the Jews of Babylonia) did not know which of the two was required, and they therefore had both of them. But we know that both of them are required, and make both of them. (See the clarification, above Emor, 195.) And everything comes out by the way of truth.

360 He began by quoting: "Blow the horn at the new moon, in concealment for our feast day. For it is a statute for Israel, an ordinance of the God of Jacob" (Psalms 81:4-5.) What is `at the new moon?' It means the lenient judgment, that is called new moon. And what is `in concealment?' This is harsh judgment, which is also termed `the fear of Isaac.' (For the source of this expression, see Genesis 31:42). The word used here for `in concealment' is *keseh*, and it therefore refers to a judgment that is covered [*m'khuseh*] permanently, i.e. the Lock, which is not judgment openly, for it is concealed in the upper three *Sfirot*, as above. `For it is a statute' refers to lenient judgment, which is the secret of the Key, which is ostensible. `Ordinance' refers to judgment mixed with compassion, and the two of them are there together, as in the paragraph above, and this is why there are two days of *Rosh haShanah*, both of which are in the same secret.

361 "Happy is the people that knows *teru'ah*" (Psalms 89:15). It does not say "that hears *teru'ah*," nor does it say "that sounds *teru'ah*," but "that knows" This is because only the sages who dwell in the atmosphere of the holy land are the ones who know *teru'ah* (and those who live elsewhere, e.g. in Babylonia, do not know it). The secret of the *teru'ah* is as it is written: "You shall break them [*tero'em*] with a rod of iron" (Psalms 2:9). (This matter is clarified in what is written above, Emor, 195.) What people is there like Israel, who know the heavenly secrets of their Master and enter in before Him and associate with Him. And all those who know the secret of the *teru'ah* will draw near and walk in the light of the countenance of the Holy One, blessed be He, because this is the first light that the Holy One, blessed be He, hid for the righteous. This is why it is necessary to know it, the *teru'ah*.

THE LOBE OF THE LIVER, GALL, TRACHEA, ESOPHAGUS, AND SHOFAR

362 It is written: "The lobe of the liver..." (Leviticus 9:10), and also: "the lobe above the liver..." (ibid., 3:4). `The lobe of the liver' means a woman of debauchery, that is Lillith, who goes and emerges from liver, that is Samael, to mislead the world and denounce them, and she leaves the male to practice prostitution. And that is why it is written: `the lobe of the liver' [the word here rendered `of, min, also means `from' `Lobe above the liver' means that, after making her adulterous union, she boasts about it (see 378 for further elaboration). She has "a harlot's forehead" (Jeremiah 3:3) and subdues her husband, who is Samael, who is called liver, in the anger of gall, which is a quarrelsome wife who rules in her husband's home. Thus "The harlot's forehead" has control over the liver, which is Samael, because she is a woman of quarrel and anger and is therefore called "lobe over the liver."

363 "Lobe of the liver:" Because she emerges from the liver, which, as explained above, is Samael her husband, in order to harm the whole world and practice adultery with all. She then mounts the male, with "a harlot's forehead," audaciously, and she is then over the liver. Again, she is called `lobe over the liver,' from another point of view, for after she has gone out to play prostitute with all, she gives the leftovers to her husband, and this is the meaning of `lobe of the liver' (for the word for lobe, comes from a root meaning `excess,' `more').

Commentary:

The lobe of the liver is from the aspect of Samael, which is the judgments of the Male, but, because she fornicates with others, judgments of the Female are also caught up in her.

364 From the liver and the lobe, which are Samael and Lillith, emerges gall, which is the sword of the Angel of Death, from which come bitter drops to kill human beings. It is written: "Her end is bitter [*marah,* also meaning 'gall'] as wormwood" (Proverbs 5:4). And the gall is hanging on the liver, all sickness and death being dependent on it, on the shell that is called gall. And on that day of *Rosh haShanah,* she prowls through the world, collecting up all the sins that are in the world. And then all the parts, which are Israel, are in trouble, for Israel is composed of the parts of the *Shekhinah,* as it is said: "The spirit of man is the lamp of the Lord" (Proverbs 20:27), which means that the spirit of man is from the lamp of the Lord, which is the holy *Shekhinah.* And then, on *Rosh haShanah,* all Israel is in trouble, so they take a shofar to awaken with those calls: *teki'ah, shevarim, teru'ah.*

THE FAITHFUL SHEPHERD

365 Said the Faithful Shepherd: Certain it is that since the limbs and the arteries of the heart, that are likened to Israel, are in trouble, they have to awaken in the trachea, which is the secret of the *shofar,* this being the windpipe connected to the lung. Since the wings of the lung are unable to quiet the anger of the gall, which overcomes the arteries of the heart and all the arteries of the limbs of the body, that spirit (or breath of air), which is the secret of *ḥasadim* that breathes in them, rises in the trachea, which is *shofar,* i.e. the next world. For *shofar* is the secret of *Binah* that is called the next world. And so it has been taught: The esophagus is like this

world, which is the secret of *Malkhut*, for there is eating and drinking in it, i.e. the intelligences of *ḥasadim* and *Ḥokhmah* that are termed eating and drinking. The trachea is likened to the next world, which is *Binah*, for there is no eating and drinking in it, for those intelligences are not disclosed there in *Binah*, but in *Malkhut*.

366 And after the *vav* of trachea [*veshet*: *vav shin tet*] has wandered off [*shat*: *shin tet*], because of the great amount of eating that it robbed, it grew longer, and the *vav* became a nun [the form of the latter letter is as that of the former, but extended to below the line and the trachea [*veshet*: *vav* shin tet] becomes Satan [*shin tet nun*], who caused that "the people wandered about [*shatu*] and gathered..." (Numbers 11:8), where the word for 'wandered about', '*shatu*', can be derived from the word '*sh'tut*' (stupidity). For it was Satan who brought about their stupidity in that they intermingled with a "mixed multitude" (Exodus 12:38 and Numbers 11:4) of stupid people whose craving was for food and drink and robbery and violence, for oppression of the poor and moaning of the needy. They went astray with a bent *nun* (as used at the beginning or in the middle of a word), for they ate without grinding it. [This refers to the quail, see Numbers 11:32; in contra distinction, the people did grind the manna, see ibid, v.8]. And what is written about them? "While the flesh (of the quail) was yet between their teeth, before it was chewed, the anger of the Lord was kindled against the people" (Numbers 11:33). For the *vav* of *shatu* [*shin tet vav*, wandered about to gather the manna] grew and became a *nun* (in its straight form, as used at the end of words), thus making Satan [*shin tet nun*]. And he whose spirit is bowed down is as a bent *nun*, that is to say that the sanctity had become a bent *nun*, but the evil forces are a straight *nun*. And the result of this was that Satan spread into the eating and drinking and overcame all the limbs and the arteries with the 365 negative precepts, for all

365 days of the (solar) year. And this is as the numerical value of *haSatan* (the Satan) [*hey shin tet nun*, 5 + 300 + 9 + 50 = 364], less one. And the one that is omitted is the Day of Atonement, on which there is no eating and drinking. Thus Satan has no control on the Day of Atonement, and is short one day of the full count of 365.

C o m m e n t a r y :

The inclusion of *Ḥokhmah* in *ḥasadim*, in *Netzaḥ* and *Hod*, is called grinding, in the secret of the powder into which the manna is ground for the righteous. And the mixed multitude increases the left, and continue their eating and drinking from the left, without the right, and this is without grinding. And on the text: They went astray with a bent *nun* ate without grinding: Because they ate without grinding, Satan joined them, and their sanctity became a bent *nun*, for the holy spirit flew away from them.

367 And the Day of Atonement is like the trachea of the lung, which is *Binah* and the next world, as above. And it is *vav*, the son of *Yah*, i.e. *bet-nun yud-hei*, the letters, rearranged, of *Binah*. And in respect thereof, the sages of the Mishnah taught: "If one sees a reed (*kaneh, kuf nun hei*, same word as used for trachea) in a dream, he may hope for wisdom, for it says "Get [*k'neh*] wisdom" (Proverbs 4:5). [Different readings of the verse, i.e. different vowels in the same consonants, allow the rendering: A reed (or trachea) is wisdom]. (cf. *Talmud Bavli, Berakhot*, 56b.) For there is no *kaneh* that is less than two, namely: *yud Ḥokhmah, hei Binah*, for there is no *Binah* without *Ḥokhmah* and no *Ḥokhmah* without *Binah*. And this is why they should awaken the *shofar*, for it is a trachea, as above, which is the next world, a long world, that receives *Arikh*

***Anpin*, from whom come the 13 attributes of Mercy, because in the letter *vav* [spelled out in full: *vav* aleph vav] the *aleph* is the secret of long [*arokh*: *aleph resh kaf*], and the two *vavs* are the secret of *anpin* (nostrils).**

368 And Upper Mother is *teki'ah* from the side of Abraham, who is *Ḥesed*. *Shevarim* are from the side of Isaac, who is *Gvurah*. *Teru'ah* is from the side of Jacob, who is *Tiferet*. The lower *Shekhinah*, which is *Malkhut*, is the link [*kesher*: *kuf shin resh*] between them all, for it receives them all. And the word *kesher* is formed from the initial letters of *teki'ah*, *shevarim*, *teru'ah*, where *teki'ah* is *kuf*, *shevarim* is *shin*, and *teru'ah* is *resh*. And all of them are tripled in the *Shekhinah*, as it is written: "They proclaim you thrice holy" (*Mussaf Amidah*, Sephardi version). For the voice cannot come out of the body other than through the mouth. So here, too, the *Shekhinah* must not be separated from the Holy One, blessed be He, for about the Holy One, blessed be He, it is said: "The voice of the Lord hews out flames of fire" (Psalms 29:7). And the *Shekhinah* is "the prayer of every mouth." And these are the mnemonics: *kuf shin resh kuf*; *kuf shin kuf*; *kuf resh kuf* (for the order of the *shofar* calls) and the *teki'ot* are clarified above (Emor, 195).

369 The *shofar* is taken in order to awaken with it *teru'ah* and *teki'ah*, which are harsh Judgment with Mercy, for the *teru'ah* is harsh Judgment, and *teki'ah* is Mercy. And *shevarim teki'ah* is lenient Judgment with Mercy, since *shevarim* is lenient Judgment (as above, 360) and *teki'ah* is Mercy. And then they thus awaken on high and intermingle with each other, that is, Judgment with Mercy and Mercy with Judgment.

THE FAITHFUL SHEPHERD

370 And in the first section, the Faithful Shepherd said that, where Satan was sweetened and the final *nun* of *veshet* [*vav shin tet*, esophagus], was folded and it returned to be a *vav*. Where the esophagus [*veshet*] became Satan (as

above, 368), it is now put back, and becomes *veshet* again, as it was. This is because "the voice is the voice of Jacob" (Genesis 27:22), for Israel has no staying power at eating and drinking, as do the other nations who inherit this world, for their strength is in eating and drinking. But as for Israel, their strength is in the voice, which is the next world, a long world that was created with the letter *yud;* and the voice of the shofar (which is the secret of the intelligences of *Zeir Anpin* that are called voice, which receives from shofar), which is *Binah,* emerges from it, from the yud which is *Ḥokhmah.* The rabbis said: "They may not recite less than... ten *shofar* verses" (*Mishnah, Rosh haShanah* 4,6), i.e. parallel to the letter *yud* (whose numerical value is 10). For with the letter *yud* is certainly made a long world, which is *vav,* the next world, i.e. that is receives intelligences of the next world, as above. And with the letter *hei* He created this world, which is small *hei,* i.e. *Malkhut,* in which there is eating and drinking of Torah, i.e. the intelligences of *Ḥokhmah* and *ḥasadim* that are called eating and drinking.

371 And there is yet another secret. For after the decree is enacted in the two letters *hei hei,* which are the two courts of *Binah* and of *Malkhut,* who is able to rescind the decree of both of them, if not the *yud vav* of the Tetragrammaton [*yud hei vav* and *hei*]. For the letter *hei* of the Tetragrammaton is Upper Mother, *Binah,* and *yud.* And what is written? "Every vow and every binding oath to afflict the soul [which is *hei* that is called soul, *nefesh*], her husband may let it stand or her husband may make it void" (Numbers 30:14). Here *yud* is the husband of the first *hei,* which is *Binah,* and *vav* is the husband of the second *hei,* which is *Malkhut.* Thus the *yud* and *vav* can rescind the decree of the two *heis,* the two courts. It is thus necessary to awaken the voice, that is *vav,* which is *Zeir Anpin,* with the ten *shofar* verses, that is *yud,* in order to annul the judgments of the two courts, which are *Binah* and

***Malkhut*. And the main thing is that each of the mnemonics should be sounded in one breath, in the mouth, which is the tenth part of ten, the mnemonics being *kuf shin resh kuf* (standing for the *shofar* calls: *teki'ah, shevarim, teru'ah, teki'ah*); *kuf shin kuf* (standing for the calls: *teki'ah, shevarim, teki'ah*); and *kuf resh kuf* (standing for *teki'ah, teru'ah, teki'ah*).**

372 Immediately on hearing these matters, Rabbi Shimon and the comrades exclaimed: Blessed be God that we have been privileged to hear such matters from him (the Faithful Shepherd, Moses), who is called the Master of all the prophets, Master of all the sages, Master of all the ministering angels, through whose mouth the Holy One, blessed be He, and His Divine Presence (the *Shekhinah*) speak, and by whose hands He wrote these secrets, the like of which have not been heard since the revelation of the Torah.

373 The Faithful Shepherd said to Rabbi Shimon: Holy Luminary, complete the matters of the secrets of the first part, by expounding on them, for the heads of all of the academies on high and the heads of all the academies below are ready to hear these things from your mouth, with your clarifications, for thereby will rejoicing and redemption awaken in heaven above and on the earth below. "Give no rest" (Isaiah 62:7), neither you nor any of your comrades.

LIVER AND HEART

374 With *teru'ah* and *teki'ah* and *shevarim*, everything is perfumed, one with the other, for all of the judgments are mitigated, and everything that the liver is holding it sacrifices to the heart, which is the King, to nourish him. And it is neither the way of that heart, nor its desire, to foul up the deeds of His people, but He takes everything that is clear and pure, namely, the merits and the good deeds, while all the foulness the filth and the dirt, which are the bad deeds He leaves for the liver, which is Samael, about whom it is said: "Esau... is a hairy [*s'ir*] man"

(Genesis 27:11). And all its arteries, which are the other peoples, the idol worshippers, are as it is written: "And the goat [*s'ir*] shall bear upon him all their iniquities" (Leviticus 16:22). What is meant by "all their iniquities" [*avonotam*: *ayin vav* nun (*vav*) *tav mem*]? The letters, re-arranged, spell *avonot tam* [*ayin vav* nun *vav* tav (*tav*) *mem*], i.e the iniquities of a tam, a complete man, the reference being to the same one about whom it is said: "And Jacob was a complete man" (Genesis 25:27). And the iniquities of His people are in the arteries and sinews that pulsate in the heart.

375 And this is why boils and leprosy and skin sores of all the limbs are to be found in the liver, deriving from the filth that remains there. From the heart comes health for all the limbs, for that is how it is: since the heart took all the pure, clean, and bright, the liver takes what is left over there of the dirt and the filth and distributes it to all the other limbs, which are the other nations, the idol-worshippers, without their wanting it. And from the garbage, the refuse of the liver, the spleen, which is Lillith, takes, about whom it is said: "Let there be lights" (Genesis 1:14), where the word `lights' is written in the abbreviated form [*m'orot*: *mem aleph resh tav*], which can also be read as *m'erat*, `the curse of,' because Lillith was created, as in the verse: "The curse of the Lord is in the house of the wicked" (Proverbs 3:33). (See above, *Bereshith Aleph*, 393)

THE FAITHFUL SHEPHERD
SPLEEN AND GALL

376 More was said in this section. Said the Faithful Shepherd: Did not the rabbis teach about it: The spleen laughs (cf. *Talmud Bavli, Berakhot* 61b, top), and this is "the laughter of the fool" (Ecclesiastes 7:6)? For this reason the sages of the Mishnah taught: Woe to him whom time laughs. [This quotation does not appear to be from the Mishnah, nor is it to be found as a *Baraita* anywhere in the Talmud!] For he receives his world during his lifetime. And

Ecclesiastes said: "Anger is better than laugher" (Ecclesiastes 7:3). The meaning of this is: The anger of the liver, which is the gall, the whiplash of the Holy One, blessed be He, is a whip with which to beat the righteous in this world with bad illnesses and plagues. And this is better than the laughter with which the spleen (which is Lillith), laughs at us, with the dirt of this world: and better than the laughter of time, i.e. wealth. For they receive in this world the reward of the good deeds that they did, so that they should utterly perish from the next world, while the righteous receive the punishment for the sins they have committed in this world so that they will inherit the next world. Again, venom of the spleen is a reptile of the dust, which is stronger than the venom of the gall.

377 And since the mixed multitude (cf. Exodus 12:38) are the leaven in the dough, i.e. they intermingled with Israel as leaven in the dough [that ferments trouble and the nations of the world are like chaff, the mixed multitude delays Israel in exile more than do the idol-worshipping nations, as the sages taught. "R. Alexandri, on concluding his prayer, used to add the following: Sovereign of the Universe, it is known full well to You that our will is to perform Your will, but what prevents us? The leaven in the dough (i.e. the evil impulse that causes a ferment in the heart)" (*Talmud Bavli, Berakhot* 17a). For the mixed multitude stick to Israel as does the leaven to the dough, but the nations of the world are no more than "like the chaff which the wind drives away (Psalms 1:4).

THE SCAPEGOAT, LIVER AND HEART

378 Again: "And the goat shall bear upon him all their iniquities" (Leviticus 16:22). When Satan wants to inform against Israel before the Holy One, blessed be He, and he bears all the sins that he can carry, until he becomes heavy [kaved, which word also means liver] a heavy burden they [the iniquities that he

bears on his shoulders] are too heavy for him (Psalms 38:4). What does he do? He like an ass, ascends a high mountain, and when he gets near the top and wants to climb up that little bit more that is left for him, the weight of the burden overcomes him, and he falls, and tumbles down to the bottom, and what with the weight of the burden pressing on him, all his bones are broken into pieces, until not a single limb in him remains whole. Thus, too, did it happen to Samael and Serpent, which are liver and the lobe of the liver, the evil inclination and its partner, harlot, whence every daughter of a strange god is called a harlot.

Commentary:

The secret of the scapegoat has already been well explained above (*Aḥarey Mot*, 116), but here the Faithful Shepherd adds another secret. For the root of all the evil forces are Samael and Serpent, which are Male and Female, the meaning of which is that Samael is drawn down from the Judgments of the Male, that is to say that all the punishments that are derived from the sins that are extensions of the Judgments of the Male are administered by Samael. And the Serpent, i.e. his female, is the Judgments of the Female, for all the punishments that are derived from sins that are extensions of the Judgments of the Female are administered by her. And it is known that these two types of Judgments are the roots for all types of sin that there are in the world. And the secret of the scapegoat mentioned above, says the Faithful Shepherd, is that it is the total quantity of accusations that Samael and Serpent carry to bring before the Holy One, blessed be He, so that He will give them permission to punish Israel, from the two aspects of their Judgments. And the scapegoat is likened to a burden-bearing ass. Thus, the scapegoat bears upon himself all the informings of Samael and Serpent, whose roots are in the two types of Judgments mentioned above. And it was explained there (*Aḥarey Mot*, 116) that, should these two types of Judgments join together, they would be able to destroy the whole world. And the correction for them is by means of the central column, by which the Judgments of the Female annul the Judgments of the Male, by means of its curtain of Ḥirik that rescinds the first three *Sfirot* of the illumination of the left. (Study that passage well.) On the text: When Satan wants to inform against Israel, etc. That is, when Samael and Serpent sent the upper scapegoat to inform on Israel. [The Aramaic word here rendered as `to inform' comes from a word meaning `destruction.' The translation `inform' is based on the text in *Talmud Bavli*, e.g. *Gittin* 56a top: `I will go and inform against them to the Government.' cf. also the use of the word in the Aramaic translation of the Book of Proverbs (the *Targum*), paralleling the English `talebearer'. Proverbs 11:13 and 20:19.] And on the text: And he bears all the sins that he can carry until he becomes heavy: i.e. both the Judgments of the Male and the Judgments of the Female, that are too heavy to bear. What does he do? He ascends a high mountain to awaken the Judgments of the Male, for he ascends the left column, which is called a high mountain, for the three columns are called mountains. When he gets near the top i.e. when he is already on the left column, in the aspect of the six *Sfirot* of the left, and wants to climb up that little bit more that is left for him: i.e. he wants to ascend to the upper three *Sfirot* of the left, where there is no unity of the right, and all the Judgments of the Male are drawn down from there, the weight of the burden overcomes him and he falls: that is to say that the Judgments of the Female that are in his burden press down upon him in the place of the upper three *Sfirot* of the left, to the extent of annulling them by the force of the central column that corrects this by force of the sending of the scapegoat into the wilderness, as is done by Israel below. And then: (He) tumbles down to the bottom, for he throws himself down below the whole length of the left column, that is to say, he does not want to receive even the six *Sfirot* of the left that the central column leaves, for the evil forces flee from the central column and its corrections. Thus, too, did it happen to Samael and Serpent, for they are the ones sent with the scapegoat and they are the evil inclinations and its partner, harlot, for Samael is the evil inclination, and the Serpent, his partner, is a harlot. For male and female have to be of the same species, and since Samael is of the Judgments of the Male, his partner should also have been of these Judgments. She is, however, of the Judgments of the Female, as explained above. And from where does she obtain these Judgments since her husband, Samael, does not give them to her? She practices harlotry with other upper forces, and from them receives judgments of the Female. For this reason Samael and his partner are called the evil inclination and harlot. And on the text: 'Whence every daughter of a strange god is called a harlot.' For the Female of Samael is the source of all the prostitution that is in the world, and the daughter of a strange god receives it from her. And this is the secret (of what he says, above, 362): 'Lobe above the liver' is because after making her adulterous union she boasts about it... and subdues her husband. For after she has prostituted herself with other forces from whom she receives the judgments of the Female, she subsequently subdues her husband, Samael, for the judgments of the Female are harsher than those of the Male

379 Rabbi Pinḥas said to Rabbi Shimon: This path was ordained for me to hear these things from the Ancient of Days. Happy is the world in which you reside. Woe to the world where orphans remain without knowing matters of Torah properly. For it is certainly like that: the liver, which is Samael, takes everything, good and bad, and although he moves around and gathers in all the sins of Israel, he likewise gathers up their merits, too, for the liar has to speak some truth at the beginning for people to

believe him. And he sacrifices everything, both merits and demerits, to the heart, and the way of the heart is not to take anything but the purest, clearest and brightest of all, i.e. the merits, as you have said, and the remaining filth and dirt, which are the iniquities, he returns to the liver, who has no choice but to take everything, as it is written: "And the goat shall bear upon him all their iniquities" (Leviticus 16:22) (as explained in the previous paragraph). I am going over this matter again, although you have already stated it, so that it will be sweet in my mouth as the sweetness of honey. Happy is my portion that I have been privileged for this.

380 He, too, began by quoting: "Lord, my heart is not haughty, nor my eyes lofty" (Psalms 131:1). David spoke this verse when he was walking on the bank of the river, and said: Master of the Universe, has there ever been a man in the world who gave thanks and praised his Master as I have? A frog chanced by and said to him: David you have no cause to be proud, for I have achieved more than you, for I have put my body at my Master's command, as it is written: "And the river shall swarm with frogs" (Exodus 7:28). And this, indeed, is how it has been interpreted. (cf. *Talmud Bavli, Pesaḥim*, 53b). And also, I (the frog) give praises and sing day and night, without interruption. Then said David: "Lord, my heart is not haughty, nor my eyes lofty" (Psalms 131:1). Lord, my heart is not haughty. (The continuation is omitted).

THE ROSE

381 (The beginning of the section is omitted.) This is a sacrifice that is on every day and at every time to the Holy One, blessed be He, in which the *Shekhinah* is included among all her other crowds, who are Israel. And all these Services remove her from among the thorns, i.e. from among the other nations. So it is with Israel. So long as they are hard-hearted and do not make a start repenting, they do not send up an aroma, and there is none to remove them from amongst the thorns. But when they open their hearts in repentance, they immediately emit an aroma, and He removes them from amongst the thorns. And the Jewish People [*K'nesset Yisrael*], which is *Malkhut*, obtains pleasure from them, as it is written: "Open to me, my sister, my love" (Song of Songs 5:2), for so long as the rose is closed, it gives off no aroma and does not rise above the thorns but sits amongst them, as they have said. And the only reason that the Holy One, blessed be He, sent us along this path was so that we should learn these matters.

THE EAGLE

382 While they were still sitting there, an eagle came, flew low and took one rose from amongst them and went. They said: From here on we shall go on our way. They arose and went. And so far they had all gone in the way of Rabbi Pinḥas, for Rabbi Shimon went together with Rabbi Elazar and the other companions, and Rabbi Pinḥas was with the other companions.

383 Rabbi Pinḥas began by quoting about this, about the eagle that took the rose: "For the Leader; upon *Shushan Eduth; Mikhtam* of David, to teach" (Psalms 60:1). What is the meaning of 'to teach?' It is to teach wisdom [*Ḥokhmah*] to mortal man, and we have already expounded this. '*Shushan Eduth*' refers to the Great Sanhedrin, which is *Malkhut* that attires *Binah*, for, the intelligences of *Binah* are called *Eduth* (testimony). *Mikhtam* of David refers to a sign that was shown to David that he would win the war, when he sent Joab to Aram-Naharaim and Aram gathered an army to make war against them (See II Samuel 10). Said Rabbi Pinḥas: The *Shushan Eduth* that is mentioned here is when the stars that are in the heavens and the *Shekhinah* are over us, and with it the upper levels, i.e. the intelligences of *Binah* that are called eduth, and it is a holy courtyard for extolling praises. This is Shushan, in perfection, as is fitting.

They arose and went on their way, some in one direction, others in a different direction. Rabbi Pinḥas went to the village of Aquimin and stayed overnight, and Rabbi Isaac and Rabbi Ḥiyya were with him.

384 They got up early to leave, then sat to wait for the morning light. Rabbi Ḥiyya looked up and saw those comets: i.e. stars that carry along a tail of light, behind them, running about (in the sky). He said: A number of times have I asked about those stars. What do they allude to?

385 Rabbi Pinḥas said: These stars of the Milky Way are known in the understanding of the companions, for the Holy One, blessed be He, created all these stars of the firmament, both great and small, and they all give thanks and praise to the Holy One, blessed be He, and when their time to sing praises arrives, the Holy One, blessed be He, calls them by name, as it is written: "He calls them all by name" (Isaiah 40:26). And they then run and hold out a scepter of light to go and praise their Master in the same place where they were numbered, as it is written: "Lift up your eyes on high and see: Who has created these? He who brings out their host by numbers" (Isaiah 40:26). Meanwhile the light dawned. They arose and went.

Commentary:

All the stages that are found in the upper three *Sfirot* are called stars, or the stars of the heavens. And it is impossible to draw down the illumination of *Ḥokhmah*, termed number or account (as above, *Pikudei* 28), from them, downwards from above. And this is the secret of the verse: "Look now toward heaven and count the stars, if you are able to count them" (Genesis 15:5). Indeed the Holy One, blessed be He, Himself reveals in them the aspect of number and account, which is the illumination of *Ḥokhmah*, only they illuminate upwards from below. And this is the secret of the verse: "He counts the number of the stars" (Psalms 147:4). For the Holy One, blessed be He, Himself counts the number: "He calls them all by name" (Isaiah 40:26). `Name' is the secret of perception, for what we do not perceive we are unable to call by name. And at that time when the Holy One, blessed be He, gathers them together to reveal through them the number, in the secret of "He counts the number of the stars," then, because of the great amount of light, they send back reflected light upwards from below, and this is like a scepter, i.e. a flow of light, and about them is the allusion in the terrestrial level, to the secret of the comets. And the reference is to the text: "(they) hold out a scepter of light to go and praise their Master in the same place where they are numbered".

A LARGE EAGLE AND KING SOLOMON

386 While they were walking along, a large eagle came and circled their heads, remaining over them. Said Rabbi Pinḥas: This is certainly a desirable time, right now, and the Gates of Mercy are open for all those who are on a sickbed, and this is the time to heal them. And although they are the prisoners of the king, for they are confined to their beds, this eagle is a sign of Mercy, for the countenance of the eagle is the secret of the central column, which is Mercy.

387 He began by quoting: "As an eagle that stirs up its nest, hovering over its young" (Deuteronomy 32:11). There is none in the world that has mercy over its children as does the eagle. This we have already learnt [there are a number of references in rabbinic literature to the eagle's mercy for its offspring as it is written: "And the children of the eagle shall eat it" (Proverbs 30:17), for he is merciful to his children. And since now is the time of mercy, this eagle has come and circled us. This is the time of mercy for all those who are ill and lying

on their beds, and this is as is written: "O Lord, in the morning shall you hear my voice" (Psalms 5:4), this being the morning of Abraham, which is the secret of *Ḥesed*, and the awakening of *Ḥesed*.

388 While he was speaking, the eagle flew in a circle and went ahead of them. Rabbi Pinḥas said: Eagle, eagle, what are you doing here with us? If you have come on a mission from your Master, behold, we are here. If you have come for something else, behold, we are here, ready. The eagle flew upwards and disappeared from their sight, and they sat down.

389 Rabbi Ḥiyya said: This matter of King Solomon is wondrous, for we have learned: A large eagle used to come to King Solomon every day, and King Solomon would ride on the wings, and they would travel 400 parasangs in one hour (i.e. about 1,600 miles). Where did the eagle take him? "To Tarmod in the wilderness" (I Kings 9:18), in the hills. There is a certain place amongst the Mountains of Darkness that is called 'Tarmod in the wilderness,' and this is not the place where the Tarmodites live, but Tarmod that is in the wilderness in the hills, where all the spirits and evil forces gather. And that eagle would fly there in one hour.

390 Since the eagle stood over that place, Tarmod, the eagle drew itself up, and Solomon wrote a note and threw it down there, and thereby was saved from those spirits. And the eagle used to look into the darkness of the mountains, to the place where Uzza and Azael were imprisoned by chains of iron, thrust in the depths, and there is no man in the world that has the ability to enter there, not even birds of the heaven, with the exception of Balaam.

391 And since the eagle used to look into the great darkness, he flew down low and took King Solomon under his left wing and covered him. And the eagle stood upon those chains of Uzza and Azael, and drew near to them. Solomon then took

out a ring, on which he had engraved the Holy Name, and placed it in the eagle's mouth. And immediately they (Uzza and Azael) would say everything that Solomon wanted, and from there Solomon knew wisdom (cf. Proverbs 1:2). This is as it is written: "And Solomon built... Tarmod in the wilderness, in the land" (I Kings 9:17-18). Did he really put up a building in the land? No! So what is meaning of "And Solomon built..." [*Vayiven*]? *Vayiven* comes from the word *havanah* (understanding, comprehension), for he looked with understanding and knew that place (*Tarmod*), and there knew wisdom. (An elucidation of this section will be found above, *Mishpatim*, 345.)

THE ROSE (B)

392 And while they were still sitting there, the eagle came back to them, with one rose in its mouth, which he dropped in front of them, and went. They saw it and rejoiced. Said Rabbi Pinḥas: Did I not tell you that this eagle is on a mission from its Master? This rose [*shoshanah*] is an allusion to *Shushan Eduth* (Psalm 60:1), as I said, and the Holy One, blessed be He, sent it to us.

393 He began again as before and said: "For the Leader; upon *Shushan Eduth; Mikhtam* of David, to teach" (Psalm 60:1). Does this mean that *Shushan* is testimony [*eduth*]? What is the testimony to which it testifies? The answer is that this *Shushan* is witness to the Work of Creation, and is witness to the peoplehood of Israel [*Knesset Yisrael*], and is witness to the heavenly unity. And this is so because in a rose [*shoshanah*] there are thirteen petals, all of them on one root, and there are five strong petals on the outside that cover this rose and protect it.

394 And it is all in the secret of *Ḥokhmah*, for the thirteen leaves allude to the thirteen attributes of Mercy that the Congregation of Israel [knesset Yisrael], which is *Malkhut*, inherit from above, from the thirteen attributes of *Arikh Anpin*, and all of them are

attached to one root, which is one covenant, i.e. *Yesod* of *Zeir Anpin*, by whose means *Malkhut* receives the thirteen attributes of mercy of *Arikh Anpin*, and thus the root of the thirteen leaves of the rose that are beneath them is an example of the covenant which is the foundation [*Yesod*] of everything. The five strong leaves that surround it are the fifty gates, i.e. *Ḥesed*, *Gvurah*, *Tiferet*, *Netzaḥ*, and *Hod*, of *Binah*, each one of which is composed of ten. And they are five hundred years that the Tree of Life, which is *Zeir Anpin*, goes in, for he receives them in the place of *Binah*, whose *Sfirot* are in the secret of hundreds, and they are five hundred years.

395 The rose is witness to the Work of Creation (as above, 393), for all the Works of Creation are words known with understanding and that stand in the account of God of the Work of Creation, which is *Binah*. And there is a vision above and a vision below. A vision above, i.e. in the secret of the next world, which is *Binah*, and a vision below in the secret of the People of Israel [*Knesset Yisrael*], which is *Malkhut*.

396 The rose is witness to the Work of Creation, for it has all these signs, i.e. the thirteen attributes of mercy and the five *Sfirot* of *Ḥesed*, *Gvurah*, *Tiferet*, *Netzaḥ*, and *Hod*. For it is written: "In the beginning God created..." (Genesis 1:11). This is the rose, which is *Binah* and which is *Malkhut*, because there is a vision above and a vision below, as above in the preceding section. The thirteen leaves are the thirteen words from "In the beginning God" (Genesis 1:1) until "...the spirit of God" (ibid., v.2), namely: ...(1) the (2) heaven (3) and the (4) earth. (5) Now the earth (6) was (7) unformed (8) and void (9) and darkness was (10) upon (11) the face of (12) the deep (13). And the spirit... These, then, are the thirteen leaves of the rose that allude to the thirteen attributes. The five stronger leaves that surround these thirteen are: (1) hovered (2) over (3) the face of (4) the

waters. (5) And (God) said from the word 'God' in the expression "And the spirit of God" until "God" in the expression, 'And God said' (v.3), exclusively. For there are five others that allude to the five *Sfirot*: *Ḥesed*, *Gvurah*, *Tiferet*, *Netzaḥ*, and *Hod*, as explained above. After this comes "Let there be light" (ibid., v.3), this being the main thing and the root of the rose, for all the stages are included in and attached to it. (And see the beginning of the Introduction to the *Sefer haZohar*.)

397 The rose is witness to the unity (as above, 393), for the five strong leaves are the roots and the unity by which these thirteen leaves are attached to them. The five words, "Hear, O-Israel, the-Lord our-God the-Lord", parallel the five leaves of the rose, while "is-one" is the main thing and the root to which all of them are attached, for the word *Eḥad* (one) is a secret, having the numerical value of thirteen [*Eḥad*: *aleph ḥet dalet*, 1 + 8 + 4 = 13]. And this is the King's ring.

C o m m e n t a r y :

The growth of the rose is with thirteen internal leaves and five external leaves, and the text says (393) that this *Shushan* is, in its two aspects of 13 and of 5, testimony to the Work of Creation, which is the secret of *Binah*, and testimony to the Peoplehood of Israel, which is the secret of *Malkhut*, and is testimony to the upper unity, which is the secret of *Zeir Anpin* and *Malkhut*. He then goes on to explain (394) that it is testimony to the Peoplehood of Israel, which is *Malkhut*, for in *Malkhut* are these two aspects; the five *Sfirot* of *Ḥesed*, *Gvurah*, *Tiferet*, *Netzaḥ*, and *Hod* that it receives from *Binah*, and within them the intelligence of greatness drawn down from the thirteen attributes of Mercy. And so the growth of the rose is testimony to the stages of *Malkhut*. Next he clarifies (395) how the rose is testimony to the Work of Creation, for these two aspects are also alluded to in the Work of Creation. The word `God' occurs there three times, namely: `God created' (v.1) `the spirit of God' (v.2), and `And God said' (v.3). Between `God created' and `the spirit of God' there are thirteen words that allude to the energies of greatness. Between `the spirit of God' and `And God said' there are five words, alluding to the five *Sfirot*: *Ḥesed*, *Gvurah*, *Tiferet*, *Netzaḥ*, and *Hod*. Thus both forms of growth of the rose (the thirteen inner leaves and the five external leaves) are testimony to the Work of Creation. Then he explains (397) how the two aspects of the rose are testimony to the unity of *Zeir Anpin* and *Malkhut*. Paralleling the five (outer) leaves of the rose are the five words of the *Shema Yisrael*: "Hear, O-Israel, the-Lord our-God, the-Lord", which are the *Sfirot*: *Ḥesed*, *Gvurah*, *Tiferet*, *Netzaḥ*, and *Hod*, since `hear' and `O Israel' are *Netzaḥ* and *Hod*, and `the-Lord' `our-God' and `the-Lord' are *Ḥesed*, *Gvurah*, and *Tiferet*. *Eḥad* (`one,' but with the numerical value of 13, as explained above) is the secret of *Malkhut* that joins together with *Ḥesed*, *Gvurah*, *Tiferet*, *Netzaḥ*, and *Hod* of *Zeir Anpin*. And by their unity (of *Malkhut* and *Zeir Anpin*) with each other are revealed the thirteen attributes of Mercy, which are the secret of the intelligences of greatness. And so he notes that *Eḥad* (one) has the numerical value of thirteen. And on the text: The five words: "Hear, O-Israel, the Lord our-God the-Lord" parallel the five leaves of the rose for these five words parallel the five strong (outer) leaves that grow on the rose, and they are themselves *Ḥesed*, *Gvurah*, *Tiferet*, *Netzaḥ*, and *Hod* of *Zeir Anpin* this being the main thing and the root to which all is attached. [i.e. *Malkhut*, with which all five *Sfirot* of *Zeir Anpin* become united.] `Is the secret, having the numerical value of thirteen': For with the uniting of *Malkhut* with *Zeir Anpin*, the thirteen attributes of Mercy are revealed. `The King's ring,' for therefore *Malkhut* is called the King's ring, i.e. His seal, inasmuch as the perfection of His illumination is dependent on *Malkhut*.

398 **Come and see: As "a rose among the thorns" (Song of Songs 2:2), so is Israel among the idol-worshipping nations and so is *Knesset Yisrael* (the Peoplehood of Israel), which is *Malkhut* among the many other angels appointed over the nations. So long as the rose stands there closed, unopened, it has no fragrance and one does not lift it out and remove it from among the thorns. When the rose is open and gives off a fragrance, then one takes it out from among the thorns. And *Knesset Yisrael* will benefit from them, as it is said: "Open to me, my sister, my love" (Song of Songs 5:2). And the Holy One, blessed be He, only sent to us the eagle who brought the rose (as above, 392) so that we should continue on our journey with the *Shekhinah*.**

Commentary:

Malkhut, when receiving from the left column, is closed and has no fragrance, that is, no illumination of *Ḥokhmah*, because the *Ḥokhmah* in it is lacking *ḥasadim*, and *Ḥokhmah* cannot illuminate without *ḥasadim* (as above, *Bereshith Aleph*, page 47, q.v.). But after it receives strength from *Zeir Anpin*, which is the central column, it then opens up from having been closed and gives off a good fragrance, which is the secret of the illumination of *Ḥokhmah* attired in the *ḥasadim* of *Zeir Anpin*, and this is the secret of the verse: "Open to me, my sister, my love" (Song of Songs 5:2)

INTERNAL ORGANS

399 **Rabbi Elazar said to his father: We have already heard the exposition of the closed organs, i.e. the external limbs, in the secret of the sacrifice, but what is the secret of the other organs, the inner ones? Said Rabbi Shimon to Rabbi Elazar: Elazar, my son, all the other organs that are internal have a supreme secret.**

400 Come and see: About the heart we have already learned: The heart is a burning fire, and if the Supreme King had not arranged for it the wings of the lung that bring to it a breeze from the wind that blows with the upper spices, i.e. from the upper three *Sfirot* of *Zeir Anpin*, the heart would burn up the whole world in a single moment.

Commentary:

For the left column of *Binah* controls the heart, which, from lack of ḥasadim, can burn up the world. And the lung, which is the secret of the right column, which is the secret of *Ḥesed*, and therefore of the wind, which is the secret of the *Ḥesed* of the right that is drawn down from the upper three *Sfirot* of *Zeir Anpin*, sweetens it. (And see below in the Commentator's Interpolation, Paragraph 3).

401 He began by quoting: "Then the Lord caused to rain upon Sodom and upon Gomorrah brimstone and fire" (Genesis 19:24). Why did he burn them? Because at that time the wings of the lung did not blow a wind on the illumination of the left that is in the heart. And thus it was the illumination of the left that burnt them up. And the secret of these wings of the lung is the secret of the verse: "The wings of the dove are covered with silver" (Psalms 68:14). For 'dove,' which is the secret of *Malkhut*, which moved from the left of *Binah*, from the aspect of the heart, has to be covered with silver, which is the secret of *ḥasadim*. And when it is covered with silver it is the secret of the angels Raphael and Tzidkiel, which are drawn down from it for the health and salvation of the world. And it is said about them: "Who makes winds His messengers" (Psalms 104:4), i.e. permanently to blow on the heart, i.e to illuminate with *ḥasadim*.

THE FAITHFUL SHEPHERD

402 And in the first section, the Faithful Shepherd said to Rabbi Shimon: Holy Luminary, everything that you have said is good, but the brain is water, ie. *Ḥokhmah* that is on the right, which is the secret of *ḥasadim*, (as above 204, q.v.); the heart is fire, which is the secret of the *Ḥokhmah* which is in the left column of *Binah*, which is the secret of Judgments, and the two of them are Mercy and Judgment. This, the brain, is the Throne of Mercy, while the other, the heart, is the Throne of Judgment. And the Holy One, blessed be He, is the King who stands up from the Throne of Judgment which is the heart, and sits down on the Throne of Mercy which is the brain.

403 When iniquities multiply in the organs and in the arteries of the heart, which is the Throne of Judgment, it is said of the heart: "And the king arose in his wrath from the banquet of wine" (Esther 7:7), which is the wine of the Torah. But when the wings of the lung blow on the heart, it is said: "Then the king's anger was assuaged" (ibid., v.10), for the two wings of the lung are the secret of the verse: "And the *Kr'uvim* shall spread out their wings, screening the ark-cover with their wings" (Exodus 25:20). This is the atonement of the heart.

Commentary:

The heart [lev: lamed bet, 30 + 2 = 32] is the secret of the 32 paths of *Ḥokhmah*, i.e. *Ḥokhmah* of the left of *Binah*, and this is a burning fire, as above. Because at the time of revelations of *Ḥokhmah*, harsh Judgments accompany it to burn up the wicked and the external ones and all those who want to come close and draw down the *Ḥokhmah*, downwards from above (as above, *Idra Rabba*, 219), and the Judgments are not quieted until the control of ḥasadim commences, i.e. the secret of the wind blowing in the two wings of the lung, as above. And this is the secret of the verse, "And the king arose" (Esther 7:7), for the illumination of *Ḥokhmah* is called arising. And Scripture says that "the king arose in his wrath" (ibid.,) i.e. with the revelation of the harsh Judgments that are with the illumination of *Ḥokhmah*. "And he arose from the banquet of wine", for this arising is from the aspect of the banquet of wine, which is *Ḥokhmah* that is on the left (as above, *Bereshith Bet*, page 37, q.v.). And on the text: And in the arteries of the heart, which is the Throne of Judgment, it is said of the heart: "And the king arose in his wrath from the banquet of wine" (Esther 7:7). For the illumination of *Ḥokhmah* that is in the heart, which is the secret of the illumination of *Ḥokhmah* that is on the left of *Binah*, does not illuminate except at the time of the appearance of harsh Judgments. This is the secret of "And the king arose" (in the illumination of *Ḥokhmah*) "in his wrath" (with harsh Judgments). And on the text: "From the banquet of wine," which is the wine of the Torah: This teaches that the discussion is about the illumination of *Ḥokhmah*, for *Zeir Anpin*, who is called Torah, draws it down. For it is the *Ḥokhmah* of the left of *Binah*, and, as above, the Judgments are not quieted until the control of ḥasadim commences. And on the text: But when the wings of the lung blow on the heart, it is said: "Then the king's anger was assuaged" (Esther 7:10), i.e. when the wind of the wings of the lung, which is *Ḥesed*, is in control.

404 And in what way was the king's anger assuaged? It was because "And he heard the Voice" (Numbers 7:89), this being the voice of the Torah, the voice of the recital of the *Shema Yisrael*, which is the central column, which is *ḥasadim*, that unites the right and the left with each other under the control of the ḥasadim. And then the Judgments are quieted, as explained in the previous paragraph. "And he spoke to Him" (ibid.), which is the secret to the revelation of *Ḥokhmah* that is in

Malkhut, **which is called speech, and this is in the prayer that is formulated in the mouth, which is "O Lord, open my lips, and my mouth will declare Your praise" [Psalms 51:17 this being the verse that is said silently by the reader prior to the recital of the *Shemoneh Esreh* which is *Malkhut.*]**

405 And that wind that blows in the wings of the lung, i.e. the *ḥasadim* that are revealed by *Ḥokhmah* of the right, as above in the preceding paragraph, carries the voice out through the trachea, which is "Get wisdom, get knowledge" (Proverbs 4:5). [This verse could also be rendered: The pipe of *Ḥokhmah,* the pipe of *Binah,* in reference to the windpipe, the trachea — tr.]. For the voice, which is *Zeir Anpin,* i.e. *vav,* is *Ben Yah* (the son of *Yah*), which are *Ḥokhmah* and *Binah.* And about this it is said: "Thus says the Lord God: Come from the four winds [*ruaḥ*], O breath [*ruaḥ*]" (Ezekiel 37:9). And the four are the four letters of the holy Name (Tetragrammaton) [*yud hei vav* and *hei*] of *Zeir Anpin.* And this is the wind that bangs on all the arteries of the heart, about which it is said: "Whither the spirit (wind) was to go, they went" (Ezekiel 1:12).

406 The Holy Luminary said to the Faithful Shepherd: Certainly, O Faithful Shepherd, it is your level at which it is said: "And the anger of the king was assuaged" (Esther 7:10), for the level of the Faithful Shepherd is the central column, which is *Zeir Anpin,* that is called voice, by which the Judgments are quieted, as above. And the proof of this is as follows: The word 'assuaged' is *shakhakhah* [*shin kaf kaf hei*]. The word for 'that is in such a case' in the verse: "Happy is the people that is in such a case" (Psalms 144:15) is *shakhakhah* [*shin kaf kaf hei*], and the numerical value of these two words, of identical consonantal spelling, is 300 + 20 + 20 + 5 = 345, which is the same as the numerical value of the letters of the name Moses (i.e. the Faithful Shepherd) [*Mosheh*: *mem shin hei,* 40 + 300 + 5 = 345] The Faithful Shepherd said to

him (to Rabbi Shimon): Blessed are you, O Holy Luminary, for you are the lamp that burns before the King and His matron. The lamp of the Lord is your soul. cf. "The spirit of man is the lamp of the Lord" (Proverbs 20:27).

407 Rabbi Shimon said to the Faithful Shepherd: You have given an explanation for the brain, the heart, and the wings of the lungs, but what about the two kidneys? What are they? Replied the Faithful Shepherd: We learned about the wings of the lungs: "Who makes winds His messengers" (Psalms 104:4), this being the secret of *ḥasadim,* which are called winds. The kidneys are "The flaming fire, His ministers" (ibid.), i.e. Judgments, and the two wings of the lung with the two kidneys stand for the four beings of the Throne, where the wings of the lung are lion and eagle, which are *ḥasadim,* and the two kidneys are ox and man, which are *Gvuroth.* And the Throne is the heart that is in the middle, which is the Throne of Judgment.

408 And so, too, does the brain have four beings, for the brain is the Throne of Mercy. And who might they be? They are sight, hearing, smell, and speech. Sight is lion, i.e. *Ḥokhmah.* Hearing is ox, i.e. *Binah.* Smell is eagle, i.e. *Zeir Anpin,* and each of them has four countenances and four wings. Speech is man, i.e. *Malkhut.* He is attached above, i.e. on the mouth of the head, and below on the body. For about the arms of the body, it is said: "Our hands are spread forth as the eagles of the heavens." Body is man [according to the Ashlag version, the old edition of the Zohar, which reads "the body is lion," should read "the body is man"], that is to say that he is in the aspect of *Malkhut,* which clings to the central column, which is body. And about the thighs it is written: "And the sole of their feet was like the sole of a calf's foot" (Ezekiel 1:7), which incline to the face of ox, which is *Gvurah.* And about the body, which is man, it is called "the second chariot" (Genesis 41:43), i.e. the chariot of

***Malkhut*, which is called second. And the word for second is *mishneh*, but this can also be read as Mishnah, and Mishnah is *Malkhut*.**

C o m m e n t a r y :

What we have here is the clarification of three chariots.

a) The Chariot of the brain, which is the Throne of Mercy, whose four beings, *Ḥokhmah*, *Binah*, *Tiferet*, and *Malkhut*, are sight, hearing, smell, and speech.

b) The Chariot of the heart, which is the Throne of Judgment, whose four beings, *Ḥesed*, *Gvurah*, *Tiferet*, and *Malkhut* are the two wings of the lung, both of which are *ḥasadim*, (but the right and left of *ḥasadim*), and the two kidneys, both of which are *Gvurah*, (but the right and the left of *Gvurah*).

c) The Chariot of the body, that contains the two subdivisions in the secret of the arms, both of which are Mercy, and are both, therefore, called eagles of the heavens. And they are similar to the previously mentioned wings of the lung. And the Chariot of the Body also has two thighs, both of which are *Gvurah*, similar to the two kidneys, and it is therefore said about both of them: "And the sole of their feet is like the sole of a calf's foot" (Ezekiel 1:7), which is ox, *Gvurah*. And the body which includes all of them is the secret of *Malkhut*, which is the face of man that is superimposed on the arms and the thighs. And the text says that the body is therefore called the second chariot, although it is in fact the third, as there is a play on the words *mishneh* (second) Mishnah, the latter of which is a synonym for *Malkhut*, and he does not really mean to say that it is the second chariot. And the reason why he does not consider *Zeir Anpin* to be a chariot is because there is no innovation in it. For he considers that the first Throne, which is the brain, which is the Throne of Mercy, *Zeir Anpin* is in this aspect. The second Throne is the Throne of Judgment, which is *Binah*, for the root of the left column is in it. The Third Throne is the Throne of Majesty (*Malkhut*), for in it the left column is corrected by the central column. Thus all the aspects are clarified, and there is no more to consider.

409 What is the spleen? The Holy Luminary, i.e. Rabbi Shimon, began: "I considered all the oppressions that are done under the sun; and behold the tears of those who are oppressed" (Ecclesiastes 4:1). Who are those who are oppressed? They are the children who are still in need of their mother when the Angel of Death takes them from the world. And is it indeed the case that the Angel of Death kills them, that he oppresses them? Not really, for Scripture adds: "and on the side of their oppressors there was power, but they had no comforter" (ibid.). Then who is that power that kills them? The answer to this is to be found in the verse: "Let there be lights [*meoroth*: *mem aleph resh tav*] in the firmament of heaven" (Genesis 1:14). And the word "*meoroth*" is written in the abbreviated spelling, i.e. without a *vav*, and can be read *meerath* (the curse of) (See 325, above). The reference, therefore, is to Lillith, who is appointed over that oppressor.

410 And Lillith, is called spleen, and she goes to play with the children, later killing them, and makes of them anger and tears, to bewail them. The spleen goes to the kind of the liver, which is Samael, who is the Angel of Death. This, i.e. the liver, was created on the second day of the Work of Creation, while the other, i.e. the spleen, was created on the fourth day of the Work of Creation. And for this reason it is not a good omen to commence something on Mondays (the second day of the week) or on

Wednesdays (the fourth day of the week). Liver is death for adults; spleen is death for children.

Commentary:

The second day of Creation is *Gvurah*, i.e. the left column, about which it is said: "Sin couches at the door" (Genesis 4:7). For at the end of the left column emerged Samael, who is the Angel of Death, and who is called liver, and with the gall that is in the liver takes the souls of men and puts them to death, for the gall is the sword of the Angel of Death (as above, 364). The liver is the Judgments of the Male and the gall is the aspect of the Judgments of the Lock, from which is death (as above, *Vayetze*, page 16), and this emerged at the end of the left column, which is the second day of the Work of Creation. And the fourth day of the Work of Creation, on which *Malkhut* emanated and emerged initially in the aspect of the left column, in the secret of the "two great lights" (Genesis 1:16), was like the second day, which is the secret of the first state of *Malkhut*. And subsequently it was diminished to a point under *Yesod* and was re-built from the aspect of the chest and below of *Zeir Anpin*, as stated above (*Bereshith Aleph* 110-115). And from the diminishment of the moon that took place emerged the shell that is called Lillith. And Lillith is under *Malkhut*, as Samael is under the left column.

And those children who are still in need of their mother are the secret of those who received intelligences from the first state of *Malkhut*, which are the secret of the energies of *Yenikah* (suckling), for in control thereof were the upper three *Sfirot* of the left column, which is the secret of the upper three *Sfirot* of *Ḥokhmah*, which Lillith overcomes at the time of the diminution of the moon, killing them and taking their souls. And they are compared to those who are oppressed, for they are children in whom there is no fault, but Lillith casts her rule over them, for no other reason than because of the diminution of the moon. This is different in the case of those over whom the Angel of Death has control, because in them there is a fault from the Lock, as noted above (*Vayetze*, page 16), and therefore the verse "behold the tears of such as are oppressed" (Ecclesiastes 4:1) is referred to them, and it is called spleen.

And it follows that spleen and liver are two of a kind, for both of them come from the foulness that is the left column. The difference between them is that the liver, which is Samael and the Angel of Death, comes from the second day, which is the left column itself, while the spleen, which is Lillith, is the foulness of *Malkhut* which is constructed from the left column, and is the aspect of the fourth day. And on the text: The spleen goes to the kind of the liver, for both of them are from the foulness of the left column. This, i.e. the liver, was created on the second day, i.e. from the left column itself. The other, i.e. the spleen, was created on the fourth day, i.e. from *Malkhut* that is constructed from the left. And for this reason it is not a good omen to commence something on Mondays or Wednesdays, for both of them give rise to angels of death: the liver, which is the Angel of Death, Samael, means death for adults, i.e. puts to death all the adults, as stated. The spleen, which is Lillith, is death for children, for, as noted, it puts to death only the children who are in the aspect of intelligences of *Yenikah* (suckling).

THE FAITHFUL SHEPHERD

411 And in the first section, said the Faithful Shepherd, that is certainly how it is, for the liver is the level of Esau, and Esau is Edom (Genesis 36:1), i.e. is all blood (dam), and gathers in all blood whether pure or venous, and does not differentiate between good and bad, between impure blood and pure blood, for he makes no distinction between them. But the heart, which is Israel, does distinguish

between good and bad, between impure blood and pure blood, and takes only the clear and the clean of that blood, like one who picks food out of the waste matter. (And see Commentator's Interpolation below, paragraph 12).

412 And after the heart, which is Jacob, i.e. *Zeir Anpin*, takes the clear blood which is at the top, and the liver, which is Esau, i.e. Samael, remains in the waste matter of the blood, he is angered at him with the gall, which is Gehenna (Hell), which was created on the second day of the Work of Creation (cf. *Talmud Bavli, Pesaḥim* 54a), which is the death of all the adults (as above, 410), while the gall is the wicked Female of Samael, which is called 'a strange fire'(cf. Numbers 3:4), 'hard bondage' (cf. Deuteronomy 26:6), and idolatry. (And see Commentator's Interpolation below, paragraph 414).

413 And since the anger awakens from it, from the gall, towards the liver, the sages taught in the Mishnah: Anyone who is angry is as though he worshiped idols. [This does not occur in our text of the Mishnah, although the identical statement is quoted by others, e.g. Maimonides in his Commentary on the Mishnah; and similar statements are to be found in rabbinic literature, e.g. "For one who is angry even the *Shekhinah* appears unimportant" (*Talmud Bavli, Nedarim* 22b, top)]. And furthermore, any burning up and temperature that comes with any of the illnesses of the parts of the body is only from the gall, for, at the time of illness, it engulfs the arteries of the liver in flames and wishes to burn up the whole body. It is like a storm in the sea and its waves reach up to the skies and want to break out of their limits and destroy the world. And this would indeed happen were it not for the *Shekhinah*, which is for a sick person like the sand to the sea, surrounding it so that it should not break out. So, too, is the *Shekhinah* enwrapping the body and assisting it, as it

is written: "The Lord will support him on his sick-bed" (Psalms 41:4).

414 And for this reason the sages of the Mishnah taught: One who visits a sick person should not sit at the head of the bed because the *Shekhinah* is over his head, nor at the foot of the bed because the Angel of Death is at his feet (cf. *Talmud Bavli, Shabbat* 12b). And this is not the case for every person, but just for ordinary people. In the case of the perfectly righteous "The Lord will support him on his sick-bed" (Psalms 41:4), i.e. at his head, and the *Shekhinah* enwraps his body up to his feet. And this is why it was said about Jacob: "He gathered up his feet into the bed" (Genesis 49:33). This is the *Shekhinah,* about which it is said: "And the earth is My footstool" (Isaiah 66:1), and the *Shekhinah* is also called bed. In the case of the thoroughly wicked person, the Angel of Death surrounds him on every side, and this is the evil inclination for the Angel of Death is the evil inclination, which the Angel of Death surrounds in every side and his sword is the gall (as above, 364), whose edges turn green with one drop of the three drops that the gall sprinkles on it (as above, *Pikudei* 916), as it is written: "But her end is bitter (same word as for `gall') as wormwood, sharp as a two-edged sword" (Proverbs 5:4). Liver is Male, which is Samael, and the lobe of the liver is his Female. (And see Commentator's Interpolation below, paragraph 14.)

415 The stomach is one part in sixty of death and is called `a deep sleep' (Genesis 2:21) since "the stomach sleeps" (*Talmud Bavli, Berakhot* 61b top), and is Asirta, which is the sixth stage of the Angel of Death (as above, *Pikudei* 919); and because it came from afar it is from the side of death, but is not death itself. The hint is "sleep is one sixtieth part of death" (*Talmud Berakhot,* 57b). (See Commentator's Interpolation, paragraph 11).

THE FAITHFUL SHEPHERD

416 The Faithful Shepherd

said: Since this body is of "the tree of the knowledge of good and evil" (Genesis 2:9), there is no part of the body that does not have in it both the evil inclination and the good inclination, this being the case for ordinary mortals. In the case of the perfectly righteous, each part does indeed have two inclinations, which are male and female, but both of them are good, being like the bride and the bridegroom. The utterly wicked have in each part of their bodies two evil inclinations, male and female, from the side of Samael and Serpent.

417 And it follows from this that, in terms of the tree of knowledge of good and evil, in the case of ordinary mortals, there are in the stomach two levels: good and evil. And this indeed is what the sages taught: the stomach is sleep (*Talmud Bavli, Berakhot* 61b), and there is sleep that is one-sixtieth part of death (*Talmud Bavli, Berakhot* 57b). And there is also sleep that is one sixtieth part of prophecy (cf. *Talmud Bavli, Berakhot* 57b: A dream is one sixtieth part of prophecy). And for this reason, the heads of the Academy taught: "It is written: 'The dreams speak falsely' (Zekhariah 10:2), and it is also written: 'I (God) do speak with him in a dream'" (Numbers 12:6). There is no contradiction here. In the former case it is through a demon, i.e. the evil forces from the side of the evil in a man's sleep. And in the latter case it is through an angel, which is from the good side in a man's sleep (cf. *Talmud Bavli, Berakhot* 55b). A dream through an angel is one sixtieth part of prophecy. A dream through a demon, which is falsehood, is from the side of death, and is straw. Thus indeed was it taught: "(Said Rabbi Yoḥanan in the name of Rabbi Shimon bar Yoḥai:) Just as wheat cannot be without straw, so there cannot be a dream without some nonsense" (*Talmud Bavli, Berakhot* 55a bot).

418 The *omasum* is the peeled gizzard, i.e. it is like the peeled gizzard of a bird (see Rashi on *Talmud Bavli, Berakhot* 61b, top), and the sages taught: the gizzard grinds

(the food) (*Berakhot* 61b, top), for it takes everything and pulverizes the food, sending it to all the parts. If the parts are without iniquities, it is as the sages taught, that there are matters that delay the sacrifice, and the one who is sent by the Holy One, blessed be He, to receive His offering, the sacrifice, does not descend to accept it. For there is an offering that the Holy One, blessed be He, receives through the lion, as it is said: "And they four had the face of a lion on the right side" (Ezekiel 1:10), and the Holy One, blessed be He, rides on him, and comes down with him to receive that offering. And there is an offering that He receives through the ox, as it is said: "And they four had the face of an ox on the left side" (ibid.).

Commentary:

The word that is here translated "*omasum*" is according to the Rashi's remarks on *Berakhot* 61b. However, in *Midrash Leviticus Rabba*, chapter 3, it is written: The food goes from the gullet into the stomach and from the stomach to the omasum. The word that Rashi understands to mean `*omasum*' here means `stomach' (and it would, indeed, seem to derive from the same Greek word as the English word `stomach'). (See Commentator's Interpolation, paragraph 414).

419 And there is an offering that He receives through the eagle, as it is written: "the four also had the face of an eagle" (Ezekiel 1:10), and they are "two turtle-doves or two young pigeons" (e.g. Leviticus 5:7). And there is an offering that He receives by Man, about whom it is written: "When any man of you brings an offering to the Lord" (Leviticus 1:2), in the form of the same one about whom it is written: "As for the likeness of their faces, they had the face of a man" (Ezekiel 1:10). The

explanation here is that the four beings are the secret of the four letters of the holy Name (Tetragrammaton) [*yud hei vav* and *hei*], lion ox being *yud hei*, and eagle man being *vav* hei. For the Tetragrammaton descends on them to receive the sacrifice, which is the secret of the four beings.

420 And there are natural beings i.e. angels appointed over bodies that are of the four basic elements: fire, wind, water, and earth, and they are pure. Opposite them are four beings of prey, i.e. the angels of destruction, who, being impure, are appointed over the four galls, namely: white gall, red gall, green gall, black gall, who are the demons of the world (as above, 413), for all temperature in every illness comes from the gall.

421 And there are intelligent beings, namely: The four angels Michael, Gabriel, Uriel, Raphael, who surround the Throne, which is *Malkhut*. And above them and higher than they are, the divine beings from the side of Holiness, i.e. *Ḥesed, Gvurah, Tiferet,* and *Malkhut* of *Zeir Anpin*. There are also the beings of the evil forces, and they are called "other gods" (cf. Deuteronomy 5:7), while the divine beings of holiness are called "the living God" (ibid, v. 23) and those divine beings of holiness are called "Gods of Godliness", and the Prime Cause over everything is "God, the Lord over all his works" (Hymn inserted on Sabbath and Festival into the first blessing before the morning *Shema Yisrael*). Like should be attracted to like and so, since there are other gods, it is said about them: "He who sacrifices to the gods, save to the Lord only, shall be utterly destroyed." (Exodus 22:20). And this is so that the living God should not be mingled with the other gods.

422 And this gizzard takes and grinds and distributes in all directions, below, i.e. to the parts of the body, and from it are nourished the lower beings. And from those dregs all those spirits and other parties who take

their nourishment at night drink below, from those parts and fats that are burnt on the altar at night (cf. Leviticus 6:2). And the remainder is taken by the other parts, the liver taking everything and sacrificing to the heart, as we have learned (above, 374), and this is what is written: "...the face of a lion on the right side" (Ezekiel 1:10). Thus there appears on the altar a lion-like image that devours the sacrifices. (cf. *Talmud Bavli, Yoma* 21b). From here on all the other parts are in the secret of the body on the same pattern as above.

THE FAITHFUL SHEPHERD

423 Said the Faithful Shepherd to Rabbi Shimon: Holy Luminary, it is sure that *omasum* takes everything up to six hours and bakes. For the gizzard, which is the *omasum* (as above, 418), is a baker. And the lung is a steward. The heart is the King, and these two, the *omasum* and the lung, are certainly the baker and the steward who give to the King of the choicest of food and drinks, for He is the head of them all and the choicest of them all. And this is the meaning of what is written: "I have gathered my myrrh with my spice; I have eaten my honeycomb with my honey; I have drunk my wine with my milk" (Song of Songs 5:1). And the verse continues: "Eat, O companions. Drink, yea, drink abundantly, O beloved ones" (ibid.). The companions are the other parts of the body, which are the hosts and camps of the King who distributes food to them by means of the chief baker, which is the *omasum*, while the drink is by means of the chief steward, which is the lung. (See the Commentator's Interpolation, paragraph 10).

424 And the liver is on the right side of man, wherefore: "And they four had the face of a lion on the right side" (Ezekiel 1:10), i.e. to the right of the King, which is the heart. The spleen is to the left, and they are of the evil forces. For the liver is Samael, the minister of Esau, and the spleen is Lillith, as explained above. "And the face of an ox on the left side" (ibid.), refers to the pouring out of wine mixed with water before the King, for wine is of the left side. And the lion devouring the sacrifices is the liver, who collects together the food, i.e. the prayer in the stead of the sacrifices, before the King, which is the heart. He is, therefore, on the right, for eating comes from the right and the wine from the left. And all this refers to the time of Exile, as is explained below. (And see Commentator's Interpolation, paragraph 12).

425 But there is a difficulty here. If the liver is Esau, how does it arrange food for the heart, which is Jacob (as above, 411)? The answer is that the heart is certainly like Isaac, i.e. the left column, and the liver is Esau, who hunted venison. (And Esau said to Isaac:) "Let my father arise and eat of his son's venison" (Genesis 27:31). This refers to the prayers of the poor that are sent away and are not accepted on high. And Isaac suffers trouble and anguish because they do not know how to direct the prayer. This is why Esau did not say "eat of my venison" but "eat of his son's venison," i.e. of Israel, as it is written: "Israel is My son, My first-born" (Exodus 4:22). Likewise, Israel in Exile has no food except through the nations of the world. (And see Commentator's Interpolation, paragraph 13).

426 But when they are in the Land of Israel, their food is through the *Shekhinah*, and the two wings of the lung will give drink to the nation of Israel, for they are the chief butler, as above. And the two kidneys, which are the chief baker, cook the seed that descends from the brain and cook the water that they receive from the wings of the lung. And after the King, which is the heart, has eaten, it is said of its two kidneys: "Eat, O companions" (Song of Songs 5:1), and of the two wings of the lung: "Drink, yea, drink abundantly, O beloved ones" (ibid.). (And see Commentator's Interpolation, paragraph 21).

427 For the heart is the Throne of Judgment, and the four beings that are its messengers are the two wings of the lung and the two kidneys, namely: *Ḥesed, Gvurah, Netzaḥ,* and *Hod,* for the wings of the lung are the secret of "Their faces and their wings were stretched upwards" (Ezekiel 1:17) to welcome the King, which is "The spirit of wisdom and understanding, the spirit of counsel and might, the spirit of knowledge and of the fear of the Lord" (Isaiah 11:2) (as above, 310), for it is He who sits on the Throne, which is the heart, which is the Throne of Judgment, and all the pulse beats follow after it as soldiers after their king. (And see Commentator's Interpolation, paragraph 22).

428 And the wind that blows from the wings of the lung blows through the two orifices of the nose (and see above, 206), and it is cold and chilled on the left and warm on the right. And from the point of view of the brain, which is the Throne of Mercy, the cold wind is to the right, which is *Ḥesed,* and the warm is to the left, which is *Gvurah,* for that is where the heart is. And the brain is tempered between the two of them, the right and the left, and so the heart is blended of cold and hot, i.e. by means of the wind of the wings of the lung that blows on it, and the brain also is blended of cold and hot, for the brain and the heart receive from each other.

429 And the spleen, with its camps, which are the bondmen and bondwomen, takes the dregs of everything. And Solomon said about them: "I acquired men-servants and maid-servants" (Ecclesiastes 11:7). The two kidneys are called fire-offerings, named after the heavenly fire-offerings, about which it is said: "They shall eat the offerings of the Lord made by fire, and His inheritance" (Leviticus 18:1).

430 And in the trachea there are six cartilage rings, about which it is said: "Ascribe unto the Lord, O sons of might" (Psalms 29:1), for ascending through them is the voice that subdivides into the six voices of the *Shekhinah*, while the seventh ascends to the mouth, which is the Throne. And the six cartilage rings of the trachea are like the six steps of the King's Throne, which is the mouth, and the trachea is a ladder with "the angels of God ascending and descending on it" (Genesis 28:12), for the angels of God are the vapors that ascend from the heart, while the spirits of air descend into the heart to cool its heat, so that it should not burn the body up.

431 And when the spirit descends, it does so in a number of spirits, like a king with the soldiers, and the wings of the lung welcome the spirit which is as a king over them, as I have noted: "And their faces and their wings were stretched out" (Ezekiel 1:17), this being in order to welcome the King over them (as above, 427), and also: "And the *Kr'uvim* shall spread out their wings on high" (Exodus 25:20).

432 If the parts of man are meritorious in keeping the precepts of the Supreme King, who is the Holy Spirit descending on the ladder (which is the throat) in a number of holy spirits (about which it is said: "Who makes winds His messengers" [Psalms 104:4]), the Supreme King will descend to accept the vapors that are in the heart, about which it is said: "The flaming fire His ministers" (ibid.). And it is also said about them: "The voice of the Lord hews out flames of fire" (Psalms 29:7), because the heart is 'The Lord' [*aleph dalet nun yud*], from whom ascend the flames of fire in the mouth, which is the Tetragrammaton [*yud hei vav* and *hei*]. For a number of spirits of holiness descend with him, that is from the four letters of the Tetragrammaton [*yud hei vav* and *hei*], concerning which it is said: "Come from the four winds, O breath" (Ezekiel 37:9). (See Commentator's Interpolation, paragraph 17).

433 The trachea [*kaneh*: *kuf nun hei*] is "Get [*kaneh*: *kuf nun hei*] wisdom [*Ḥokhmah*], get [*kaneh*: *kuf nun hei*] understanding [*Binah*]" (Proverbs 4:5), for they are to the right of the trachea, which is *Ḥesed*, this being the secret of "Get wisdom", and to the left of the trachea, which is *Gvurah*, this being the secret of "Get understanding." *Tiferet* is in the middle of the trachea, and is a ladder and the secret of *Da'at*. And the body has six extremities, namely: The two arms which are *Ḥesed* and *Gvurah*, the torso and the covenant which are *Tiferet* and *Yesod*, and the two thighs which are *Netzaḥ* and *Hod*. And the six extremities of the body parallel the six cartilage rings of the trachea. (See Commentator's Interpolation, paragraph 18).

434 And when the Tetragrammaton [*yud hei vav* and *hei*] descends to the heart, to 'The Lord' [*aleph dalet nun yud*], Judgment joins with Mercy in the heart, making: *yud aleph hei dalet vav* nun hei yud [the combination of the letters of the Tetragrammaton and of 'The Lord']. And when 'The Lord' ascends to the mouth at "Lord, open my lips" (Psalms 51:17 and introduction to the *Shemoneh Esreh*) to welcome the Tetragrammaton in the mouth, the two names become there one union, namely: *yud aleph hei dalet vav* nun hei yud, just as they were combined in the heart. For this reason the sages of the Mishnah taught: "No one whose character does not correspond to his exterior may enter the study house" (*Talmud Bavli, Berakhot* 28a in the name of Rabban Gamliel), i.e. who does not have mouth and heart the same [that is, saying one thing and thinking something else]. For just as there is a unity of the Tetragrammaton and 'The Lord' in the heart, there will also be a unity of the Tetragrammaton and 'The Lord' in the mouth. (See Commentator's Interpolation, paragraph 17).

435 The six cartilage rings of the trachea are combined together, and they are called "the sons of might" [*elim*: *aleph lamed yud mem*] (Psalms 29:1).

And they give forth a wind to blow over the world, and they come from the side of *Gvurah* (might), and when they join together they are like a *shofar*, which is the secret of *Binah*, and they are called *shofar*, which is the secret of the *shofar* (horn) of Isaac's ram [*ayil*: *aleph yud lamed*] (cf. Genesis 22:13). And they are "rams [*elim*] of the breed of Bashan" (Deuteronomy 32:14). As it is written: "Ascribe to the Lord, O sons of might [*elim*]" (Psalms 29:1), for they are the *elim* (rams/mighty ones) of Isaac that bring forth spirit and voice. And that voice goes out and meets with rain clouds and is heard by the creatures of the outside. It is thus written: "But the thunder of his mighty deeds who can understand?" (Job 26:14), for they certainly come from the side of *Gvurah*. And for this reason: "The God of glory makes to thunder, even the Lord upon many waters" (Psalms 29:3). It is not written: "The God of glory thunders" but "The God of glory makes to thunder," the meaning of which is that He makes others do the thundering, namely the sons of the mighty. And there is none that knows the praise of this voice, which is why it is written "who can understand?" (Job 26:14). (See Commentator's Interpolation, paragraph 18).

THE FAITHFUL SHEPHERD

436 And in the first part, the Faithful Shepherd started by saying: Woe to those people whose hearts are closed and whose eyes are unseeing, who do not know the parts of their own body and according to what they are arranged. For the trachea is composed of three forces:
a) Vapor; [*hevel*: *hei, bet, lamed*] when letters rearranged make up "flame"; [*lahav*: *lamed, hei, bet*] which is "the flaming fire" (Psalms 104:4) that issues from the heart and which is divided into seven vapors or vanities as mentioned by Ecclesiastes.
b) Air, which enters it (the trachea) from outside.
c) Water, of the wings of the lung, which are attached to the trachea. And from these three, that is from water, wind, and

fire, is made voice, and each one is subdivided into seven, and they are seven flames, seven airs, and seven brooks. (See Commentator's #Interpolation, paragraph 19).

437 And when the flames of the heart meet with the rain clouds, which are the wings of the lung, by way of the trachea of the lung, the result is: "But the thunder of his mighty deeds who can understand?" (Job 26:14). For therein the heart understands [*mevin*] with *Binah*, which is in the heart on the left, which is *Gvurah*. And *Ḥesed* is to the right, which is the water of the wings of the lung, and *Ḥokhmah*, which is brain, is there. That is to say that *Ḥesed* and *Gvurah* ascend and become *Ḥokhmah* and *Binah*. And from it (the brain) comes "a fountain of gardens, a well of living waters, and flowing streams from Lebanon" (Song of Songs, 4:15), which is the whiteness [*lavnunit*] of the brain that flows through the trachea of the lung, after the clouds of *Binah* have ascended to the brain. (See Commentator's Interpolation, paragraph 19).

438 And the secret of the matter is in the verse: "Who is this who comes up out of the wilderness like pillars of smoke...?" (Song of Songs 3:6), for this is the smoke of the system that rises from the heart to the brain, which cannot be moved from its place by all the winds in the world. The letters of the word *Ḥokhmah* [*ḥet kaf mem hei*] form the two words *Koaḥ* [*kaf ḥet*] and *Mah* [*mem hei*], because it is *Koaḥ* (strength) in the heart and *Mah* (what) in the brain. The trachea is *Tiferet* and incorporates six *Sfirot*: *Ḥesed, Gvurah, Tiferet, Netzaḥ, Hod* and *Yesod*, which are the six stages to the Throne, which is Mother, so that *Ḥokhmah* will descend to it from the brain to the heart, for in it the heart understands. For this reason it is written: "Get [*k'neh*] wisdom [*Ḥokhmah*], get [*k'neh*] understanding [*Binah*]" (Proverbs 4:5), for Father, which is *Ḥokhmah*, descends in it, and Father ascends in it. And this is a

ladder on which two descend, for Father and Mother are incorporated in each other and descend from the brain to the heart, and ascend from the heart to the brain. (See Commentator's Interpolation, paragraph 19-20).

439 The esophagus, that swallows the food from where it (the food) enters all the parts, is the stage of offerings by fire. These offerings by fire draw near immediately, swallowing and taking everything from the upper fire that includes the offerings by fire. And this is the secret of the verse: "They shall eat the offerings of the Lord made by fire, and His inheritance" (Deuteronomy 18:1). These are the offerings by fire that devour and swallow, and the others do not so eat. (See Commentator's Interpolation, paragraph 7).

440 And all the people of the world on the outside know not how they are eaten nor do they know their secret, but the stages that are inside do know and they take from them (the offerings). For the esophagus cannot be examined from the outside, for they do not know, but on the inside they do know and take until it enters the mill and is pulverized and readied. And the liver takes everything, as we had learnt, but from those offerings by fire issue forth stages that take before the liver. And who are they? (What stages are these?) They are the molar teeth, which eat the sacrifices and grind (them). Therefore, on the destruction of the Temple, it is written: "And the grinders cease because they are few" (Ecclesiastes 12:3). The initial reference here is to the molar teeth. (And see Commentator's Interpolation, paragraph 6-7).

441 Once it (the food) has been ground, those who exercise control over them (the molar teeth) swallow and take (the food), and they are called the esophagus. Why is the esophagus [*veshet*: *vav shin tet*] so called? Because the shape of the first letter of the word, the *vav* is like a bowed-over esophagus.

The other two letters, the *shin* and the *tet*, form the word *shat*, 'went about,' for it goes about to drink wine and water, as it is written: "The people went about and gathered" (Numbers 11:8) food to eat and to drink wine and water, namely the libation of wine and the libation of water. (And see Commentator's Interpolation, paragraph 6, 8).

442 Those seraphs with their flames enter through the esophagus and are drawn into the lung, where they take a drink, and they are called lung, in one union with the lung and everything is absorbed into them. And each one of them takes as befits him. And on the destruction of the Temple, "And the grinders ceased because they were few" (Ecclesiastes 12:3), even all of them. (And see Commentator's Interpolation, 8). For their form and their food have been diminished, and there is no day that passes without a curse (*Mishnah, Sotah* 9,12). Rabbi Shimon lifted up his voice and said: Woe to Jerusalem the Holy City. Woe to the people that has lost all this goodness and the image of ministers, heroes, and officials has been reduced. The companions cried about this and said: Alas, Rabbi, when you depart from the world, who will reveal to us such deep and hidden secrets that have not been heard from the days of King Solomon until now? Happy is the generation that hears such matters! Happy is the generation amongst whom you are! Woe to the generation that will be orphaned without you!

Commentator's Interpolation

1) The sacrifice, or the prayer that is instead of the sacrifice, is the elevating of the Female Waters to unite the Female, which is 'The Lord' [*aleph dalet nun yud*], with the Tetragrammaton [*yud hei vav* and *hei*], which is *Zeir Anpin*. It is therefore discerned as eating, as it is written: "My food which is

presented unto Me for offerings" (Numbers 28:2). The body of man parallels the Tetragrammaton, incorporating all four of the worlds: *Atziluth*, *Briah*, *Yetzirah*, and *Assiah*, where from the head to the chest is *Atziluth* and *Briah*, the head paralleling *Zeir Anpin*, and the body to the chest parallels the Female, for Briah is the wife of *Atziluth*. From the chest down is *Yetzirah* and *Assiah*, and just as these two worlds of *Yetzirah* and *Assiah* are interwoven with the impure shells, so there are in the body of man, from the chest down, parts that parallel the shells of impurity, namely: the liver, the lobe of the liver, the gall, and the spleen. And the Zohar explains each one of these organs as it is in man: its root in the Tetragrammaton that is throughout *Atziluth*, *Briah*, *Yetzirah*, and *Assiah*, which is called man that is in *Atziluth*, *Briah*, *Yetzirah*, and *Assiah*, for all of the four worlds *Atziluth*, *Briah*, *Yetzirah*, and *Assiah* are considered as though one man; and the name of the Tetragrammaton as one, where *Atziluth* is the secret of *yud* (the first letter) and head, and *Briah* is the secret of *hei* (the second letter) down to the chest, and *Yetzirah* is the secret of *vav* (the third letter) and *Assiah* the secret of the final *hei* (last letter), and *Yetzirah* and *Assiah* are from the chest downwards. And having explained the root of every organ and what it is in Man of *Atziluth*, *Briah*, *Yetzirah*, and *Assiah*, he goes on to explain the act of the sacrifice that a man brings, or the prayer that he prays: how it ascends to become the Female Waters, to *Malkhut*, which is the secret of the heart, and the actions that have to be taken with the sacrifice in each of the organs until it comes to *Malkhut* in the desirable form, so that it, *Malkhut*, will be fitting for the Female Waters, for *Zeir Anpin*. And he also explains the matter of the Male Waters that *Zeir Anpin* sends down on to the Female Waters that are in *Malkhut*, and the secret of their mating.

2) First, we shall clarify the matters briefly: The sacrifice, which is the secret of the Female Waters, ascends and is dealt

with in the same way as the food and drink that come in to the body of man, through the esophagus and the other internal organs until it becomes blood, and the liver extends the blood towards the heart, and the heart takes the clear and the clean of the blood and sends it to the limbs, while the unclean blood remains in the liver. The way of the sacrifice, or the prayer that is instead of the sacrifice, is the same. It comes first to the grinders that are in the Tetragrammaton of *Atziluth*, *Briah*, *Yetzirah*, and *Assiah*, which are the secret of the molar teeth that grind the food, and when it is ground up it goes to the esophagus, from the esophagus to the *omasum* and thence to the stomach, where it is ground up a second time. And the secret of the grinding by the teeth of the sacrifice or prayer is the dispute between the two columns, the right and the left, prior to the emergence of the central column, each one of which wished to do away with the other. The right column wished to rescind the control of *Ḥokhmah* that is on the left, and put *ḥasadim* alone in control, while the left column, on the other hand, wanted to rescind the control of *ḥasadim* and place *Ḥokhmah* in control alone. And so they go and pound at each other, making each other smaller, until both of them are pulverized, and one of them remains at the end as ruler. And in the first instance, the right overcomes the left and the right controls, and this is achieved by the pounding and grinding that is in the teeth, for by this grinding the food is swallowed through the esophagus into the *omasum*. But since the Female Waters come on the inside of the body, the power of the left then awakens and starts a second grinding, which is the secret of the grinding of the *omasum*. And the dispute is there stronger, and the grinding is therefore finer, and in this grinding the left eventually overcomes, and under its control, which is the control of the *Ḥokhmah* of the left, the Female Waters are upturned and become blood, which is the secret of the light of *Ḥokhmah*, in the secret of the verse: "For the blood is the soul" (Deuteronomy 12:23), that is, the light of life, which is *Ḥokhmah*. However, in this situation, the power of death is greater than the light of life, because of the impure blood that is mixed up with it, as it is in the aspect of the upper three *Sfirot* of *Ḥokhmah*, whose judgments are most harsh and destroy the world, as is known. Therefore, after the Female Waters have become blood-like, the liver, initially as Samael, takes all of that blood, including within it both pure and impure blood, for they are intermingled, and proffers it to the heart, which is the secret of *Malkhut*, from the aspect of the building of the left of *Binah*, which is discerned as King, and the heart sorts out the clean and the clear that is in the blood, i.e. the aspect of the six ends of *Ḥokhmah*, which is ready to unite with the right; and the remainder, which is the impure blood, it leaves for the liver and its side, i.e. Samael and his faction. And then the flow of Male Waters begins to descend from *Zeir Anpin*, which is the secret of the wind, which unites with the Female Waters that are in the heart, and they become one.

3) And the Male Waters are the secret of the *ḥasadim* that are drawn down from the brain, which is the secret of the upper three *Sfirot* of *Zeir Anpin*, and from there the wind, which is the secret of the *ḥasadim*, is drawn to the nose, which is the *Tiferet* of *Zeir Anpin*, and also to the mouth, which is *Malkhut* of *Zeir Anpin*, and the wind that comes from the brain enters the two orifices of the nose, which is the secret of right and left that are included in *Tiferet* of *Zeir Anpin* (as above, *Idra*, 223). And from there it is drawn by way of the trachea into the lung, and the two wings of the lung blow the wind, which is the secret of *ḥasadim* and Male Waters, to the heart, and then the *Ḥokhmah* that is in the heart becomes attired with the *ḥasadim* that are in the wind. And *Zeir Anpin*, which is the Tetragrammaton, also unites with *Malkhut*, which is 'The Lord,' as the union of the female waters with the male waters. And in this secret it is said: "My food which is presented unto Me for offerings" (Numbers 28:2). This

teaches that from this mating the request of the offerer of the sacrifice or the worshipper is fulfilled, for additionally all the worlds receive from this mating, each one at its appropriate level, for the mating of Male and Female illuminates, in the first instance, all the worlds, while only a small beam of the illumination of the mating reaches man to satisfy his request. (For the reason, see above, Introduction to the Wisdom of the Kabbalah, 161.) And it follows that the man who offers a sacrifice or who prays not only corrects himself but also corrects all the worlds, and for this reason the structure of his body hints at the Tetragrammaton that includes all four of the worlds: *Atziluth*, *Briah*, *Yetzirah*, and *Assiah*, as above. And there is also a Tetragrammaton that includes five worlds, namely: Primordial Man, *Atziluth*, *Briah*, *Yetzirah*, and *Assiah*. (As above, in the Introduction to the Wisdom of the Kabbalah, 3). However, the deed of man does not reach to the world of Primordial man, and even in the world of *Atziluth* it only reaches as far as *Zeir Anpin* of *Atziluth*, and the head, therefore only parallels *Zeir Anpin* of *Atziluth*. From the mouth to the chest parallels *Briah* and the Female of *Zeir Anpin* of *Atziluth*, for *Briah* is the wife of *Atziluth*. From the chest downwards parallels the two worlds of *Yetzirah* and *Assiah*, as above.

4) And one has to understand here exactly how and what is the form of the prayer, and how it rises up to the Female of *Zeir Anpin*, and is transformed there into food for the Female and for *Zeir Anpin*, in the secret of the verse: "My food which is presented unto Me for offerings" (Numbers 28:2), for prayer is in the stead of the sacrifice. And the point is that the person offering the sacrifice or the prayer does so for some request that he has from the Holy One, blessed be He, in which respect it has been said: Prayer is only in the heart. And this desire attires itself in the parts of his soul and it is they, the parts of the soul, that actually ascend on high and cut through all the spheres until

they reach the Female of *Zeir Anpin* of *Atziluth* (as has been explained at length, *Vayakel*, 131). This happens in such a way that the request is attired in the parts of his soul, and the parts of his soul ascend and become Female Waters for the mating of *Zeir Anpin* with his Female, this being the secret of eating, for the mating is called bread and food, as is written: "He knew nothing except the bread which he ate" (Genesis 39:6). And from this one can also understand why the prayer or sacrifice becomes Female Waters to arouse the mating, for nothing is given on high if not through the mating of Male and Female, as is known. And so, if the Holy One, blessed be He, wishes to fulfill the desire of the worshipper, then He needs the mating. And it follows that every prayer worthy to be fulfilled arouses the mating of Male and Female so that they might emanate that fulfillment to the worshipper; and, first, the illumination of this mating reaches, of necessity, the upper worlds, until it finally comes to man who is praying (as above, in the Introduction to the Wisdom of the Kabbalah, 161). More exactly: those parts of the soul that ascended to the Female of *Zeir Anpin* and became Female Waters to arouse the mating . They themselves become a receptacle for the illumination of the mating that fulfills the request of the worshipper, and they return to Him on fulfillment of the request. This happens in such a way that the parts of the soul that ascend to the Female Waters have two roles:

a) To arouse the mating in fulfillment of the request of the prayer.

b)To be qualified to be a receptacle to receive the fulfillment of the prayer.

And both of them happen simultaneously.

5) And you already know that nothing is complete until the order of the three columns that are drawn from the three points *ḥolam* (vowel \`o'), *shuruk* (vowel \`u'), and *ḥirik* (vowel \`i') pass over it (above, *Bereshith Aleph* 38), for he says: No seed

can be sown unless in the secret of these three points. And for this reason, the Female Waters, i.e. the prayer, as above, has to come first into the body of the Female, in the aspect of grinders, for it there receives the control of the first column, the right, and from there it passes to the *omasum* and to the stomach where the Female Waters receive the control of the left column, for the Female Waters have become blood. And the liver receives them and gives them to the heart. And from the two wings of the lung that blow the wind onto the heart, the Female Waters receive the action of the central column, which is the secret of the mating. And then the Female Waters are perfected (as above, 2 and 3). And it becomes a receptacle to receive the illumination of the mating for the fulfillment of the request of the worshipper.

6) And on the text (440): "From those offerings by fire issue forth stages that take before the liver. And who are they? They are the molar teeth, which eat the sacrifices and grind (them)." After the food accepts the control of the left column, it then turns into blood, and the liver takes it first and gives it to the heart (as above, 2). However, prior to this, there is need for the control of the right column, as above, and this is the secret of the stages that are termed molar teeth, which receives the Female Waters before the liver does, which issue forth by the power of those offerings by fire that are in the right column, i.e. the judgments that are at the point of *ḥolam* (vowel `o'), from the force of *Malkhut*'s ascent to *Binah* (as above, *Bereshith Aleph*, 15). And these offerings by fire work with these teeth, and by their grinding, which is the secret of the warring of the right and the left against each other, as above, the right overcomes. And on the text: `Once it (the food) has been ground,' i.e. after the warring between right and left, that is called grinding, is terminated, and the right is victorious, then: "Those who exercise control by fire, for they were victorious and control the Female Waters. And they are called the esophagus. " Those judgments of the right column

that swallow the Female Waters are called *veshet* (esophagus).

7) And on the text (439): "The esophagus, that swallows the food and from where it enters all the parts, is the stage of offerings by fire." For, prior to the Female Waters being included in the offerings by fire of the right column, which offerings by fire are derived from the mitigation of *Malkhut* by *Binah*, they are not fitted for inclusion in the body of the Female, nor to receive of the illumination of the mating (as above, *Bereshith Aleph*, 7). This mitigating fire is, therefore, considered as swallowing, for it swallows the Female Waters and brings them into the body of the Female. And on the text: "And from where it enters all the parts" the text itself explains: "These offerings by fire draw near immediately," i.e. these offerings by fire, that are called the esophagus, draw near initially to the Female Waters. "Swallowing," which brings them into the body. "And taking everything from the upper fire that includes the offerings by fire," i.e. the fire of the point of ḥolam, from which come the offerings by fire. "And this is the secret of the verse: 'They shall eat the offerings of the Lord made by fire, and His inheritance" (Deuteronomy 18:1). For the priests, who are the aspect of the right column, are the ones who eat and receive these offerings by fire. And whoever does not have this fire of the right column is unable to welcome the Female Waters, inasmuch as he is without the sweetening of *Binah*. And on the text: "That devour and swallow," i.e. the offerings by fire that are included in the esophagus. "And the others do not so eat." For the other bodily organs, who do not have this fire of the right column, will not be able to receive the Female Waters and include them in the body, and this refers to those organs that have only the power of the left column, which are the aspect of the external intelligences; they do not receive them even though there is fire that swallows the Female Waters. And on the text (440): "And all the people of the world on the outside know not how they are eaten." For those

who are not privileged with the internal spheres do not know that there is such a thing as this mitigating fire that eats the Female Waters, as above. But the stages on the inside, i.e. those who have been privileged with the internal spheres of the intelligences, know and they take from them. They know and comprehend these offerings by fire. And this is the secret of: "For the esophagus cannot be examined from the outside, for they do not know." For from the point of view of the external spheres, there is not even any concept of the existence of this fire. And it follows that the beginning of the process of inclusion in the internal spheres of the intelligences is by an acceptance of this fire.

8) And on the text (442): "Enter through the esophagus." For the entry into the body is by the power of the fire that is in the right column, which is the esophagus. "And are drawn into the lung," that is to say, until the Female Waters come to the omasum and the liver, and to the heart on which the wings of the lung blow, and then the Female Waters are drawn in and included in the lung. "Those seraphs," i.e. the Female Waters that turn into blood in the heart, which is there as a burning fire because of the Judgments of the left column (as explained in paragraph 2). "With their flames... they take a drink," for they are included in the waters which are *ḥasadim*. "And they are called lung, in one union," i.e. the flames of the heart, which are *Ḥokhmah*, after they come into one union with the waters, which are *ḥasadim*, are together called lung. For the letters of the word `lung' [*re'ah*: *resh yud aleph hei*], when re-arranged, form the word `sight' [*r'iyah*: *resh aleph yud hei*], i.e. through them is the illumination of *Ḥokhmah* that is included in the *ḥasadim*, that is termed sight. And on the text (441): "Why is the esophagus [*veshet*: *vav* shin tet] so called?" Because the shape of the first letter of the word, the *vav*, is like a bowed-over esophagus, i.e. it has the shape of a column or line like the letter *vav*, but not a straight line, which is the central column, but rather a bent line,

i.e. the right column, which is the aspect of the six *Sfirot* without a head (as above, *Bereshith Aleph*, 15), whose top is bent over. The other two letters, the *shin* and the *tet*, form the word *shat*, `went about,' to eat. For by virtue of its being bent over it swallows the food and brings it inside the body, as above. And on the text: "And on the destruction of the Temple `And the grinders cease because they are few'" (Ecclesiastes 12:3). The Temple was destroyed because the left overcame the right, and then the grinders ceased, for the molar teeth are the secret of the warring between right and left. And with the ceasing of the right, the Female Waters, that Israel cause to rise up, no longer enter the upper body. And on the text: "For their form and their food have been diminished." The form of the right has ceased to exist and, therefore, their food dimished for the Female Waters do not enter the upper body.

9) And after the first grinding has been done by the teeth, with the right column winning out and swallowing the Female Waters in the upper body, the Female Waters descend for a second grinding to the *omasum*, and in this grinding it is the left that wins (As above, 2). And on the text (418): "The *omasum*...grinds...for it takes everything and pulverizes the food, sending it to all parts." In this grinding the left overcomes and turns it into the aspect of blood in the secret of *Ḥokhmah* of the left which is of a reddish hue, in the secret of: "For the blood is the soul" (Deuteronomy 12:23). And whatever does not turn into blood leaves the body in the secret of the waste-matter. And on the text (422): "And from those dregs...drink below...," i.e. the waste-matters.

10) However, you must know that the very eating is the illumination of the *ḥasadim*, and it only comes to the *omasum* to be ground and fall under the control of the fire of the left in order to be complemented and made up by the *Ḥokhmah* that is

on the left. And the very drinking, i.e. the drinking of the wine, is the illumination of the *Ḥokhmah* that is on the left, but it is not perfected unless it comes under the control of the right and is included in the *ḥasadim* of the right. And on the text (423): "The *omasum* takes everything up to six hours and bakes." For the female Waters that come to the *omasum* are included in the six *Sfirot*, *Ḥesed*, *Gvurah*, *Tiferet*, *Netzaḥ*, *Hod*, and *Yesod*, which are in the body of *Malkhut*, and the fire that is in the *omasum* bakes the Female Waters. The meaning of this is that, just as the baker places the bread on the fire and does not intend to burn any of the bread, but rather that the bread should become sweet from the heat of the fire, so, too, the Female Waters of eating are *ḥasadim* and they come into the fire of the left of the gizzard only for the sake of inclusion and perfection, just as in the baking of the bread on the fire. And on the text: "The gizzard...is a baker. And the lung is a butler." For the gizzard which is the *omasum* bakes the Female Waters so that its illumination of *Ḥokhmah* may be included in them. And the lung, which is the right, and is *ḥasadim*, receives the wine which is the illumination of *Ḥokhmah* in order to include the illumination of *ḥasadim* in them. The heart is the King, and these two. The gizzard and the lung are certainly the baker and the butler who give to the King, for the heart which is the very structure of *Malkhut* that is to the left of *Binah*, takes from them what is fitting for it, and after the heart has received, it gives, and distributes to all the parts. "And this is the meaning of what is written: `I have gathered my myrrh... Eat, O companions. Drink, yea, drink abundantly, O beloved ones'" (Song of Songs 5:1) The eating of the companions is through the chief baker, i.e. by a mitigation of the left that is in the *omasum*. And the drinking of the beloved is by the chief butler, i.e. by the mitigation of the right that is in the lung.

11) This does not mean that the Female Waters come

directly from the *omasum* to the heart, which is the King, but that the Female Waters descend from the *omasum* to the stomach and etc. to the liver, and the liver gives them to the heart. And the secret of the stomach alludes to the aspect of the departure of the intelligences that arrive by control of the left column, since *Ḥokhmah* is then without *ḥasadim*, and so long as the illumination of the *ḥasadim* departs, then the illumination of the *Ḥokhmah* of the left also appears as though it is departing. This is because *Ḥokhmah* is unable to illuminate without *ḥasadim* (as above, *Bereshith Aleph*, page 47). And on the text (415): "The stomach is one part in sixty of death and is called `a deep sleep'. " For wherever deep sleep is mentioned the reference is to this aspect. Asirta is the sixth stage of the Angel of Death, and there, in this aspect of deep sleep, the evil spirit that is called Asirta, which is the sixth stage of the Angel of Death, is in control (as explained above, *Pikudei*, 919, q.v.) And this Asirta is in control of those who do not want to depart from the left column, which is the secret of "sin couches at the door" (Genesis 4:7). But for those who come to cleave to the right, this power of the Angel of Death is discerned in the aspect of the correction of *Ḥokhmah*, in the secret of the verse: "I said: I will get wisdom, but it was far from me" (Ecclesiastes 7:23) (as above, *Vayigash*, 11 which passage should be well studied). And on the text: "And because it came from afar." That is to say, because this power came to correct *Ḥokhmah* that would come from afar. "It is from the side of death." It is possible to say about it only that it is from the side of the aspect of death. "But is not death itself;" but it is not actual real death. And therefore the hint that it is one sixtieth part of death, i.e. it is not death itself, as explained.

12) And after the Female Waters have been turned into blood by the gizzard and the stomach etc., the liver takes them, and you already know that the blood teaches about the illumi-

nation of *Ḥokhmah* that is from the left, in the secret of "For the blood is the soul" (Deuteronomy 12:23), for it contains the forbidden part, namely the upper three *Sfirot* of the left, and it also contains the permitted part, namely the six *Sfirot* of the left, and they are termed pure blood and impure blood. And since the heart, is the secret of the Holy *Malkhut*, the Female of *Zeir Anpin* of *Atziluth*, how is it able to come into contact with impure blood? Accordingly it needs an intermediary, from the evil forces, which is the liver, that will receive the pure and impure blood together, and give to it. And *Malkhut* selects from it the clean and clear blood, which is the secret of the six *Sfirot* of the left, and leaves the three upper *Sfirot* of the left in the liver, without touching it. And on the text (411): "That is certainly how it is, for the liver is the level of Esau." That is, the minister of Esau, which is Samael (as above 210). He "gathers in all the blood, whether clear or turbid", etc. That is, from the three upper *Sfirot* of the left, which is forbidden, which is the turbid blood, or from the six *Sfirot* of the left, which is permitted, which is the clear (blood). "The heart... is Israel..." That is to say that it is *Malkhut*, from which Israel receives. The heart distinguishes "between good and bad, between impure blood and pure blood, and takes only the clear and the clean," etc. That is, only the six *Sfirot* of *Ḥokhmah*, for they are clear and clean, as above.

13a) And on the text (425): "But there is a difficulty here. If the liver is Esau, how does it arrange food for the heart, which is Jacob?" This difficulty is semantic, for he says (425) that the liver is the level of Esau and the heart is Israel. And the difficulty is: How is it possible for the liver, which is the minister of Esau, to prepare food for the heart, which is Israel? And the answer comes (425): "The heart is certainly like Isaac," i.e. that the heart is not Israel, but the *Shekhinah* from the aspect of the left column, which is like Isaac, who is the left column of *Zeir*

Anpin. "The liver is Esau, who hunted venison." For the liver, which is the level of Esau, receives all the blood, the impure and the pure, and gives to the heart, which is the *Shekhinah.* "(And Esau said to Isaac:) 'Let my father arise and eat of his son's venison'" (Genesis 27:31). This refers to the prayers of the poor that are sent away and not accepted on high. And the meaning is: Those who do not know how to direct their prayer to request the illumination of the central column, that unites right and left in the secret of *Da'at* (knowledge), but pray for the drawing down of the upper three *Sfirot* of the left, that illuminate without the unity of the central column these are the ones who are called poor (this refers to a spiritual inadequacy), for their prayer is not acceptable, but is thrown out to the evil forces. Therefore, when the liver, which is the level of Esau, collects the impure blood and the pure blood and gives them to the heart, he says "and eat of his son's venison," i.e. that he should receive the prayers of these poor, and grant them their request that the upper three *Sfirot* of the left be illuminated in the world. For the whole motivation of the evil forces is that the *Shekhinah* should agree to illuminate the upper three *Sfirot* of the left in the worlds (as above, Noah, page 48, q.v.). And on the text: "And Isaac (which is the *Shekhinah*) suffers trouble and anguish because they do not know how to direct the prayer." For they do not know how to direct their prayer to the central column, and he is therefore in trouble and anguish because he does not receive their prayers but rather he receives from the liver only the pure blood which is the secret of the six *Sfirot* of the left; and the upper three *Sfirot* of the left, which are the prayers of the poor, chase away from him and leave in the liver as above, and the poor are forced to receive their desire from the liver, which is the minister of Esau. And on the text: "Likewise, Israel in exile has no food, except through the nations of the world." Just as the poor are forced to receive their request from the liver, which is the minister of Esau, because the *Shekhinah* cannot give them their request because it is impure blood, as above, so Israel in exile, who does not cleave to the central column but is under the authority of the left, is similarly obligated to receive their request from the ministers of the nations, for exactly the same reason as noted in the case of the poor. But (426) "when they are in the Land of Israel, i.e. cleaving to the central column, their food is through the *Shekhinah*." They are then able to receive their food from the heart, which is the *Shekhinah*, i.e. the illumination of the six *Sfirot* of the left is accepted in the heart, which is the *Shekhinah*, and they no longer receive from the liver which is Samael.

13b) And here you see how the evil forces, i.e. the liver, benefit from each sacrifice, for the heart leaves the upper three *Sfirot* of the left with him, as above, and now you will be able to understand what Rabbi Shimon said above (Noah, 118). "The end of all flesh" (Genesis 6:13), which is the evil forces, refers to those sacrifices that Israel used to offer at the altar, etc. Review entire passage, which is the secret of the sacrificial goats on *Rosh Ḥodesh* (the new moon) and the scapegoat on *Yom Kippur* (as is clarified there, 99 and 129). And on the text above (374): "Everything that the liver is holding it sacrifices to the heart, which is the King" i.e. whether impure or pure blood. "And it is neither the way of that heart, nor its desire to foul up the deeds of His people," i.e. with impure blood coming from the upper three *Sfirot* of the left; "but He takes everything that is clear and pure," i.e. the pure blood coming from the six *Sfirot* of the left, "while all the foulness, etc.," i.e. the impure blood remains for the liver, and the evil force benefit from every sacrifice, as above. And it is said: "And the goat shall bear upon him all their iniquities" (Leviticus 16:22), for this is the secret of the scapegoat, as above.

14) And it is known that at the end of the Judgments of

the left is revealed the shell from the Lock that is called sin, and death, in the secret of the verse: "sin couches at the door" (Genesis 4:7). And this shell is the secret of the gall that is attached to the liver, for the liver is the Judgments of the left that is called Samael, and, at its end, the gall is revealed, in the secret of the verse: "But its end is as bitter (same word as `gall') as wormwood" (Proverbs 5:4), for it is the sword of the Angel of Death. And on the text (412): "He is angered at him with the gall, which is Gehenna (Hell), which was created on the second day;" for the second day is the left column, and the gall is at the end of the left column. And the gall brings anger into the liver, and the liver punishes the wicked, that wish to continue suckling from the upper three *Sfirot* of the left that is in it, through the gall. "The death of the adults." For by the shell (evil husk) of the gall, death comes to adults, i.e. to all people except for the children, who die at the hand of Lillith, which is the spleen, as explained. But the death of each person is by the hand of the gall, which is the secret of the Lock, as explained above (*Vayetze*, page 67). Furthermore, it burns with the flames on the arteries of the liver and wants to inflame the entire body, this being after the liver has received the upper three *Sfirot* of the left, which is what the heart leaves for it. And then, when the gall awakens and drips a drop on the liver, then those upper three *Sfirot* depart from it, for the Lock is such that whenever it awakens, the upper three *Sfirot* depart from there (as above, *Vayetze*, page 13). And it follows that all the arteries of the liver are burnt up in the fire of the Judgments of the gall. And on the text (413): "It is like the sea when there is a storm;" for the sea is angered at the sand that restricts it. And its waves "reach up to see the skies" (Psalms 107:26) and want to break out of their limits and destroy the world. That is to say; when the left column awakens in the midst of the sea, and wants to reveal the upper three *Sfirot* of the left, this being the secret of `reach up to the sky,' in order to reveal the upper three *Sfirot*, which then would destroy the world with the Judgments of the upper three *Sfirot* of the left therefore, when the waves of the sea touch the sands that surrounds it, these waves containing the Judgments of the Lock, then immediately the upper three *Sfirot* of the left depart from those waves that touched the sand that is on the sea shore, and then "they went down to the deeps" (Psalms 107:26). For the sea is like the liver, and the waves of the sea are the secret of the upper three *Sfirot* of the left, just as in the liver. And just as when the sea wishes to reveal those upper three *Sfirot* to the world, it cannot because of the sand which removes the upper three *Sfirot* from it, so is it with the liver. When the wicked come to suckle from the liver the upper three *Sfirot* of the left that it contains, the upper three *Sfirot* are unable to be revealed because of the gall that is there, for this latter immediately awakens and removes those upper three *Sfirot*.

15) And all this concerns the wicked who want to suckle from the liver, and the gall surrounds them and restricts them so that they should not be able to suckle from the upper three *Sfirot*. But in the case of the righteous it is the *Shekhinah* that restricts them so that they should not suckle from the upper three *Sfirot*, for they always cleave to the *Shekhinah*, and just as the *Shekhinah* receives only the six *Sfirot* of the left, so is it with the righteous. And on the text (413): "Were it not for the *Shekhinah*, which is for a sick person like the sand to the sea." That is, should some sin happen to a righteous person and the power of the left, that is drawn from the liver, increase over him and he become ill, then the *Shekhinah* preserves him so that he should not fail in the upper three *Sfirot* of the left. This is just as the sand protects the sea, and as the gall protects the liver. And (414): Because the *Shekhinah* is over his head and not his feet, the Angel of Death being over his feet, means that, although the *Shekhinah* watches over him, he can nevertheless depart from it and sin again. It is understood that at the feet of the sick person

is still to be found the Angel of Death, for the end is termed feet. And on the text: But "this is not the case for every person, but just for ordinary people. In the case of the perfectly righteous `The Lord will support him on his sick-bed' (Psalms 41:4) at his head, and the *Shekhinah* enwraps his body unto his feet; for he is assured of the *Shekhinah*'s protection forever, as it is said about Jacob: "He gathered up his feet into the bed" (Genesis 49:33). And on the text: "In the case of the thoroughly wicked person, the Angel of Death surrounds him on every side, and his sword...." i.e. the gall, which is the sword of the Angel of Death, guards him so that he should not suckle from the liver, as above. "Whose inner turns green with one drop." That is to say that the upper three *Sfirot* are called inner, and they are turned green by one drop of the gall, i.e. that the upper three *Sfirot* depart because of it, as above. Liver is male and the lobe of the liver is female; i.e. the female of the liver is not the gall, but the lobe of the liver, which is composed of a mixture of the Judgments of Male and the Judgments of Female (as above, 363) because it prostitutes itself with others. (That passage should be studied). But gall is the Judgments of the Female solely, and the difference between gall and spleen is that, although both of them are Judgments of the Female, the gall is from the aspect of the Judgments of the Lock and the spleen is from the aspect of the Judgments of the Key, as is well clarified above (410).

16) And after the heart receives the clean and clear blood from the liver, which is the secret of the six *Sfirot* of *Ḥokhmah*, it is then full of Judgment, for, before *Ḥokhmah* is enclothed with *ḥasadim* that are on the right, it is all Judgment. And on the text (402): "The heart is fire," and also (403): "It is said of the heart: `And the king arose in his wrath from the banquet of wine'" (Esther 7:7). Study the commentary there well for it is fully clarified. Thus the heart, which is *Malkhut*, now needs to mate with *Zeir Anpin*, that He should emanate to

her the spirit of *ḥasadim*. And when she mates with *Zeir Anpin*, then the spirit of *ḥasadim* descends from the brain, which is the secret of the upper three *Sfirot* of *Zeir Anpin*, to the nose, which is the secret of *Tiferet* of *Zeir Anpin*, and the spirit of *ḥasadim* descends through the two orifices of the nose to the trachea of the lung, which is *Binah* of *Malkhut*, and from the trachea to the two wings of the lung which are *Ḥesed* of *Malkhut*. And from the two wings of the lung the spirit of *ḥasadim* comes to the heart. This is the lung drawing spirit to the heart. And then *Ḥokhmah* that is in the heart enclothes itself in *ḥasadim*. Thus is completed the illumination of the mating, from where it reaches to all the worlds until it arrives at the worshipper to complete for him the request that is in his prayer. And on the text (402): This (the brain) is the Throne of Mercy while the other (the heart) is the Throne of Judgment, for the brain of *Zeir Anpin* is the Throne of Mercy, and it is from there that the spirit of *ḥasadim* descend. And the heart, which is *Malkhut*, is the Throne of Judgment, because of the *Ḥokhmah* without *ḥasadim* that is there. "And the Holy One, blessed be He, is the King who stands up from the Throne of Judgment which is the heart and sits down on the Throne of Mercy which is the brain." That is to say, He mates with the heart, and then Mercy is drawn down to the heart from the brain, and it is the Throne of Mercy of the brain that is in control.

17) And on the text (432): "If the parts of man are meritorious in keeping the precepts" that his prayer is accepted "of the Supreme King, who is the Holy Spirit" i.e. the spirit of *ḥasadim* of *Zeir Anpin* "descending on the ladder (which is the throat) in a number of holy spirits" i.e. the spirit of *ḥasadim* descends from the brain to the trachea in four spirits, paralleling the four letters of the holy Name Tetragrammaton [*yud hei vav* and *hei*] "about which it is said: Who makes winds His messengers. [Psalms 104:4]" these winds are the spirits of *ḥasadim* that *Zeir Anpin* sends to *Malkhut*,

and this is why they are called messengers. "The Supreme King will descend to accept the vapors that are in the heart," for the spirits of *ḥasadim* receive the *Ḥokhmah* of the left that is in the heart, which is called vapors (as above, *Vayetze*, page 7, and *Tazria*, 97). "About which it is said: The flaming fire are His ministers (Psalms 104:4)," i.e. the Judgments that are in the vapors are the messengers of the *ḥasadim*, by which *ḥasadim* are included in the illumination of *Ḥokhmah*. And this is the secret of the mating of *Zeir Anpin* and *Malkhut*, which are brain and heart, as above. And the mating takes places in two places. One is in the mouth of the head, in the secret of the union of the head with the body which is there, in the secret of the palate and throat. And the other place is in the heart, i.e. in *Malkhut*. And in the mating that is in the heart, the *Ḥokhmah* that is in the heart is the principal, and the *ḥasadim* of *Zeir Anpin* complement it, while in the mating that is in the mouth, the *ḥasadim* are the principal, and the *Ḥokhmah* that rises up there with vapors that are in the heart only complements the *ḥasadim*. And on the text (434): "And when the Tetragrammaton [*yud hei vav* and *hei*] which is *Zeir Anpin*, descends to the heart, to `The Lord' [*aleph dalet nun yud*] which is *Malkhut*, Judgment joins with Mercy in the heart" i.e. *Ḥokhmah* of the left with *ḥasadim* of *Zeir Anpin* "making: *yud aleph hei dalet vav nun hei yud*" which teaches about the mating of *Zeir Anpin* and *Malkhut*, which are the Tetragrammaton and `The Lord' respectively, combined with each other. "And when `The Lord' ascends to the mouth...;" just as they were combined in the heart, the difference being that in the mouth the *ḥasadim* are the principal, while in the heart the *Ḥokhmah* is the principal, as above.

18) And they ascend and descend by way of the trachea, which is the secret of ladder, for the spirits of *ḥasadim* from the brain descend by way of the trachea to the heart, and the vapors of the heart, which is the secret of *Ḥokhmah*, ascend by way of the trachea to the head, while the trachea itself is the secret of

Binah of *Malkhut*, which is joined to the head, which is the secret of *Zeir Anpin*, for every lower sphere that receives from an upper sphere so receives with the purest part of it, and *Binah*, which is the trachea, is the purest vessel of all the vessels that are in *Malkhut*. And on the text (433): The trachea [*kaneh*: *kuf nun hei*] is "Get [*k'neh*: *kuf nun hei*] wisdom [*Ḥokhmah*], get [*k'neh*: *kuf nun hei*] understanding [*Binah*]" (Proverbs 4:5): That is, *Binah* includes ten *Sfirot*, namely: *Ḥokhmah*, *Binah*, *Ḥesed*, *Gvurah*, *Tiferet*, *Netzaḥ*, *Hod*, and *Yesod*. And on the text: The two arms, the torso, the covenant, and the two thighs. These are the six *Sfirot* that parallel the six cartilage rings of the trachea, while *Ḥokhmah* and *Binah* are further up, at the top of the trachea, and they are all *Sfirot* of *Binah*. And on the text (435): "The six cartilage rings of the trachea... come from the side of *Gvurah* (might)," i.e. from *Binah* which is in the left column. "And when they join together;" and when the two columns of *Binah*, right and left, come together by means of the central column, "they are like a *shofar*," which is *Binah* when it emanates *Zeir Anpin*, which is the voice that issues out of the *shofar* (as above, Introduction to the Book of the Zohar, 239), i.e. in the secret of three emerging from one and one being in three (as above, *Bereshith Aleph*, 287). And they are called *shofar*, the mighty rams of Isaac, i.e. the Judgments of the left column that are called Isaac. "That bring forth spirit and voice," which is the secret of the central column, which is *Zeir Anpin*, that is called spirit and is called voice, for he is born and emerges through the mitigation of these Judgments in *Binah*, which is called shophar. "And that voice goes out and meets with rain clouds," i.e. when the central column goes and meets the Judgments that are in *Binah*, that are called rain clouds, "and is heard by the creatures on the outside." Then the thunder of the Judgments is heard on the outside, for, before the central column comes to *Binah* to unite its right and left, the Judgments of the left column are not heard, and it is not known that they have any importance (as above, *Balak*, 174). It is thus written: "But the thunder of His mighty deeds who can understand?" (Job 26:14), for they certainly come from the side of *Gvurah*. For before the central column, that is called voice, arrives, who is there to contemplate them that they should be considered as His mighty deeds? And on the text: "It is not written 'the God of glory thunders' but 'the God of glory makes to thunder' (Psalms 29:3)," i.e. by means of the sons of the mighty (ibid., v.1). This means that he revealed the Judgments and *gevurot* of the left of *Binah*. "And there is none that knows the praise of this voice;" and there is no one who can comprehend the praise of that voice which is the central column that reveals all this. As it is written: "Who can understand?" (Job 26:14). And this is a second interpretation of the verse "Who can understand," for initially it was interpreted to mean the *gevurot* of the left of *Binah*, while he later applies it to the central column.

19) And on the text (436 in "The Faithful Shepherd"): "For the trachea is composed of three forces... fire that issues from the heart:" where the judgments of *Ḥokhmah* are; "Air," which is the spirit of *Zeir Anpin*, "which enters it from the outside," i.e. that comes into it through the orifices of the nose; and the third, "Water, of the wings of the lung, which are attached to the trachea:" namely *ḥasadim*. "And from these three:" which are *Ḥesed*, *Gvurah*, and *Tiferet* (water *Ḥesed* that is in the wings of the lung; and fire = *Gvurah*; that ascends from the heart and wind = *Tiferet*). And each one is subdivided into seven, paralleling, *Ḥesed*, *Gvurah*, *Tiferet*, *Netzaḥ*, *Hod*, *Yesod*, and *Malkhut* that is in each one of them. And on the text (437): "And when the flames of the heart (being the *Ḥokhmah* of the left that is in the heart, which are Judgments and fire from lack of *ḥasadim*) meet with rain clouds which are the wings of the lung," (which are *ḥasadim*), and the *Ḥokhmah* that is in the heart becomes enclothed in *ḥasadim* that are in the wings of the lung (by way

of the trachea of the lung, i.e by *Ḥokhmah* being enclothed in *ḥasadim*), *Ḥokhmah* is revealed in the trachea of the lung. And on the text: "For therein the heart understands [*mevin*]... and *Ḥokhmah*, which is brain, is there... and flowing streams from Lebanon" (Song of Songs 4:15), which is the whiteness [*lavnunit*] of the brain that flows through the trachea of the lung; for *ḥasadim*, which is the secret of the color white, descends by way of the trachea of the lung from the brain to the heart, as above. And, after the clouds of *Binah*, which are Judgments of the left, have ascended to the brain: i.e. after the clouds of *Binah*, which are Judgments of the left that are in the heart, have ascended to receive *ḥasadim* from the brain, for the *ḥasadim* from the brain then flow over them. And on the text (438): "And the secret of the matter is in the verse: `Who is this who comes up out of the wilderness like pillars of smoke...?' (Song of Songs 3:6), for this is the smoke of the system that rises from the heart to the brain;" for the judgments of *Ḥokhmah*, before they unite with *ḥasadim*, are called the smoke of the system, which is the secret of the cloud of *Binah* (as above, 26), and this smoke ascends to the brain to become enclothed in *ḥasadim* that are in it, and thereby the *Ḥokhmah* that is in the heart is perfected. "Which can not be moved from its place by all the winds in the worlds," for they are unable to prevent its illumination.

20) And on the text: "The letters of the word *Ḥokhmah* [*ḥet kaf mem hei*] form the two words *koaḥ* [*kaf ḥet*] and *mah* [*mem hei*] because it is *koaḥ* (strength) in the heart and *mah* (what) in the brain;" that is to say that it is perfected only by the *koaḥ*, i.e. the flames that ascend from the heart to the brain, which are the illumination of *Ḥokhmah*, and by the *ḥasadim* that descend from the brain to the heart, which is the secret of *mah* (which alludes to *ḥasadim*, in the respect of What (*mah*) do you know? What (*mah*) do you understand?, and with these two *Ḥokhmah* is perfected, as above. "The trachea is *Tiferet* and

incorporates six *Sfirot: Ḥesed, Gvurah, Tiferet, Netzaḥ, Hod,* and *Yesod,* which are the six stages to the Throne, which is Mother." For the trachea is, as a rule, the secret of *Binah,* in the secret of the verse: "Get wisdom, get understanding" (Proverbs 4:5), and includes the six *Sfirot: Ḥesed, Gvurah, Tiferet, Netzaḥ, Hod,* and *Yesod* (as above, Commentator's Interpolation, paragraph 18). Inasmuch as *Ḥesed, Gvurah, Tiferet, Netzaḥ, Hod,* and *Yesod* are included in the trachea, they are the six stages of the Throne, which is *Binah.* "So that *Hokhmah* will descend in it from the brain to the heart, for in it the heart understands;" i.e. by the descent of *Hokhmah* from the brain (which is the secret of *Hokhmah* of the right which is *ḥasadim*) in order to dress the *Hokhmah* of the left column of *Binah,* which is the heart, the perfection of the *Binah* that is in the heart is revealed, in the secret of the heart understands. "For this reason it is written: 'Get [*k'neh*] wisdom [*Hokhmah*], get [*k'neh*] understanding [*Binah*]' (Proverbs 4:5), for Father, which is *Hokhmah,* descends in it and Father ascends in it. And this is a ladder..." For Father, which is the secret of *Hokhmah* of the right, descends from the brain to the heart, and, after being included with *Hokhmah* of the left that is in the heart, returns and ascends by way of the trachea to the brain. And likewise Mother, which is the secret of *Hokhmah* that is in *Binah,* i.e. *Hokhmah* of the left that is in the heart, ascends by way of the trachea to the brain to be enclothed in *ḥasadim,* and then returns and descends to the heart. And it follows that two ascend, namely, Father and Mother, and two descend, namely Father and Mother, as explained.

21) And it was explained above (4) that two ministers serve the heart, which is the King, the wine steward, which are the two wings of the lung, and the chief baker, which is the *omasum.* And the wine steward dresses *Hokhmah* in *ḥasadim,* and the chief baker complements the *ḥasadim* with *Hokhmah.* And this is stated regarding the mating of *Zeir Anpin* and *Malkhut* to

nourish the worlds, but in the mating to give birth to souls, the two kidneys are considered as the chief baker, in the secret of their cooking the seed that descends from the brain to give birth to souls. And on the text (426): "And after the King, which is the heart, has eaten, it is said of its two kidneys: `Eat, O companions' (Song of Songs 5:1)," for they cook the seed for the birth of souls. And on the text (427): "For the heart is the Throne of Judgment, and the four beings that are its messengers are the two wings of the lung and the two kidneys," for the two wings of the lung are two beings, i.e. right and left of *Ḥesed*, which are the wine stewards, and the two kidneys are the two beings of Judgment, which are the chief baker, as above. And they bear the Throne which is the heart, i.e. serve it, as above.

22) And it was clarified above (*Vaera*, page 13) that from the aspect of the vessels it is discernible that the right column is hot and that the left column is cold. And after the central column has acted with the curtain of *ḥirik*, and united the right and the left with each other, and the energies have emerged, the right column becomes cold and the left column hot. The passage should be studied well. And on the text here (428): "And the wind that blows from the wings of the lung blows through the two orifices of the nose..., and it is cold and chilled on the left and warm on the right;" for, since the wind rises upwards from below, from the lung to the two orifices of the nose, they are discerned according to the aspect of the vessels of right and left, where the cold is on the left and the hot on the right. "And from the point of view of the brain, which is the Throne of Mercy" from whom the wind emanates downwards from above by the central column, which is the secret of the Throne of Mercy "the cold wind is to the right, which is *Ḥesed*, and the warm is to the left, which is *Gvurah*," for from the point of view of the central column, the lights are reversed, the hot being on the left and the cold on the right, as was clarified above (*Vaera* 13, q.v.).

THE FAITHFUL SHEPHERD
SEVEN HEAVENS

443 The Faithful Shepherd began by saying: It is written: "Though our lips were full of praise as the expansive firmament" (Prayer book, *Nishmat*, Sabbaths and Festivals). And the heavens are seven in number: Curtain, Firmament, Heavens, Abode, Residence, Dwelling, and Skies (*Talmud Bavli, Hagigah* 12b). Heavens [*Sheḥakim*] is so called because therein the millstones grind the mannah for the righteous, which are *Yesod* and *Malkhut* that are called righteous and righteousness. This grinding is for the future, i.e. from the emanation of *Binah* that is called the future, and the basis for the name *Sheḥakim* is the verse: "And you shall grind [*shaḥakta*] some of it very thin" (Exodus 30:36). And they are *Netzaḥ* and *Hod*, about which it is said: "And the heavens [*sheḥakim*] shall pour down righteousness" (Isaiah 45:8), which is the lower *Shekhinah*, i.e. *Malkhut*, which is called righteousness, to which the emanation pours down from the Heavens [*sheḥakim*].

444 The first heaven, which is *Malkhut*, is called Curtain, for in it is the beneficence entering in the evening, and which emanates in the morning, this being the time for emanating. And the second one to be called a heaven is *Yesod*, for in it the sun and the moon give light, for they are the central column, i.e. *Tiferet*, and the lower *Shekhinah*, i.e. *Malkhut*.

That is to say that *Yesod* unites *Zeir Anpin* and *Malkhut* with each other, and both of them illuminate through it, as it is written: "And God set them in the firmament of the heaven to give light upon the earth" (Genesis 1:17). And the righteous one, which is *Yesod*, is called "sign" when uniting *Netzaḥ* and *Hod*, but "testimony" when uniting *Tiferet* and *Malkhut*.

NETZAḤ AND HOD

445 *Netzaḥ* and *Hod* are the two halves of one body, like two twins, which is why they are called

***sheḥakim* [Heavens, the plural form of *shaḥak*]. The two of them together are the letter *vav* (spelled out: *vav* vav) of *veshet,* (esophagus) from the aspect of the left, and they are the two grinders from the view of the right.**

Commentary:

For in truth the right column and the left column contradict each other, for the right column is drawn from the aspect of the *ḥolam* (vowel `o'), which is the secret of the ascent of *Malkhut* to *Binah* and the departure of the upper three *Sfirot*, while the left column is drawn from the point of the *shuruk* (vowel `u'), the secret of which is that *Malkhut* has returned and descended from *Binah*, and the upper three *Sfirot* have left again. (As above, *Bereshith Aleph*, page 15). That being so, the right column is cancelled as though it had never been, for *Malkhut* has returned and descended from *Binah.* However, from the chest up of *Zeir Anpin*, He suckles from the parallel aspect from the chest up of *Arikh-Anpin*, for there Father and Mother are attired, for in them the yud does not emerge from the Air. (As above, *Bereshith Aleph*, page 251). This means that *Malkhut* does not descend from *Binah*, and the action of the left column is never received, and, therefore, from the chest and up of *Zeir Anpin*, although the left column emerges, it does not rescind the right column, for it suckles from the supreme Father and Mother. This is not the case from the chest down of *Zeir Anpin*, where the two columns, the right and the left, are called *Netzaḥ* and *Hod*, for they suckle from the aspect parallel to them from the chest down of *Arikh Anpin*, for there are Israel Grandfather and Understanding, in which the left column is revealed, the *yud* emerging from Air. Consequently, when the left column, which is *Hod*, appears, *Netzaḥ* immediately disappears, for when greatness returns there is certainly no more smallness there. However, even in Israel Grandfather and Understanding there is internal and external, where, in the aspect of the internal of Israel Grandfather and Understanding the right column is also in control and the yud does not emerge from Air, as in Father and Mother. And so, when *Netzaḥ* and *Hod* of *Zeir Anpin* receive from the internal of Israel Grandfather and Understanding, the right column retains its existence even after the emergence of the left column, for the right column receives strength from the right column of the internal of Israel Grandfather and Understanding.

And consequently, *Netzaḥ* and *Hod* of *Zeir Anpin* have two aspects. If they are in the aspect of external, i.e. receiving from the external of Israel Grandfather and Understanding, then *Netzaḥ* is rescinded by the emergence of *Hod*, just as greatness does away with smallness. But when they receive from the internal of Israel Grandfather and Understanding, then the right column remains in force even after the emergence of the left column.

And on the text: "*Netzaḥ* and *Hod* are the two halves of one body, like two twins," for *Netzaḥ* and *Hod* are two halves of one body, for the right column is the emergence of smallness, and the left column is the emergence of greatness, of the same body, i.e. of the same stage, and from this aspect, greatness should do away with smallness, but, nevertheless, both of them remain in control, like two twins. But this is only so from the aspect of the interior of *Netzaḥ* and *Hod*, for the right column receives its strength from the interior of Israel Grandfather and Understanding, as above. "Which is why they are called *sheḥakim*," because both of them are in control, each over itself, war against each other and pulverize each other, as above. "The two of them together are the letter *vav* [spelled out: *vav vav*] of *veshet* (esophagus), from the aspect of the left...", for from the aspect of the exterior of Israel Grandfather and Understanding, which is the left side, the two of them are considered as one stage, for the left annuls the right. And the letter *vav* of *veshet* alludes to them, for when the *vav* of *veshet* (*vav shin tet*) is lengthened, it becomes a *nun*, as in Satan (*shin tet nun*) [the letters of *veshet* re-arranged, with *nun* in place of *vav* —tr.] because it was without grinding (as above, 366). "And they are the two grinders from the view of the right," for, from the aspect of the interior of Israel Grandfather and Understanding, which is the right side, the right side, which is *Netzaḥ*, also has validity, and then they are two separate stages that are warring against each other, and they are the two grinders that grind up the mannah for the righteous.

446 "And Moses took the bones of Joseph with him" (Exodus 13:19), that is the bones of the "righteous one, the foundation [*Yesod*] of the world" (Proverbs 10:25), which is the level of Joseph the righteous. And about them, about *Netzaḥ* and *Hod*, it is said: "My food [*leḥem*] which is presented to Me for offerings made by fire" (Numbers 28:2); and by 'food' or 'bread' [*leḥem*] is meant Torah (cf. *Midrash Bereshith Rabba*, 43, 6), i.e. *Netzaḥ* and *Hod* who are warring [root: *lamed ḥet mem*, the same as the word *leḥem*] against each other, in the secret of the above-mentioned grinding. And it is said about them: "Come, eat [*laḥamu*] of my bread [*laḥami*]" (Proverbs 9:5). And they *Netzaḥ* and *Hod*, are the bunches of grapes that are bestowed by the righteous one, which is *Yesod*. And the righteous one, which is *Yesod*, is called a fruit-tree, and for it is it said: "And they bore it upon a pole [*Mot*] between two" (Numbers 13:23). And why on a pole? Why does it not say "And they bore it upon a tree?" It is because the righteous one, who is called tree, was not there, for *Yesod*, which is the central column, did not unite the two bunches of grapes, which are *Netzaḥ* and *Hod*, so that they might be included in each other, and they therefore bore on a pole between two, without the inclusion of the righteous one.

447 And because *Netzaḥ* and *Hod* should not be separated, it is said about the righteous one, which is *Yesod*: "He will never suffer the righteous to collapse [*mot*]" (Psalms 55:23). [This verse can also be rendered: He will never give a pole (*mot*) to the righteous one —tr.]. That is, *Yesod* will never cease uniting *Netzaḥ* and *Hod*, and it is tree, about which it is said: "Whether there is a tree in it or not" (Numbers 13:20). But those (the spies) who spread an evil report of the land (cf. ibid. v.32) uprooted this tree, which is righteous one, which is *Yesod*, and gave rise to "And they bore it upon a pole between two" (ibid. v. 23) on a pole and not on a tree. And the two are *Netzaḥ* and *Hod*, in the aspects of *vav vav* without the unity of *Yesod*, for the righteous one is collapsed [*mot*] because they spread an evil report on the land. [Wherever the Hebrew word "*etz*" (tree) is used in a verse, this indicates the inclusion of "*Yesod*" (central column). Where another but similar word is used in a verse, this indicates the exclusion of the central column —tr.].

448 And about *Netzaḥ* and *Hod* it was said, in connection with the sin of the tree of knowledge (cf. Genesis 11:17), that Eve squeezed grapes (cf. *Midrash Bereshith Rabba* 19, 5). [In *Midrash Bereshith Rabba* 15, 7 R. Judah b. R. Ila'i is quoted as saying that the fruit of the tree was grapes —tr.] And she gave to him, for *Netzaḥ* and *Hod* are called bunches of grapes (as above, 446), and grapes are the secret of the illumination of *Ḥokhmah* that is on the left, for it is forbidden to draw it down, from above downwards (as above *Bereshith Aleph*, page 60), and its being drawn down from above is compared to the squeezing of grapes, which is the secret of the sin of the tree of knowledge. The righteous one, which is *Yesod*, contains a secret (*sod*), [the root of *Yesod*: *yud samekh vav* dalet, includes the Hebrew word for secret (*sod*) *samekh vav dalet* — tr.] which is cellaret wine from its grapes, from the Six Days of Creation, for *Yesod* guards the grapes which is the secret of the illumination of *Ḥokhmah*, so that they would not be squeezed, i.e. that it should not be drawn down from above, but only upwards from below; and the Six Days of Creation are the six levels of *Ḥesed*, *Gvurah*, *Tiferet*, *Netzaḥ*, *Hod*, and *Yesod*, of the letter *vav* [whose numerical value is six —tr.] which is *Tiferet*, the central column, which is to say that *Yesod* receives its power of protection from it (as above, *Bereshith Aleph*, page 60). And they are called seraphim when they are *vav vav* without unity, as it is written: "... the seraphim, each one had six wings" (Isaiah 6:2). [The structure of the Hebrew of this verse is: six wings, six wings for each —tr.]. That is, six, [the numerical value of *vav* —tr.] is mentioned twice. And they are called seraphim from the aspect of the left that is in them, and they extract water from the aspect of the right that is in them, and they are thirsty because of the flame that is in them from the side of *Gvurah*, i.e. from the left side, and they draw water from the side of *Ḥesed*.

449 About *Netzaḥ* and *Hod* it is said: "Who makes winds (spirits) His messengers" (Psalms 104:4), i.e. from the side of the central column, which is *Zeir Anpin*. That is to say that they are the winds that are drawn down from *Zeir Anpin* to within the wings of the lung (as above, in the Commentator's Interpolation, paragraph 3), that blow on the heart, which is the tenth level of the Holy Spirit, i.e. *Malkhut*, which is between them, i.e. between *Netzaḥ* and *Hod*; and this is *Yesod*, which is the letter *vav* (whose numerical value is 6), which is a sign in his hosts that includes the six joints of the two legs, which are *Netzaḥ* and *Hod*, each one of which has three joints, because it is the central column. For it is written about them: "His legs are as pillars of marble [*shesh*]" (Song of Songs 5:15) [as well as meaning 'marble,' the word *shesh* means six —tr.]. And this is the righteous one, the sign of the covenant that includes the six of *Netzaḥ* and *Hod*.

450 The upper *vav* of the two *vavs* in the name of

the letter *vav* (spelled out: *vav vav*) is *Tiferet*, because it is the central column between the six joints of the two arms, and because this is body and covenant, namely *Tiferet* and *Yesod*, which is called *vav vav*, i.e. the two *vavs* of the letter *vav* written out in full: *vav vav*, and we consider them one. And they, *Netzaḥ* and *Hod*, "spread out their wings on high" (Exodus 25:20) towards the heavenly *vav* that is above them, namely *Tiferet*; and by its side, *Netzaḥ* and *Hod* are called the true prophets, for *Tiferet* is called truth. "*Netzaḥ* and *Hod* screen with their wings" (Exodus 25:20) the covenant, i.e. *Yesod*, which is the second *vav*, which is "the righteous one, foundation of the world" (Proverbs 10:25). And this is why *Netzaḥ* and *Hod* grind up the manna for the righteous who are from the side of "the righteous one, foundation of the world," which is between them, for the righteous one, which is *Yesod*, is the central column between *Netzaḥ* and *Hod*, and receives from the manna that they grind, and this is why *Netzaḥ* and *Hod* are called grinders.

451 And from the side of *veshet* (esophagus), which had a prior grinding in the teeth, it is said: "The people went about [*shatu*: *shin tet vav*, the letters of *veshet*, re-arranged] and gathered it" (Numbers 11:8), it being the collection of judgments that is in the Mishnah, i.e. the Female Waters that Israel causes to rise up by engaging in Torah and Mishnah, which ascend to the secret of the upper *veshet* (esophagus) for *shatu*: *shin tet vav* re-arranged make up the word *veshet*: *vav shin tet* (esophagus) (as above in the Commentator's Interpolation, paragraph 7, q.v.). "And (they) ground it in mills" (Numbers 11:8). It follows that whoever brings out of his mouth words of Torah, must grind them in his teeth, i.e. clarify them completely, in order to express complete words, and these words are called complete or perfect. But as

for the others, the words that are scorned, these words are eaten greedily, without being ground in their molars and their teeth, i.e. they do not clarify fully the words of the Torah that they bring out of their mouths, and about them it is written: "While the flesh was yet between their teeth... and the anger of the Lord was kindled against the people" (Numbers 11:33). This is because they come from the root of he (Esau) who said: "Let me swallow down, I pray you..." (Genesis 25:30), i.e. the wicked Esau. And *Netzaḥ* and *Hod* are called *K'ruvim*, whence the verse: "And the *K'ruvim* shall spread out their wings on high" (Exodus 25:20), which refers to *Netzaḥ* and *Hod*, as explained in the preceding paragraph.

SAID THE SABBATH: YOU HAVE GIVEN ME NO MATE

452 There are eight *Sfirot*: *Ḥokhmah, Binah, Gedulah, Gvurah, Tiferet, Malkhut, Netzaḥ, Hod*. *Tzadik* ('righteous one'), which is *Yesod*, has a diadem on His head, for it has no mate. What is the meaning of His diadem? It refers to the upper *Keter* (crown). And in respect thereof the sages of the Mishnah taught: In the next world there is no eating or drinking, but the righteous sit with their diadems upon their heads (cf. *Talmud Bavli, Berakhot* 17a). And this is as they taught: The Sabbath pleaded before the Holy One, blessed be He: "To all the days You gave a partner, but to me You gave no partner" (*Midrash Bereshith Rabba*, 11, 8 in the name of Rabbi Shimon bar Yoḥai).

Commentary:

It is clarified that there are two *Malkhut*, namely: The Key and the Lock. The meaning of the Key is *Malkhut*, as sweetened by *Binah* and called the diadem of *Yesod*, it being part of the upper nine *Sfirot* and not of *Malkhut* itself (as above in the Introduction to the *Sefer haZohar*, pages 44 & 45). And the other is the Lock, which is *Malkhut* proper. And it is hidden away at the head of the Ancient One, and there is nothing of it in Atziluth except the aspect of an insignificant illumination and this, too, is only in the upper three *Sfirot* of the *Partsufim* (configuration), i.e. from the chest and upwards, while from the chest and downwards there is no mention of it (as above, Introduction to the *Sefer haZohar*, page 44, which passage should be well studied). Consequently, it is noted that the aspect of *Malkhut* is only from the chest upwards, which is the secret of the face of man. But from the chest and downwards, after *Yesod*, there is nothing but the Key, i.e. the diadem of *Yesod*, which is the aspect of *Malkhut*, mollified by *Binah*, while from the aspect of the Lock, which is the true *Malkhut*, there is nothing. It is also known that *Malkhut* of the Lock is not included in any *sfirah*, since its location is under *Yesod* and not above it. But *Malkhut* of the Key, which is *Malkhut* that ascended to *Binah*, becomes female of the left column of the *Sfirot*, i.e. in *Binah*, *Gvurah* and *Hod*. Because *Malkhut* ascended to *Binah*, *Binah* became the Female of *Ḥokhmah*. Likewise, *Gvurah* became the Female of *Ḥesed*, and *Hod* became the Female of *Netzaḥ*.

And on the text: There are eight, *Sfirot*, i.e. four pairs. *Ḥokhmah Binah* are the first pair. Gedulah *Gvurah* are the second pair. *Tiferet Malkhut* are the third pair, i.e. the *Malkhut* that is above the chest and contains the illumination from the Lock, as above. *Netzaḥ Hod* are the fourth pair. But the righteous one, which is *Yesod*, has a diadem on His head, for it has no mate. For the partner of *Yesod* should have been *Malkhut* of the Lock, whose place is at the end of the nine *Sfirot*, but it is hidden away and is not there, as above. Nevertheless, the diadem of *Yesod* serves in its place. What is the meaning of His diadem? It refers to the upper *Keter* (crown), for which is the Key, the aspect of *Binah* that is called upper crown. And this is not *Yesod*'s partner, for only *Malkhut* of the Lock is its mate. In the next world, which is *Binah*, the righteous sit with their diadems on their heads. For when *Zeir Anpin* ascends to *Binah*, which is the next world, *Malkhut* of the key becomes a diadem on its head, in the secret of the verse: "A virtuous woman is a diadem to her husband" (Proverbs 12:4). For *Malkhut* of the Key is not the mate of *Yesod*, but upper crown is. And so it is taught: The Sabbath, which is *Yesod*, pleaded before the Holy One, blessed be He. To all the days, i.e. to all the *Sfirot* from *Ḥokhmah* to *Hod*, You gave a partner, as above, but to me, to *Yesod*, You gave no partner. For its partner is *Malkhut* of the Lock which was hidden away, as above.

THE LETTER AYIN OF THE WORD SHEMA (HEAR) AND THE LETTER DALET OF THE WORD EḤAD (ONE) IN THE SHEMA YISRAEL.

453 Rabbi Shimon began by quoting: "Hear, O Israel, the Lord our God, the Lord is One" (Deuteronomy 6:4). (In the Torah scroll) the letter *ayin* in the word *Shema* (Hear) is written larger, and so is the letter *dalet* in the word *Eḥad* (one). And these two letters, the *ayin* and the *dalet*, form the word '*ed*', meaning a witness, as is written: "The Lord is witness against you" (I Samuel 12:5). And from the word *shema* [*shin mem ayin*], the letters *shin mem* remain, the *mem* being medial (i.e. that form of the letter that is used at the beginning or in the middle of words). What is the reason that the *mem* is not final? (i.e. the form of the same letter used when it is the last letter of a word.) What is the difference between a medial mem and a final *mem*? It is that the final *mem* is the upper *Melekh* (king), i.e. *Binah*, while the medial *mem* alludes to the lower *Melekh* (king), i.e. *Malkhut*. And the letters *shin mem* of the word *Shema* allude to *Malkhut*. And the other letters of the *Eḥad* [*aleph ḥet dalet*, one] that remain are: *aleph ḥet* [*aḥ*, brother]. "It is the glory of God to conceal a thing" (Proverbs 25:2), it is written.

Commentary:

It is known that *Malkhut* has two states:

a) When it is developed like *Zeir Anpin* and enclothes the left column of *Binah*, then it is the sealed or final mem as is *Binah*, i.e. its lights are blocked off (as above, *Bereshith Aleph*, page 247); and in this state *Zeir Anpin* and *Malkhut* are called brother and sister, for both of them are then the children of *Binah*, for *Zeir Anpin* attires the right column of *Binah* and *Malkhut* in the left column of *Binah*.

b) And the second state is after it has been diminished to the aspect of from the chest and downwards of *Zeir Anpin*, and has descended to below the level of *Zeir Anpin*, and has become the aspect of the wife of *Zeir Anpin*, i.e. as one who receives from *Zeir Anpin*; but its lights are on and it illuminates to those below in all perfection (as explained above, *Bereshith Aleph*, from 110-116, q.v.). And it is then called an open or medial mem, for it is opened from its blockage. Three combinations can be made from the letters of the two words *shema* [*shin mem ayin*] and *Eḥad* [*aleph ḥet dalet*], namely: *Shin mem* [*shem*, name]; *ayin dalet* [*ed*, witness]; *aleph ḥet* [*aḥ*, brother]. *Shin mem* is *Malkhut* that is called *shem* (name). *Ayin dalet* is *Zeir Anpin*, as it is written: "The Lord is witness [*ed*, *ayin dalet*]" (Samuel I 12:5). *aleph ḥet* [*aḥ*, brother] is also *Zeir Anpin*, as it is written: "Open to me, my sister" (Song of Songs 5:2). And the difference between witness and brother (both of which are *Zeir Anpin*) is that witness is when *Zeir Anpin* emanates to *Malkhut* revealed energies from the upper Eden, and brother is when *Zeir Anpin* is in the aspect of rear with *Malkhut*, i.e. in the first state, for then *Zeir Anpin* and *Malkhut* are comparable to a brother and sister. And on the text: "The letter *ayin* in the word *shema* (hear) is written larger, and so is the letter *dalet* in the word *Eḥad* (one)." This refers to the revealed energies of *Zeir Anpin*, for *Zeir Anpin* is then called: "The Lord is witness [*ed*, *ayin dalet*]" (Samuel I 12:5). From the word *shema*, [*shin mem ayin*], the letters *shin mem* remain, the *mem* being medial, for this refers to *Malkhut* in the second state, when its lights have already opened, because she received developed energies of *Zeir Anpin*, called *ed* (witness). And this happens in such a way that both the combinations *shin mem* and *ayin dalet* reflect the mating of *Zeir Anpin* and *Malkhut* in the second state, where *Malkhut* is a medial mem. And on the text: "What is the reason that the *mem* is not final?" That is to say: why is *Malkhut* not sealed? And the answer is given: The final *mem* is the upper king, i.e. *Malkhut* is called final (or sealed) *mem* when it attires the upper king which is *Binah*, i.e. in the first state. Medial *mem* alludes to lower king, i.e. when *Malkhut* is in the aspect of itself, which is below *Zeir Anpin*, and is then called medial *mem*. And because here *Malkhut* receives from *Zeir Anpin* in the concept of (*ed*), witness which is within the framework of the open *mem*. And the combination *aleph ḥet* [*aḥ*, `brother,' the two remaining letters of the word *Eḥad*, one, after the *dalet* is removed for `*ed*', `witness'], refers to the level of *Zeir Anpin* that is in the first state of *Malkhut*, but now, in the second state, it remains without action. And on the text: "And the other letters of the *Eḥad* [*aleph ḥet dalet*, one] that remain are: *aleph ḥet* [*aḥ*, brother]." That is to say they have remained without action, for *Malkhut* is now already diminished and hidden from being in the aspect of a sister to *Zeir Anpin*, which is the secret of the verse: "It is the glory of God to conceal a thing" (Proverbs 25:2). For, although in the first state *Zeir Anpin* and *Malkhut* were in the aspect of two large lights, a brother and sister, this was not to *Malkhut*'s honor, for its lights were blocked off, but now in the second state, although it [*Malkhut*] is diminished and hidden from its large stage, for this very reason its lights are opened in the secret of the mating *shin mem ayin dalet*, and it emanates to all the worlds, this being "the glory of God," and all this happened because of "concealing a thing."

454 I have found it (written) in the book of Rabbi Hammuna Sava: Everyone who makes this unity (i.e. recites the *Shema Yisrael*) each day, rejoicing is prepared for him on high, in the secret of the letters *shin mem* of the word *shema* (Hear) at the beginning of the verse, and *aleph ḥet* of the word *Eḥad* (one) at the end of the verse. And he starts to join them together, i.e. the *aleph* of the *aleph ḥet* (from *Eḥad,* one) at the end of the verse is placed before the *shin* of the *shin mem* (from *shema,* hear) at the beginning of the verse; and he continues, i.e. the *mem* of the *shin mem* (from *shema,* hear), and subsequently the *ḥet* of the *aleph ḥet* (from *Eḥad,* one). The four letters so arranged, i.e. *aleph shin mem ḥet,* make the word *esmaḥ,* as in the verse: "I will rejoice [*esmaḥ*] in the Lord" (Psalm 104:34). And this is so literally, for it is the holy unity, alluded to in the letters *ayin dalet* (*'ed',* witness) for the letters of the two words *Shema* (hear) and *Eḥad* (one), when re-arranged as above, form the two words *esmaḥ* (I will rejoice) *'ed'* (witness) and this is only right. And thus is it (written) in the Book of Enokh, who similarly said that whoever makes this unity (i.e. recites the *Shema Yisrael*) each day, rejoicing from above is extended to him).

455 Furthermore, let us reflect upon the word *shema* (hear), for it includes the two letters *shin mem,* together with the large *ayin* [and *shin mem* spells the word *shem,* name —tr.]. These are the seventy [the numerical value of the letter *ayin* —tr.] names that are in the secret of the holy patriarchs, i.e. the 72 names in *Ḥesed, Gvurah,* and *Tiferet* that are called patriarchs (as above, *Beshallaḥ,* 173), of which there are seventy main names in the secret of the 70 (members of) the Sanhedrin [the supreme court and legislature of rabbinic times — tr.] and the 2 witnesses (ibid 163), and this is the secret of *shema* (hear): *shema* [*shin mem ayin*] is *shem* [*shin mem*] *ayin* (=70), i.e. the name of 70, where *shem* (name) is

Malkhut that is composed of the 70 names. (And the ensuing four words of the *Shema Yisrael* are) O-Israel, the-Lord our-God, the-Lord, these being the four compartments of the phylacteries, which are the four intelligences: *Ḥokhmah*, *Binah*, the right of *Da'at*, and the left that is in *Da'at*, to which the two letters *aleph ḥet* (*aḥ*, brother) from the word *Eḥad* (*aleph ḥet dalet*, one) are attached. And *Eḥad* refers to the one who said: "Open to me, my sister, my love" (Song of Songs 5:2), namely: *Zeir Anpin*. And the letter *dalet* from the word *Eḥad* is the knot of the head phylacteries, which is the shape of the letter *dalet*, for *Malkhut* is attached to them. And the secret was given to the sages, but not to be revealed. Rabbi Shimon fell silent. He cried, then laughed and said: I shall tell the secret, for it is certainly the Heavenly Will, for there will be no generation such as this one until the King Messiah comes, in which permission will be granted to reveal it.

THE STRAPS AND THE KNOT OF THE HAND PHYLACTERIES

456 Two straps come out of each side, i.e. from the right and the left, this being the secret of the two thighs that are from the chest and downwards of that (*aḥ*, *aleph ḥet*) brother, which is *Zeir Anpin*, i.e. *Netzaḥ* and *Hod* of *Zeir Anpin*, onto which the prophets of truth hold. For above, on the head, two straps come out, which are the secret of the two arms that surround the head from the right and from the left, which are the secret of *Ḥesed* and *Gvurah*, and to which the *dalet*, which is *Malkhut*, is attached, in the secret of the knot of the head phylactery. Later *Malkhut* descends, and the straps, which are the secret of the thighs below, fall loose. For, since it (*Malkhut*) is attached above, with the *dalet* of the knot of the head phylactery, as is proper, it descends below to *Netzaḥ*, *Hod*, and *Yesod*, to hold on with her Hosts and becomes attached in Her Host which means sharing beneficence to the dwellers of the worlds of

Briah, Yetzirah, and Assiah. It is so attached at the end of the thighs, and the imprint of the *yud*, which is the holy covenant, i.e. *Yesod*, is on it from above, and it then unites in one unity with *Zeir Anpin*.

Commentary:

Although in the first state *Malkhut* is blocked and congealed, as above, and is able to illuminate only after it comes into the second state (as above, 453), nevertheless the vessels of the second state are fitting for the receipt of *ḥasadim* only and not to *Ḥokhmah*. And therefore, so that *Malkhut* should also be able to receive *Ḥokhmah*, it is necessary first to awaken the building of *Malkhut* from the aspect of the first stage, in order to receive from there vessels for the acceptance of *Ḥokhmah*, and, subsequently, so that *Malkhut* would be able to receive the lights and emanate, it is brought down to the second stage. And on the text: For above, on the head, two straps come out; these are the secret of *Ḥesed* and *Gvurah* that are above the chest of *Zeir Anpin*. And to which the *dalet* is attached; this is the secret of the awakening of the first state of *Malkhut*, whose stature is equivalent to *Ḥesed*, *Gvurah*, and *Tiferet* of *Zeir Anpin*, that attire the right column of *Binah*, while *Malkhut* attires the left column of *Binah*. And then *Malkhut* is called *dalet*, in the meaning of impoverished [*dalah*] and poor, for its lights are congealed and it is unable to emanate to the worlds of *Briah*, *Yetzirah*, and *Assiah*. However, from this state the perfect tools that are fitting for the receipt of *Ḥokhmah* are drawn to it (to *Malkhut*), and so that it should be able to emanate properly to the worlds of *Briah*, *Yetzirah*, and *Assiah*, it is necessary to draw it down to the second state, i.e. to reduce it to the aspect of "from the chest and downwards of *Zeir Anpin*" so that it should be the bottom level, under *Yesod* of *Zeir Anpin*. And then it will be able to render beneficence (as above,

453). And on the text: And since it is attached above, as is proper, it descends below: For after the unity has been effected above from the chest as is proper, in the secret of the dalet of the knot of the phylacteries, drawing down perfect tools to her, *Malkhut* has to be continued below from the chest of *Zeir Anpin*, in order to take hold of its hosts, so that it should be able to render bestowal to the dwellers in the worlds of *Briah*, *Yetzirah*, and *Assiah*. For in the first state it was blocked up and unable to bestow anything, while this second state is its main perfection. And on the text: "And when it is attached there... it is so attached at the end of the thighs, and the imprint of the *yud*, which is the holy covenant, is on it from above," i.e. after it has been reduced and becomes the stage under *Netzaḥ*, *Hod*, and *Yesod* of *Zeir Anpin*, which is the secret of the second state, it then unites in one unity, which was not the case above in the secret of the unity of the *dalet* of the knot of the phylacteries, which alludes to the first state, where *Zeir Anpin* and *Malkhut* were not in one unity, but were rather in the aspect of back to back.

457 *Yud* is the secret of the covenant, i.e. *Yesod*, for everyone who keeps this covenant will be saved in heaven and on earth. Because Pinḥas [*pei nun ḥet samekh*] was zealous for this covenant, he was saved from the heavenly judgment and from earthly judgment, which is why the letter yud was added into his name, as it is written: *Piynḥas* [*pei yud nun ḥet samekh*]" (Numbers 25:11).

458 This *yud* has to be such that it will never move from the hand phylactery, i.e. the knot of the hand phylactery that is in the shape of the letter *yud*, which alludes to *Yesod*, as above. This is that there should be no separation between *Yesod*, which is *yud*, and the hand phylactery, which is *Malkhut*. And the whole of *Malkhut*'s rejoicing is with this *yud*, which is *Yesod*. And this *yud* is to be

found in the Male but not in the Female, for the Male, *Yesod,* is called righteous one [*tzadik*: *tzadi dalet yud kuf*], while the Female, *Malkhut,* is called righteousness [*tzedek*: *tzadi dalet kuf*], without *yud,* for *yud* is to be found with the Male and not with the Female. And this is why the *yud* is close to it on the hand phylactery, and whoever moves the *yud,* which is *Yesod,* away from this place, from *Malkhut,* which is the hand phylactery, will himself be far from the delights of the next world, i.e. he will not be privileged to receive the emanation coming from the mating of *Yesod* and *Malkhut* that is drawn down from the upper Eden, which is called the next world.

459 In the Male is righteous one [*tzadik*: *tzadi dalet yud kuf*], while the Female is righteousness [*tzedek*: *tzadi dalet kuf*], without a *yud.* Similarly *ish* (a man, *aleph yud shin*) is written with a *yud,* while *ishah* (a woman, *aleph shin hei*) is written without a *yud.* This is why it is her rejoicing to come close to the *yud* so that it will delight (root: Eden) with her in the mating. Whoever removes this delighting is himself removed from Eden on high. And thus it is written: "For them that honor Me, I will honor" (I Samuel 2:30).

NOW WHEN PINḤAS... SAW... AND TOOK A SPEAR IN HIS HAND

460 Come and see: Pinḥas stood before the strong judgment of Isaac and blocked up the breach, i.e. halted the plague which came from the harsh judgments of the left that is called *Yitzḥak.* For this reason, the letter *yud* was added to Pinḥas' name, giving it the same numerical value as the name *Yitzḥak.* He stood in the breach as it is written: "Then stood up Pinḥas and wrought judgment, and so the plague was stayed" (Psalms 106:30), Pinḥas here being written with a *yud,* i.e. *Piynḥas.* He stood in the breach against the judgment of Isaac in order to defend Israel, which is why their names have the same numerical value, e.g. *Yitzḥak* [*yud tzadi ḥet kuf,* 10 + 90 + 8 + 100 = 208] and *Piynḥas* [*pei yud nun*

ḥet samekh, 80 + 10 + 50 + 8 + 60 = 208].

461 Should you suggest that the matching of numerical equivalent, which is the secret of *Ḥokhmah* (as above, *Pikudei,* 28), is dependent on none but its eyes, i.e. on the illumination of *Ḥokhmah* that is in *Malkhut,* for eyes are *Ḥokhmah,* and *Ḥokhmah* is revealed only in *Malkhut* and not in any other *sfirah* (as above, *Bereshith Aleph,* page 276), while here (contrary to this rule) you have matched numerical equivalents higher up, at Isaac, which is the left column of *Zeir Anpin,* then I should reply that you are certainly right, but there is an explanation. The matching of numerical equivalents, which is the secret of *Ḥokhmah,* is here made at the level of Isaac, since Isaac depends upon and is drawn from the place that is called eyes, i.e. it is drawn to *Ḥokhmah* that is in *Malkhut,* where the judgments of the whole world are judged, for all the judgments that are in the world have their root in the judgments of *Ḥokhmah,* for its eyes (an eye = *ayin,* which letter has the numerical value of 70) are the 70 Thrones of Judgment, which is where the judgments that are in the world are, and they are called the seventy (members) of the Sanhedrin [the name of the supreme court and legislature in rabbinic times —tr.] and the number 70 [*ayin*] is because they are drawn from its eyes [*eynayim,* in the singular: *ayin*]. Thus everything is one, because Isaac and the eyes of *Malkhut* go together, for *Malkhut* is built up from Isaac and its eyes are derived from him, i.e. from the left column, and so the two of them are really one, and everything fits.

462 So Pinḥas is Isaac, for Pinḥas stood up and judged the case of Zimri and Cozbi (see Numbers 25), and put on the strong *Gvurah* (might), which is left and is called Isaac. And because of this deed [the spearing of Zimri and Cozbi —tr.], Pinḥas merited the right, i.e. he earned the priesthood, which is *Ḥesed,* left being here included in the right. "Pinḥas, the son of Elazar, the son of Aaron

the priest, has turned My wrath away from the children of Israel" (Numbers 25:11). What is the meaning of "turned My wrath away?" The answer is that this refers to the three officials in Gehenna (Hell) who are called Destruction, Anger, and Wrath. For Pinḥas saw that wrath spreading and being drawn down from the side of Isaac. What did he do? He put on the level of Isaac, which is the root of wrath, and then he took hold of that wrath as one who takes hold of his fellow and pushes him back.

Commentary:

Wrath is the Judgment of the Male, which is the secret of the judgments that are drawn down from the left column which is Isaac. Since Israel sinned with idolatry, which is the secret of the drawing down of the left, downwards from above, the wrath spread over them. Pinḥas then attired himself in the left, which is Isaac, which is the root of wrath, and so the text says that he gripped it as a man takes hold of his fellow and pushes him back, as we shall explain further below.

463 And then he judged the case and passed judgment. He judged the case according to the rule: If a man makes an Aramean woman his paramour [as did Zimri see Numbers 25:6], the zealots (like Pinḥas) may fall upon him and it was permitted to strike Zimri (Mishnah, Sanhedrin 9, 6). And he passed judgment, as it is written: "And thrust both of them through" (Numbers 25:8). Wherefore it is written: "Has turned My wrath away" (ibid. v. 11), while elsewhere it is written: "He has turned back His right hand from before the enemy" (Lamentations 2:3). Just as in the one case (of His right hand), the turning [*heshiv*] is back, so also in the other case (of My wrath), the turning [*heshiv*] is back.

And thus the *yud* that was added here to the name of Pinḥas is the *yud* that is in Isaac, which alludes to *Yesod* (as above, 457). And it is all "away from the Children of Israel" (Numbers 25:11), for when he (Pinḥas) saw that wrath, he saw it as it was descending on the heads of children of Israel, and it is therefore written: "...has turned My wrath away (literally: from over) from the Children of Israel", (ibid.).

Commentary:

It is not said that he removed or annulled [*hesir*] My wrath, but that he turned it away (re-directed it). This teaches that he did not anul it altogether, but removed it from the internal aspect only, while leaving it in the aspect of the rear ones. For this is the secret of the harsh judgments that are drawn down with *Ḥokhmah* in order to expel the external and wicked ones who want to draw down from it, downwards from above. (As above in the *Idra Rabba*, 219). And the text brings a proof of this from the verse: "He has turned back His right hand" (Lamentations 2:3), where the turning [*heshiv*] could not mean, heaven forbid, that he annulled the right, but only that he turned it away, re-directed it to the rear. The same word [*heshiv*] is used here (Numbers 25) for turning away the wrath, and so the meaning here too is not that he annulled it, but that he re-directed it to the rear [this is deduced using the exegetical principle of *gezerah shavah* inference by analogy]. And the wrath remains there in order to expel the external and wicked ones. It is therefore written: "Away (literally: from over) the Children of Israel" (ibid.), for he turned the wrath away only from the Children of Israel who cleave to the internal aspect, and not to the wicked who cleave to the rear.

THE LETTERS MEM VAV TAV ARE A SIGN OF THE ANGEL OF DEATH

464 It is written: "And when Pinḥas...saw..." (Numbers 25:7). What did he see? He saw a letter *mem* flying through the

sky, and this letter is a sign of the Angel of Death, for the *mem* wants to be built up with the letter *vav* and the letter *tav* to form the word *mem vav tav, Mavet*, 'death.' What did Pinḥas do, for he was then attired with Isaac? He then took that letter mem and snatched it away from the Angel of Death, and it joined him. And when the Angel of Death saw that Pinḥas had taken the letter *mem* to himself (to Pinḥas), he (the Angel of Death) immediately retired to the rear.

465 But what is the reason behind all this? The answer to this question is that when Pinḥas was zealous in his heart, he attired himself with Isaac [i.e. the letter *yud* was added to his name: Pinḥas. And he rose up to become *resh ḥet* (200 + 8 = 208), which is the numerical value of the letters of *Piynḥas* [*pei yud nun ḥet samekh*, 80 + 10 + 50 + 8 + 60 = 208]. It is also the numerical value of Isaac [*yud tzadi ḥet kuf*, 10 + 90 + 8 + 100 = 208] (as above, 460). And since he saw the letter mem flying in the sky, he snatched it and joined it to himself, and immediately became *resh mem ḥet*, (*romaḥ*, a spear). That is, the letter *mem* joined the numerical value of Pinḥas' name, *resh ḥet* [208] and formed the word *romaḥ*, a spear, as it is written: "...took a spear in his hand" (Numbers 25:7).

466 The letter *mem* was the first sign for Adam that death was ordained over the world, because this letter flew over Adam's head at the time when, as is written: "She took of [*mi*, i.e. the letter *mem*] the fruit thereof" (Genesis 3:6), and this *mem* was waiting for the letters *vav* and *tav*, as is written: "...and did eat [the word 'eat' starts *vav tav*]; and she gave [the word starts *vav tav*] also to her husband with her, and he did eat. And the eyes of them both were opened [the word starts *vav tav*] (Ibid., vv. 6-7). And thus was death [*mavet*: *mem vav tav*] established over the world.

467 And now Pinḥas saw that same letter *mem* that was flying over the heads

of the Children of Israel. And how did he see it? He saw the shape of a medial *mem* [the form used at the beginning or in the middle of words —tr.] covered in blood. When he saw it, he said: This is certainly a sign of the Angel of Death. He immediately snatched it, mentioned over it the Name of Names [i.e. the Tetragrammaton in its original pronunciation — tr.] and brought that letter down to himself. And the numerical value of *Piynḥas* [*pei yud nun ḥet samekh*, 80 + 10 + 50 + 8 + 60 = 208] is that of the letters *resh ḥet* (200 + 8 = 208), and the *mem* combined with the resh ḥet to form *resh mem ḥet* (*romaḥ*, a spear), as it is written: "And took a spear [*romaḥ*: *resh mem ḥet*] in his hand" (Numbers 25:7). And this is why it is also written: "Has turned My wrath away from over the Children of Israel, in that he was very zealous for My sake" (Numbers 25:11), for he (Pinḥas) was zealous for the Holy Name, for they had joined it (the Holy Name) to another dominion. "He was very zealous for My sake among them" (ibid.). What is the meaning of "among them"? The answer is that he went in amongst a number of hordes and a number of great ones and gave himself over to death for their sake, in order to save them. Therefore it is written: "Among them" (ibid.). But the real secret of "among them" is as follows: The letters of "among them" [*b'tokham*] are *bet tav vav kaf mem*, which can be read as two words, namely: *b'tokh* [*bet tav vav kaf*] *mem*, i.e. within *mem*, for the zealousness that he showed was with a *mem*.

Commentary:

The matter of the letters *mem vav tav* has already been thoroughly explained above (in the Introduction to the *Sefer haZohar*, 212-213, q.v.) where the *mem* is the aspect of the Male of the evil forces, i.e. the judgments of the Male that are revealed with *Ḥokhmah*, and the *tav* is the judgments of the Female, i.e.

the judgments of the Lock, from which death comes, and the *vav* is the basis [*Yesod*] that joins the *mem* with the *tav*. And death was not decreed on the world until after the mating of these two letters *mem* and *tav* through the *vav*, for at that point the Lock received strength to kill what was alive.

And on the text (466): "The letter *mem* was the first sign for Adam that death was ordained over the world, because this letter flew over Adam's head at the time when, as is written: 'She took of [*mi*, i.e. the letter *mem*] the fruit thereof' (Genesis 3:6);" for the tree of knowledge is the secret of *Malkhut* from the aspect of the left, and the secret of the sin was that he drew down the *Ḥokhmah* in it, downwards from above, according to the desire of Samael and Serpent who enticed him. And since it started to be drawn down, immediately revealed were the laws of the Male of the evil forces, which is the secret of the *mem* that flew over Adam's head, i.e. over the upper three *Sfirot* of Adam (= man) that are called head. And on the text: "At the time when, as is written: 'She took of [*mi*, i.e. the letter *mem*] the fruit thereof' (Genesis 3:6);" that is, at the time when he began to draw down *Ḥokhmah*, which is the secret of the fruit, on the advice of the Serpent, the *mem* was revealed. However, the male of the shell does not yet have the ability to kill, for death comes from the side of the *tav*, which is the Lock. And on the text: "And this *mem* was waiting for the letters *vav* and *tav*." The *mem* was waiting for the letters *vav tav*, which are the Female of the evil forces, from which comes death after the mating with the *mem*. And on the text: "As it is written: '...and did eat...and she gave...' And thus was death established over the world." For on conclusion of the eating [of the fruit of the tree —tr.], i.e. at the end of the drawing down, the letters *vav tav* were revealed, in the secret of the verse: "Sin couches at the door" (Genesis 4:7). And then the *mem* mated with the *vav tav*, and death came to the world.

And on the text (467): "Pinḥas saw the shape of a medial

mem covered in blood:" i.e. covered in impure blood, this being the secret of drawing down, from above downwards, which is called impure blood, i.e. because of the iniquity of Peor (see Numbers 25:3), and there he would see the shape of a *mem*, which is the judgments of the Male of the evil forces that wait to mate with the Female of the evil forces, which is *vav tav*, and to bring death. "He immediately snatched it." i.e. he snatched it away from the evil forces, and joined it (the *mem*) to holiness. Because when the *mem* and the impure blood that is on it are in the internal aspect, i.e. the desire is to draw it down, from above downwards, although it is full of Judgments, it is then at the disposal of the evil forces, and the evil forces draw death out of it, as above. However, if the *mem*, together with the impure blood that is on it, is placed in the aspect of the rear, i.e. this drawing down is rejected, then, because of the Judgments that are in it, it returns to holiness, for it becomes a guardian over holiness that the wicked ones should not draw from it, downwards from above (as above, in *Idra Rabba*, 219). And on the text: And "mentioned over it the Name of Names... and brought that letter down to himself." The central column, which is *Zeir Anpin*, is the secret of the Name of Names, i.e. the four-letter Tetragrammaton. And it is known that the central column reduces the upper three *Sfirot* of the left, onto which the evil forces and the wicked hold. Therefore, so that the letter *mem* might be corrected in order to be a guardian over the holiness, it was first necessary to mention over it the Name of the Names of *Zeir Anpin*, in order to reduce the upper three *Sfirot* of the left. And then: "And brought that letter down to himself." i.e. it descended and became a part of holiness. And on the text: "And the numerical value of Pinḥas... is that of the letters *resh ḥet* (208)," i.e. Pinḥas attired himself in the *Ḥokhmah* of the left of holiness, being also the numerical value of the name Isaac (208), in order to have control over the *mem* (as above, 464). And "the *mem* combined with *resh ḥet* to form *resh mem ḥet* (*romaḥ*, a spear)" and became the aspect of a spear, which, with the Judgments that are in it, killed Zimri and Cozbi, for this was achieved by the spear that reduced the upper three *Sfirot* of the left and stayed the plague (see Numbers 25:7 8). And on the text: "For he (Pinḥas) was zealous for the Holy Name, for the *mem* had been joined in another dominion," for the mem which had been in the hands of the evil forces did in truth belong to the Holy name, to protect *Ḥokhmah* from the suckling of the wicked, as above. And on the text: "For the zealousness that he showed was with a *mem*." For he (Pinḥas) was zealous because the *mem* was in the hands of the evil forces, as explained.

And on the text (464): "And when the Angel of Death saw that Pinḥas had taken the letter *mem* to himself (to Pinḥas), he (the Angel of Death) immediately retired to the rear." That is to say: Since Pinḥas had pushed the *mem* to the rear, i.e. had stopped it from being inside, i.e. had annulled its drawing down (as above, in the Commentary to 467), and since this *mem* is the whole power of the Angel of Death, so the Angel of Death was also pushed to the rear with it (with the *mem*), i.e. it was not capable of inflicting death. On the text: "Immediately retired to the rear" it is written: "So the plague was stayed" (Numbers 25:8).

468 It can be asked: What is the reason that he was zealous over the *mem*? The answer is that it is a sign of death; a sign of the forty lashes (cf. *Mishnah Makkot*, 1, 1-3); and a sign of four forms of capital punishment (i.e. stoning, burning, beheading, and strangulation, and see *Mishnah Sanhedrin* 7, 1). And from there it ascends and descends, descends and ascends. When it rises in number it is 40 [*mem*], and when it drops it is 4 [*dalet*]. It descends to 4, i.e. the four winds that separate out from the male and female of impurity, they being the reason for there being four forms of capital punishment. And

from there they ascend to 40 [*mem*], the *mem* being a sign and tools for the Angel of Death. And it was this that Pinḥas took, and arose "among them," i.e. within *mem*, as above, wherefore it is written: "So that I consumed not the Children of Israel in My jealousy" (Numbers 25:11).

Commentary:

The *mem* is the secret of the Judgments of the Male that are drawn down with the revelation of *Ḥokhmah*, downwards from above. And these Judgments are not yet in the aspect of death, but only of lashes and punishments. However, at the end of those Judgments, awakens the Lock, which is the secret of death, this being the hidden meaning of the verse: "Sin couches at the door" (Genesis 4:7), as in the previous paragraph. And on the text: "It [*mem*] is a sign of death," for death descends and drops down from it, in the secret of the verse: "Sin couches at the door" (ibid.). It is a sign of the forty lashes... and a sign of the four forms of capital punishment...." That is to say that the *mem* contains these two aspects, that of lashes and that of the four forms of capital punishment, as above. "And from there [from the *mem*] it ascends and descends, descends and ascends." It rises to 40 and drops to 4. That is to say on high, where the mem is revealed, it is only lashes and does not contain death. And on the text: "When it rises in number it is 40 [*mem*]." That is, when it rises in its place, it is only forty lashes and not death. But "when it drops it is four," for when it descends, i.e. at its lower end, the four forms of capital punishment coming from the Lock are revealed, in the secret of the verse: "Sin couches at the door" (Genesis 4:7). And therefore: "The *mem* being a sign and tools for the Angel of Death." Since the *mem* descends to the bottom, where it is in the aspect of the four forms of capital punishment, the Angel of Death therefore uses it to activate death with it. And on the text: "And it was this that Pinḥas took," this *mem* in its upper aspect, while it was there with the evil forces in the aspect of 40 lashes only this was the aspect that Pinḥas took, and he joined it together with holiness, as in the adjoining paragraph. And on the text: "And arose 'among them,' i.e. within *mem*," i.e. he joined it to holiness in the aspect of the *Ḥokhmah* of holiness, that it should be a guard against the external ones, as above in the adjoining paragraph. And the illumination of *Ḥokhmah* is called arising. And on the text: "And arose," i.e. he received the illumination of *Ḥokhmah*. "Within *mem*," this means that the *mem* was protecting *Ḥokhmah* all around from the external ones, for in this way he placed it in holiness.

469 How can it be said that Pinḥas turned away the wrath of the Holy One, blessed be He, when it is written: "And those that died by the plague were twenty and four thousand: (Numbers 25:9)? Had not even one of them died, I could have said "has turned away My wrath," but since so many died it does not make sense to say "turned away My wrath... so that I consumed not the Children of Israel: The answer is that the matter certainly needs clarification, as follows: Woe to the person who faults his own seed (cf. *Talmud Bavli, Kiddushin* 70a). Woe to the one who does not guard his seed properly, for these are they who died in the plague. But heaven forbid, not even one of Israel died, with the exception of the tribe of Shimon. When the mixed multitude came, they intermingled with the women of the tribe of Shimon, after they had converted, and bore them sons, some of whom died at the Golden Calf episode (see Exodus 32:35): "And the Lord smote the people because they made the calf" and others died in the plague (after the spies returned, see Numbers 14:37) "Even those men that bring up an evil report of the land, died by the plague before the Lord"); while those who remained alive died here, as it is written: "And those

that died by the plague were twenty and four thousand" (Numbers 25:9). Scripture does not say "which had died" (i.e. using a verbal form) but rather "the dead ones" (i.e. using a noun form), which teaches that they were already considered dead, for the wicked are called dead.

470 And because Israel, all of whom are holy seed, were careful, they were all counted and not one of them was missing, wherefore it is written: "I consumed not the Children of Israel" (Numbers 25:11). The inference here is that He did consume others who were not of the Children of Israel. And so, too: "Turned away My wrath from over the Children of Israel" (ibid., v.11). He turned away from over the Children of Israel, but he did not turn it away from the others, who were a mixed multitude. And therefore Scripture explicitly states: "From over the Children of Israel." This is why the Children of Israel were counted and the Holy One blessed be he joined them to himself again as formerly (see Numbers 26:2): "Take the sum of all the congregation of the Children of Israel." Something similar happened in the case of the Golden Calf, as it is written: "And there fell of the people that day about three thousand men" (Exodus 32:28). All of these were from the mixed multitude (cf. *Midrash Exodus Rabba* 42, 6). To prove the point that they were not of the Children of Israel, Scripture later says: "And Moses assembled all the congregation of the Children of Israel" (Exodus 35:1), which shows that none of the Children of Israel had been amongst those who had died because all of them were complete.

TAKE AN OFFERING FROM AMONG YOU AND NOT FROM THE MIXED MULTITUDE

471 Come and see: In the first instance it is written: "From every man whose heart makes him willing, you shall take My offering" (Exodus 25:2). That is, from absolutely anyone, even the mixed multitude. Since the mixed multitude had made the Golden Calf, and those of them who

had died (i.e. were wicked) had died, the Holy One, blessed be He, wanted to be reconciled with Israel. He said to them: Join yourselves together, all of you, to one side, as it is written: "And Moses assembled all the congregation of the Children of Israel" (Exodus 35:1) by themselves. He said to them: My sons, I want to rest upon you; My tabernacle shall be amongst you. And so it is written: "Take an offering from among you" (ibid., v.5) from you and not from anyone else. I do not want the others to have any connection with Me nor with you. And this is why all of the mixed multitude were destroyed. And so also here. All those about whom it is written "And those that died..." (Numbers 25:9) were of a bad stock, i.e. they were the offspring of the mixed multitude who had intermarried with the tribe of Shimon, as above. Those who died were certainly already dead, for they were of the mixed multitude who are called dead even during their lifetime, as above, and not of Israel. And this is why he counted them, as it is written: "Take the sum of the congregation of the Children of Israel" (Numbers 26:2), the literal translation of which is: "Lift up the head of the congregation of the Children of Israel", i.e. raise up their heads.

472 Rabbi Elazar said: Father, what you have said would have been most beautiful if there had not been an internal contradiction. He said to him: My son, please tell me. And he replied: It is written: "And Israel joined himself [Hebrew root: *tzadi mem dalet*] to the Baal of Peor" (Numbers 25:3), and we have learnt that Israel was joined to the Baal of Peor as a bracelet [Hebrew root: *tzadi mem dalet*] is joined or attached to a person amongst his jewelry. (cf. *Midrash Numbers Rabba*, 20, 23.) That is: It is quite clear in this case that Israel also sinned, and not only the mixed multitude, as you have implied. He (Rabbi Shimon) said to him (Rabbi Elazar): So it is indeed that "Israel joined himself to the Baal of Peor," but I did not say that Israel was innocent of that sin. All I said was that they were cleared of the

death penalty, that death should not rest on them.

473 He said to him: But it is also written: "Take all the chiefs of the people and hang them" (Numbers 25:4), and the reference is clearly to Israel. He (Rabbi Shimon) said to him (Rabbi Elazar): It does indeed say "the chiefs of the people," i.e. the mixed multitude who are called people without further epithet. It does not say: The chiefs of the Children of Israel. And from the use of the term "the people" we can learn that wherever Scripture uses 'the people' the reference is to the mixed multitude. Here (Numbers 25:4) it is written "the people," and elsewhere it is written: "And when the people saw that Moses delayed" (Exodus 32:1) and: "The people gathered themselves together" (ibid.), and: "And there fell of the people..." (ibid. v. 28). In all these cases, 'the people' means the mixed multitude. But come and see: All that is written is "And Israel joined himself to the Baal of Peor" (Numbers 25:3). It does not say that they worshiped the Baal of Peor, as it does in the preceding verse about 'the people,' as is written: "And the people did eat and bowed down to their gods" (ibid. v.2). Scripture does not say that Israel ate and bowed down, but that the people did eat and bowed down! And since it is written "And Israel joined...," what is the meaning of "And the people did eat...?" Scripture should have said: And Israel did eat. What, therefore, was the sin of Israel? It was that bad stock, i.e. the mixed multitude who married Israelite wives.

474 Another comment. Take the verse: "And Israel joined himself to the Baal of Peor" (Numbers 25: 3). Come and see: "And Israel joined himself at the Baal of Peor" is not written, but rather "to the Baal of Peor." This is so because they gave only embellishment and strength to the Baal of Peor, without awareness. Because the worship of Peor consisted of uncovering oneself and depositing in front of him hot faces, which worship used to give him pleasure and he grew strong from it. Israel, when they saw this, thought that they were thereby scorning him and disgracing him, for about idolatry it is written: "You shall say to it: Go out [tse']" (Isaiah 30:22), and the word for faces [tso'ah] comes from the same root. So they, Israel, uncovered themselves and answered the call of nature in order to deride the idolatry, without awareness. And it was for these that Pinḥas made atonement and stopped the plague from them, as it is written: "And he made atonement over the Children of Israel."

THE FAITHFUL SHEPHERD

475 Said the Faithful Shepherd: It is written: "Turned away My wrath" (Numbers 25:11). What is the meaning of "turned away My wrath?" The answer is that this refers to three officials over Gehenna (Hell). One is over bloodshed, another over incest, and the third over idolatry, and they are called Destruction, Anger and Wrath. And the latter, Wrath, was flying through the world, and about it is said: "Turned away My wrath." He said: "Turned away My wrath from the Children of Israel," but He did not say "from the people," which would refer to the mixed multitude. For it is said: "And there fell of the people that day about three thousand men" (Exodus 32:28), where the meaning of `the people' is the mixed multitude. But here (in Numbers 25) it does not say "turned away My wrath from the people," but rather from "the Children of Israel." This is to teach that the wrath was not turned away from the mixed multitude. For this is how we have taught, and we asked the Holy Luminary, that is, Rabbi Shimon.

476 What does Scripture say? "Take an offering from among you to the Lord" (Exodus 35:5). It explicitly says `from among you' and not from the mixed multitude, for Israel was not called a community and a union until the mixed multitude had been removed from them. When the mixed multitude was intermingled amongst them, as it were, it was as though they were not one people. That is why it says: "Take an offering from among

you" and not from any other partnership, i.e. not from the mixed multitude, for I (i.e. the Holy One, blessed be He) do not want to involve others in the relationship between Me and you.

477 And not only that, but when the mixed multitude were intermingled with Israel, what is written? "Her adversaries are become the head" (Lamentations 1:5). And after the mixed multitude have been removed from Israel, what is written? "Take the sum of all the congregation of the Children of Israel" (Numbers 26: 2) [the literal translation of which verse is: 'Lift up the head of all the congregation of the Children of Israel']. And not only that, but the Holy One, blessed be He, said: I want to dwell with them, this being what is written: "And let them make Me a sanctuary that I may dwell among them" (Exodus 25: 8).

478 And not only that, but when the Children of Israel are in exile it is said about them: What prevents (them from doing God's will)? The yeast in the dough (cf. *Talmud Bavli, Berakhot* 17a), for the sages of the Mishnah have taught: When the mixed multitude are the heads over Israel, as it were, it is as though the rule of the Holy One, blessed be He, was removed and they had come under the rule of the jurisdiction of the stars and planets. This is why they cry out, saying: "O Lord our God," other Lords beside You have had dominion over us" (Isaiah, 26:13).

479 Another explanation of the verse "Pinḥas..." (Numbers 25:11): Arise, O Holy Luminary, and say things in the presence of the *Shekhinah*. The Holy Luminary, that is Rabbi Shimon, arose and said: In the first part it was said: Come and see: Pinḥas arose before the strong judgment of Isaac and stood before the gap, i.e. broke the plague, as it is written: "Then stood up Pinḥas and wrought judgment, and so the plague was stayed" (Psalms 106:30), and this he did in order to protect Israel. This is the reason why Pinḥas [*pei yud nun ḥet*

samekh, 80 + 10 + 50 + 8 + 60 = 208] and Isaac [*yud tzadi ḥet kuf*, 10 + 90 + 8 + 100 = 208] have the same numerical value. And now new things have to be said.

480 He began by saying: Elijah, the beloved of the divine King, i.e. Pinḥas, for Elijah is Pinḥas, saw the letter *mem* from the word *mavet* (death) flying in the air, snatched it down and joined it to *resh ḥet* (200 + 8 = 208), which is the numerical value of both Isaac and Pinḥas, and, with the *mem*, completed the combination *resh mem ḥet* (*romaḥ*, a spear). Subsequently, he saw the letter *vav* from the word *mavet* [*mem vav tav*] (death) flying in the sky, and he snatched it down also and placed it with the *resh mem ḥet*, thus completing the word: *resh vav mem ḥet* [*romaḥ*], a spear now in the fuller spelling, as it is written: "And he took a spear in his hand" (Numbers 25:7) [This has already been explained above, 467, q.v.].

481 And with what was he able to snatch down these two letters, the *mem* and the *vav*? He used the two spirits that were preserved for him on high, for they make up Pinḥas [*pei yud nun ḥet samekh*], namely *Pnei Ḥas* [i.e. the letters of *Piynḥas*, re-arranged: *Pei nun yud ḥet samekh*] (the meaning of which is: 'the countenance of pity'), for, with these two countenances, he had pity on Israel that they should not be lost in the strength to those two, Zimri and Cozbi, "and he thrust both of them through" (ibid. v.8) with the two letters, the *mem* and the *vav*, which is as is written: "...in that he was very zealous for My sake among them" (ibid. v.11).

482 Why did Pinḥas associate himself with Isaac? It was because Isaac gave himself over to death, which is why he joined himself to Isaac, that he should help him. For from the side of the two fawns of the does, Abraham and Jacob for support participated in him, for Abraham, whose level is that of *Ḥesed* (loving kindness) participated in the *ḥet samekh* (*Ḥas*, pity) of

Pinḥas, while Jacob is the remaining letters (rearranged) *Pnei* [*pei nun yud*], because it is said about him (about Jacob): "As he passed over Peniel [*Pei nun yud aleph lamed*]" (Genesis 32:32). And the letters of Peniel can be read as two words: *Pnei El*, the face of God. For, whenever the world is in trouble, but there is a righteous man in the world who is zealous for the covenant, then the patriarchs combine with him. And for their sake, Moses said, when Israel was in trouble [when God wanted to destroy them after the episode with the Golden Calf "Remember Abraham, Isaac and Israel, Your servants" (Exodus 32:13)]. And with the last three letters [i.e. *yud hei vav*] of Elijah [*aleph lamed yud hei vav*], which are the secret of Abraham, Isaac, Jacob, he earned the *hei*, which is *Malkhut*, of *ha-navi* (*hey nun bet yud aleph*, the prophet), and this is: Elijah the prophet [*Eliyahu ha-navi,'* or *El YHVH navi*], and thus the *yud hei vav* and *hei* (of the Tetragrammaton) come together in him.

Commentary:

You already know that the *mem* of *mavet* (*mem vav tav*, death) is the Judgments of the Male that come from *Ḥokhmah*, while the *vav* of *mavet* is the secret of *Yesod* that joins the Lock to the *mem* and becomes the combination: *Mavet*. For death comes from the Lock. However, the *vav* of *mavet* is also the aspect of the Lock, but is the aspect of the Judgments of the Female in general, and the Lock is not discernible in it, but in the *tav*. Nevertheless, the *vav* is able to awaken the *tav*, which is the Lock, and is therefore the aspect of *Yesod* in joining the *mem* with the *tav*. And it is impossible to join the *tav* of *mavet* to Holiness, for it is the secret of *Malkhut* that has been hidden away. But the *mem vav* belong to the corrections of Holiness, for the *mem*, which is the Judgments of the Male, is required to safeguard *Ḥokhmah* (as above, 467), while the *vav*, which is the Judgments of the Female, is needed for reducing the upper three *Sfirot* of the left, from which comes all the strength of the evil forces. And on the text (480): "...saw the letter *mem* from the word *mavet*...and joined it to *resh ḥet*..., which is the numerical value of both Isaac and Pinḥas: For *resh ḥet* (200 + 8 = 208) has the same numerical value as Isaac [*yud tzadi ḥet kuf*, 10 + 90 + 8 + 100 = 208], which refers to *Ḥokhmah* that is in the left column, with which the *mem* joined in order to protect the *resh ḥet*, which is *Ḥokhmah*, from the external ones and the wicked ones, as above. And "with the *mem*, completed the combination: *resh mem ḥet*," for *resh ḥet* together with *mem* makes *resh mem ḥet*. "Subsequently, he saw the letter *vav* from the word *mavet*," this being the Judgments of the Female that reduce the upper three *Sfirot* of *Ḥokhmah* of the left, which is all the life force of the external ones, as above. "Thus completing the word: *resh vav mem ḥet* (*romaḥ*, a spear);" and with this spear he thrust Zimri and Cozbi through, for he took all their life force, which is the upper three *Sfirot* of the left, to which the evil forces cleave, and from which they live. And on the text (481): "And with what was he able to snatch down these two letters...?" The question is: What force did he use to uproot them from the evil forces, i.e. from the combination *mem vav tav* (*mavet*, death) that enforced the plague, and return them to Holiness? And the answer is given: With the two spirits *Pnei* and *Ḥas*, where *Pnei* is the secret of the central column which snatched the *mem* and returned it to the back, and thereby drew down the energies of *Panim* (front), which is the secret of *Pnei* [literally: `the front of'. The *vav* was snatched by *Ḥas*, which is the secret of the right column, where are included the Judgments of the Female that are in this *vav*, in order to increase the power of the right over the left, for this *vav* decreases the upper three *Sfirot* of the left. And on the text: "With these two countenances, he had pity on Israel that they should not be lost...;" i.e. with the power of these two columns, the right and the central, that drew the *mem vav* down and joined them to the *resh ḥet*. And on the text: "In the strength of those two...." For two forces are needed, the *mem* is required for guarding and the *vav* for reducing the upper three *Sfirot* of the left so that they should not again become powerful. And on the text (482): "Why did Pinḥas associate himself with Isaac?" The answer is given: Because Isaac gave himself over to death. The meaning of this is that he allowed himself to be bound on the altar (see Genesis 22), for there the upper three *Sfirot* of his left become smaller (as above, *Vayikra*, 304) and he attained the six ends of *Ḥokhmah*, which is the secret of the interior intelligences. Which is why he joined himself to Isaac, for support, for he had to attire himself with the six ends of *Ḥokhmah*, which is the secret of the *resh ḥet* of *resh vav mem ḥet* (*romaḥ*, a spear). "For from the side of the two fawns of the does," this being the secret of the Male and Female Judgments that control the does, the secret of which is *Malkhut* (as above, *Metzora*, 61-62). "Abraham and Jacob participated in him," this is the secret of the right column and the central column, as above. For "Abraham, whose level is that of *Ḥesed* (loving kindness) participated in the *ḥet samekh* (*Ḥas*, pity) of Pinḥas;" and it was he who snatched the *vav* of *mavet*, as above; while Jacob is *Pnei* of Pinḥas, and it was he who snatched the *mem* of *mavet* (death). And from this it follows that all three columns were attired with Pinḥas, for *Pnei* and *Ḥas* are Abraham and Jacob, while the numerical value of Pinḥas (208) is Isaac. And on the text: "Whenever the world is in trouble, but there is a righteous man in the world who is zealous of the covenant, that the patriarchs combine with him," that is, the three patriarchs who are the secret the three columns, just as they attired themselves in Pinḥas who was zealous for the covenant. And these three columns are the secret of the three letters *yud hei vav* of the Tetragrammaton [*yud hei vav* and *hei*], which emanate towards the final letter of the Tetragrammaton, the *hei*, that completes it.

And on the text: "And with the last three letters [i.e. *yud hei vav*] of Elijah [*Eliyahu*: *aleph lamed yud hei vav*];" for Elijah (who is Pinḥas) earned the three columns which are the secret of the *yud hei vav* that joined together to form his name: *Eliyahu*. "Earned the *hei*... of *ha-navi* (*hey nun bet yud aleph*, the prophet): He also earned the final *hei* of the Tetragrammaton, which is *Malkhut*, and the *hei* from *ha-navi* is joined to *Eliyahu*, thus making: *EL YHWH, navi*, and thus the *yud hei vav hei* of the Tetragrammaton come together and are completed in him."

483 The *yud* that Pinḥas earned (where his name is written out in full with a *yud*: *Piynḥas*) was because he was zealous for the covenant, and thus merited the covenant, for the *yud* that was added to his name teaches of the covenant. There are two *yuds*, upper *yud* from the Tetragrammaton [*yud hei vav* and *hei*], with which He made the covenant with Abraham between the ten (numerical value of *yud*) fingers of the hands, and small *yud* which is from 'The Lord' [*aleph dalet nun yud*], with which He made the covenant between the ten (numerical value of *yud*) toes to the feet. And it is a holy letter that is adorned by the upper inceptive *hei*.

Commentary:

The sign of the covenant includes two things: Circumcision and uncovering [of the corona in circumcision — tr.] which means the removal of the foreskin and the drawing down of the energies — and this is the secret of the *yud* that Pinḥas earned. And the text explains: There are two *yuds*, for just as there is a sign of the covenant below in the diadem of *Yesod*, which is the secret of the central column, so there is a sign of the covenant on high in the upper three *Sfirot* in the secret of *Da'at*, which is the central column, i.e. in the curtain of *Ḥirik* that is in it, which reduces the upper three *Sfirot* of the left, this being the aspect of circumcision, and unites the left with the right, when the energies of *Ḥokhmah*, *Binah*, and *Da'at*, which are *yud hei*, are revealed. For this is the uncovering [*peri'ah*: *pei resh yud ayin hei*], the letters of which can be re-arranged to make two words: *para' Yah* [*pei resh ayin*, *yud hei*], meaning: He uncovered *Yah*. And this is the secret of the upper *yud*, with which He made the covenant with Abraham between the ten fingers of the hands, which is the secret of the covenant of the tongue, which is *Da'at*. For the hands are *Ḥokhmah* and *Binah*, in the secret of "Lift up your hands to the sanctuary" (Psalms 134:2), and the tongue is the secret of *Da'at* (knowledge), i.e. the central column, in which is the curtain of *Ḥirik*, which is the secret of the sign of the covenant. And this is the secret of *yud*, (the first letter) of the Tetragrammaton [*yud hei vav* and *hei*], which is the secret of upper *Ḥokhmah*. Small *yud* is from 'The Lord,' with which He made the covenant between the ten toes of the feet, i.e. the diadem of *Yesod*, which is the secret of the central column of the feet, namely: *Netzaḥ* and *Hod*. And through circumcision and uncovering, lower *Ḥokhmah* is revealed in it to *Malkhut*. And it is a holy letter that is adorned by the upper inceptive, which is the diadem that adorns upper *Yesod*, i.e. *Yesod* of *Zeir Anpin*.

484 This small *yud* is always ever recorded, that is to say that it is noted in all the stages of the energies, for without it no stage is revealed. It is the sign of Sabbath, the sign of the phylacteries, the sign of the festival days, the sign of the Almighty [*Shaddai*] that is recorded "on the doorposts of your house and on your gates" (Deuteronomy 6:9), which is the secret of the *yud* of *Shaddai* [*shin dalet yud*], and Israel is impressed with it in their straps, i.e. in the knot of the hand phylactery which has the

shape of the letter *yud*. And in their covenant, i.e. the circumcision, it is noted of them that they are the sons of *Malkhut*, courtiers in the palace of the Holy King, which is *Malkhut*, called palace. This means that they should receive the energies of lower *Ḥokhmah* which are drawn down from *Malkhut*, and this they merit by keeping the covenant. And by engaging in the Torah, they are recorded with the upper yud of the Tetragrammaton [*yud hei vav* and *hei*], i.e. they merit upper *Ḥokhmah*, for they are the sons of the divine King. It is as we have taught, and so it is said: "You are the children of the Lord your God" (Deuteronomy 14:1) the secret of their receiving from yud of the Tetragrammaton [*yud hei vav* and *hei*], which is from *Zeir Anpin*, who is called *yud hei vav* and *hei*.

485 And the letter *yud* of *Shaddai* (*shin dalet yud*, the Almighty) is the sign of the covenant and a halter that is lowered onto the neck of the demon, which is the evil inclination, for the letters of *Shaddai* [*shin dalet yud*] make two words *shed* [*shin dalet*], a demon, and *yud*, i.e. the *yud* prevents the demon [*shed*] from harming man. And this is as David said: "Deliver my soul from the sword; my only one from the power of the dog" (Psalms 22:21), for the evil inclination is serpent, dog, lion, about which David said: "He lies in wait in a secret place as a lion in his lair" (Psalms 10:9), or, in the words of the prophet, a bear, as it is written: "He is to me a bear lying in wait, as a lion in secret places" (Lamentations 3:10). And it (the evil inclination) is likened to all the animals, i.e. is likened to all the beasts of prey, and the likeness is drawn for each person according to his sins. That is, according to a person's sins so is the evil inclination called lion or bear and so on but this has already been clarified.

486 And this, the evil inclination, is dog, and serpent, and braying donkey, onto which the soul is mounted, and, as soon as it is known that one on it is wicked, it is written

about it: "And his rider falls backward" (Genesis 49:17), and the secret of the matter is: "Should any man fall from it" (Deuteronomy 22:8). And for this reason, Job said: "I am not inferior to you" (Job 12:3). (The literal rendering of this verse is: 'I do not fall from you'. But the righteous person who rides on it binds it with the knot of the phylactery straps, the sign of the phylacteries, which is the *yud* of *Shaddai* [*shin dalet yud*], being the ring, the halter on the neck, while the *shin* of the phylacteries is a chain on the neck.

487 And Elijah rode on the evil inclination when he ascended into the heavens, as it is written: "And Elijah went up by a whirlwind into heaven" (Kings II 2:11). Also: "Then the Lord answered Job out of the whirlwind" (Job 38:1). And this is why the sages of the Mishnah taught: Who is mighty? He that subdues his (evil) inclination. (*Mishnah Pirke Avot*, 4, 1.) And there are those for whom it (the evil inclination) becomes a donkey that causes no trouble for its rider, and they are the ones who make efforts at exposition by inference from minor to major. And this is why it is written about Abraham: "And he saddled his donkey" (Genesis 22:3). And this is also why it is said about the Messiah: "Lowly and riding upon a donkey" (Zekhariah 9:9).

C o m m e n t a r y :

The evil inclination receives its power to harm and provoke man from the left column, and the wicked person, by his iniquities, increases the power to the left over the right, which thus falls under the authority of the evil inclination, which has many nomenclatures according to the seriousness of man's sin. On the text (485): "For the evil inclination is serpent, dog, or lion..." The evil inclination is likened to all the animals according to a person's sins, for it is named according to the category of iniquity that a man commits. And on the text (486): "And the letter *yud* of *Shaddai* is the sign of the covenant and a halter that is lowered onto the neck of the demon, which is the evil inclination." For the *yud* of *Shaddai* [*shin dalet yud*] is the secret of the sign of the covenant, the secret of the central column, in which the curtain of *Ḥirik* reduces the upper three *Sfirot* of the left. These three *Sfirot* represent the total strength of the evil inclination, but the righteous person who keeps the covenant binds it (the evil inclination) so that it will not be able to make him sin. It is as though he threw a noose around the neck (of the evil inclination) and controlled him. The *shin* [the form of the letter is with three arms —tr.] of the phylacteries is as a chain [*shalshelet*] on the neck, this refers to the three [*shalosh*] columns. And on the text (486): "And this, the evil inclination, is dog, and serpent, and braying donkey, onto which the soul is mounted," for every person is given an evil inclination for him to subdue and mount, and all perfection comes by means of the evil inclination, should he subdue it, as the sages of blessed memory taught: "With all your heart" (Deuteronomy 6:5), i.e. with both your inclinations, your good inclination and your bad inclination [since the word 'heart' is here written not *lev* (*lamed bet*) but *levav* (*lamed bet bet*, i.e. with the two *bets*] (*Mishnah*, *Berakhot* 9, 5). And it follows that if a man is privileged to surmount his evil inclination, then he merits everything. And on the text (487): "And Elijah rode on the evil inclination when he ascended into the heavens," for the whirlwind is the evil inclination, which he subdued and surmounted and was privileged to ascend into heaven. Also: "Then the Lord answered Job out of the whirlwind" (Job 38:1) because Job was privileged to subdue the whirlwind, that is, his evil inclination. "And this is why the sages of the Mishnah taught, who is mighty? He that subdues his (evil) inclination (*Mishnah*, *Pirke Avot*, 4, 1). For if he subdues it he earns all the above-mentioned perfection. "And there are those for whom it (the evil inclination) becomes a donkey that causes no trouble for its rider." That is, whoever is able to subdue it to a certain extent, the evil inclination becomes for him a donkey to ride on and the evil inclination will never again give him any trouble. And these are the ones who make efforts at exposition by inference from minor to major [*ḥomer*: *ḥet vav mem resh*], who keep the easy precepts as they do the difficult ones, and then the evil inclination becomes for them a donkey [*ḥamor*: *ḥet mem vav resh*] whose letters are the same as those of the word *ḥomer* (major). And this is why it is written about Abraham: "And he saddled his donkey" (Genesis 22:3). And this is also why it is said about the Messiah: "Lowly and riding upon a donkey" (Zekhariah 9:9): for they both managed to subdue their evil inclination, until it became a donkey for them to ride on, bringing them to perfection.

488 And for this reason, all demons and devil spirits are fearful of the *yud* of *Shaddai* [*shin dalet yud*], i.e. the sign of the covenant, which is the noose that is the secret of the curtain that is in the central column (as above, in the preceding paragraph), since it reduces the upper three *Sfirot* of the left which is their total life-force, and immediately on seeing the *yud* of *Shaddai* on the doorposts of the gates they flee, for about the *yud* of *Shaddai* it is said: "To bind their kings with chains, and their nobles with fetters of iron" (Psalms 149:8). And even more do they flee away when they see it (the *yud*) on the phylacteries that are on the arms, i.e. in the knot of the hand phylactery. And of those who are marked with it with the sign of the covenant in their own flesh, it is said: "And the stranger that comes near shall be put to death" (Numbers 1: 51); i.e. the evil inclination that is called stranger shall be put to death, for stranger [*zar*: *zayin resh*] is the evil inclination [*yetzer*: *yud tzadi resh*, where *zayin* and *tzadi* are phonetically similar —tr.] that is similar to all the beasts and birds of prey, as above.

489 And for this reason: "Remember, I pray you,

whoever perished, being innocent?" (Job 4:7). This refers to Pinḥas, who was zealous for the covenant, since the letters of the word innocent [*naki*: *nun kuf yud*], when re-arranged, spell *kenei* [*kuf nun yud*] (which is the Aramaic equivalent of the Hebrew: *kanei* (*kuf nun aleph*), meaning to be zealous. And it is recorded of him that he is the son of the King and the Queen, for when he was zealous in thought, he earned the letter yud of the Tetragrammaton [*yud hei vav* and *hei*], which is the secret of the upper *Ḥokhmah*, and he became the son of the King. And when he was zealous in deed, he earned the letter *yud* of 'The Lord' [*aleph dalet nun yud*], which is lower *Ḥokhmah*, and he became the son of the Queen. And this is *Ḥokhmah* at the beginning of the combination *yud aleph hei dalet vav nun hei yud*, which is the *yud* of the Tetragrammaton [*yud hei vav* and *hei*], and *Ḥokhmah* at the end of the combination *yud aleph hei dalet vav nun hei yud*, which is the *yud* of 'The Lord' [*aleph dalet nun yud*]. And since Adam was marked with these two *yuds*, the sages taught about him that he (Man) is the first in thought but the last in deed (i.e. the last of the created). (cf. *Midrash Leviticus Rabba* 14, 1.) For the Tetragrammaton is the secret of thought and 'The Lord' is the secret of deed. And while he was still saying these things, he disappeared from their sight. Said Rabbi Elazar: Happy is our portion that we have been privileged to hear these matters from the sons of the next world.

490 And in the first part, he said: "Wherefore, say" (Numbers 25: 12), i.e. this being what the Holy One, blessed be He, said to Moses: An oath upon you: Whether you want to say to him "Behold, I give to him My covenant of peace" (ibid.), or whether you don't want to say it to him, nevertheless, say it. This was what Rabbi Pinḥas ben Yair said, for 'wherefore' is the language of an oath. The same shadow came and smote Rabbi Abba in the eyes and said to him: Did the Holy One, blessed be He, really not know if

Moses wanted to say this to Pinḥas or not? Did he really have to say it to him with some doubt: Either way...say! He said to him: Even if it is apparent to the Holy One, blessed be He, who says that it is apparent to others? Therefore He said to him: "Wherefore, say" (ibid.) vis-a-vis the others.

ISRAEL IS COMPOSED OF PARTS OF THE SHEKHINAH

491 And it was also said in the first part: "For the Leader; upon *Shushan Eduth; Mikhtam* of David" (Psalms 60:1). David was shown a sign in a rose that he would win the war when he sent Joab to Aram Naharaim and Aram Zobah to make war against them (see II Samuel 8 and above, 383). Said the Faithful Shepherd: *Shushan Eduth* is the *Eduth* (testimony) of the *Shekhinah,* which is called *Shushan Eduth* because it is testimony, standing over us and testifying on us before the King, and the holy upper levels are with it, and it is holy help for us to offer praises; therefore, it is called *Shushan Eduth*. Said the Faithful Shepherd: It is called *Shushan Eduth* because the *Shekhinah* is *Eduth* (testimony) about Israel, for they are its (bodily) parts and it is their soul. It is help from heaven, about which is written: "You, in heaven, will hear" (I Kings 8: 32). It is holy assistance, about which it has been said: Here is Tanya' [i.e. a Baraitha, i.e. a teaching of the Mishnaic period that was not included in the Mishnah that can help you [this being a formula used in rabbinic literature to introduce a quotation in support of an opinion] for the *Shekhinah* is called *tanya*.

492 "Though firm be your dwelling-place, and though your nest be set in the rock" (Numbers 24:21). The word for 'firm,' *eitan* [*aleph yud tav nun*] is written with the letters, rearranged, of *tanya* [*tav nun yud aleph*], i.e. *Mishnah* and *Baraitha* [both being teachings from the same period, the difference being that the former was included in the official compilation, the *Mishnah,* while the latter was excluded. '*Baraitha*'

comes from a word meaning 'outside.'] *Mishnah* and *Baraitha*, is the nest of the upper eagle, which is the *Shekhinah*, and about it is said: "As an eagle that stirs up its nest, hovering over its young" (Deuteronomy 32:11). And those who teach *Halakhah* and *Mishnah* are called the young of the eagle. And each speech that emerges out of the mouth of that *tanya*, i.e. the teachers of *Mishnah*, whether for the sake of the Tetragrammaton and whether in Torah, prayer, blessing, or in any one of the precepts what is written about it? "Spreading abroad its wings" (ibid.), i.e. that same eagle that is speech, for the *Shekhinah* is called speech, with which the Tetragrammaton, i.e. *Zeir Anpin* who is called voice, will spread its wings.

493 "Takes it and bears it on its pinion" (Deuteronomy 32:11). The question is asked: What is the meaning of 'on its pinion?' And the answer is given: On that part of man with which he performed a precept of the Tetragrammaton, called a limb of the *Shekhinah*. Thus: "Bears it on its pinion" (ibid.). And the meaning of 'bear it' or 'lift it up' is as in the verse: "The Lord lift up His countenance upon you and bless you" (Numbers 6:26 the priestly benediction).

494 And what is the meaning of "though your nest be set in the rock" (Numbers 24:21)? But David said about the *Shekhinah*: "The Lord is my rock and fortress" (II Samuel 22:2). So also for the *tanna*, i.e. the student of *Mishnah*, whose *halakhah* (legal tradition) is as firm as a rock that no hammer can break with all the objections in the world. It is here that the eagle, i.e. the *Shekhinah*, makes its nest. And all the students are called nests of the *Shekhinah*, therefore: "If a bird's nest chance to be before you" (Deuteronomy 22:6), where it is the *Shekhinah* that is called a bird, i.e. by pure chance, once, as a visitor, as a wayfarer who just happens to come to the inn.

495 And there are students of the *Mishnah*, in

whose *Mishnah* the *Shekhinah* has a permanent home, as it is written: "And the Children of Israel shall keep the Sabbath, to observe the Sabbath throughout their generations" (Exodus 31:16). The word `throughout their generations,' *l'dorotam,* is written in the abbreviated spelling *lamed dalet resh tav mem,* and can, therefore, equally be read: *l'diratam,* `for their home.' And indeed, there are sages of the *Mishnah,* whose *Torah,* is such that the *Shekhinah* does not move from them all their days. But those about whom the Scripture speaks in the verse "If a bird's nest chance to be before you" (Deuteronomy 22:6) are those to whom the *Shekhinah* comes by chance, at one time resting on them and being with them and at another not being with them.

496 And the secret of the matter is: The times when the *Shekhinah* is with them is when it is said: "You shall not take the mother bird with the young" (ibid.), but he does not let the mother bird, which is the *Shekhinah,* go. And the times when the *Shekhinah* is not with them is when it is said: "You will surely let the mother bird go" (ibid. v. 7), for they are not fitting for her to be with them. "The young ones" (ibid v. 6) are the sages of the Mishnah; "or eggs" (ibid.) are the sages of the Bible. About those who do not study regularly it is said: "You will surely let the mother bird go" (ibid. v.7), while about those who do study regularly it is said: "You shall not take the mother bird with the young" (ibid. v. 6); they do not let her go. And there are sages of *Halakhah* (legal tradition) who are like the stars, as it is written: "They that turn the many to righteousness (shall shine) as the stars for ever and ever" (Daniel 12:3). But they are not as the stars (that we see in our sky), about which it is written: "And all their hosts shall wither away" (Isaiah 34:4), but rather as though they were the stars of the next world that remain always for ever and ever, and to which is applied the verse: "They that turn many to righteousness (shall shine) as

the stars forever and ever" (Daniel 12:3)."

LETS US MAKE MAN IN OUR IMAGE AFTER OUR LIKENESS" (GENESIS 1:26)

497 "And God said: Let us make man in our image, after our likeness" (Genesis 1:26). After each craftsman had completed his work, the Holy One, blessed be He, said to them: One craft remains for Me to undertake, and all of us shall be partners in it. Let all join together, and let each one do his share, and I shall join in with you, to give it My share. For this is what is written: "Let us make man in our image, after our likeness." And the sages taught that only the people of Israel are referred to as *adam* (man) (cf. *Talmud Bavli, Baba Metsia,* 114b), as it is written: "And you My sheep, the sheep of My pasture, are men" (Ezekiel 34:31). That is: You are men, but the idolators are not, and therefore is it written: "Let Israel rejoice in his Maker" (Psalms 149:2).

498 Said the Holy Luminary, that is, Rabbi Shimon: This must certainly have been said by that same *tanna* (teacher of the Mishnaic period) who hid in the rock of the Serpent, for it is written about him: "Though firm be your dwelling-place, and though your nest be set in the rock" (Numbers 24:21). For the three patriarchs are called `the firm ones' (cf. *Talmud Bavli, Rosh haShanah* 11a), and the fourth one, that is, Moses, who is "Firm be your dwelling place," for in him the *Halakhah,* which is the *Shekhinah,* takes shape, as in the expression `A law given to Moses from Sinai,' (cf. *Mishnah, Peah* 2, 6) [This expression is a formula denoting a very old tradition which is not derived from the Written Torah.] And he spreads over the six hundred thousand of Israel and gives them light with the Torah as the sun which is hidden by night but gives light to all the stars and constellations. So it is with Moses: had he not hidden in that rock, he would have been unable to give light to Israel. And night always refers to the Exile, as in "Watchman, what of the night? Watchman, what of

the night?" (Isaiah 21:11). This refers to the Exile, for then Moses hides in the rock and appears by day, at the time of the Redemption, about which it is said: "As soon as the morning was light" (Genesis 44:3), which is the morning of Abraham, about which is said: "And in the morning, then you shall see the glory of the Lord" (Exodus 16:7). "As the Lord lives, lie down until the morning" (Ruth 3:13).

499 While he was yet speaking, behold, the Faithful Shepherd came out from that rock and appeared to Rabbi Shimon. He said to him: Holy Luminary, what good did it do me to hide from you, for I have not left a place that I did not enter to hide from you, and I have found that I can not hide from you in it. That being so, there is no sense in my continuing to hide from you.

500 The Holy Luminary said to the Faithful Shepherd: After Scripture records: "Let us make man in our image, after our likeness" (Genesis 1:26), what is the meaning of the verse that is written later: "And God created man in His own image" (ibid. v. 27)? He replied: This is what the sages of the Mishnah taught: He asked the ministering angels whether to create man or not. Some said: Let him be created, while others urged: Let him not be created. And the Holy One, blessed be He, created him, as it is written: "And God created man in His own image" (cf. *Midrash Bereshith Rabba,* 8, 5). He said to him: If that is so, then he did not place in him (in man) one part from the ministering angels, and he was not made after their form, but after the form of the King, in His image, in His likeness, which is the image of the likeness of His form alone. He noted: That is the meaning of what you say.

501 Said the Faithful Shepherd: Heaven forbid that (you should think that) I said that he is not made up of any of the angels and creatures. What I said to you was that he (man) was created from all the angels and creatures,

and was made to rule over all the creatures. Just consider what would have happened had each one given his share to man, for, when he was angry with him (with man), each one could have come back and taken his share away from him. "For how little is he to be accounted" (Isaiah 2:22).

502 But the Holy One, blessed be He, created him in His image, which is the holy *Malkhut* that is called image, which is the picture of everything, for all the inhabitants of the worlds of *Briah*, *Yetzirah*, and *Assiah* are included in it. And the Holy One, blessed be He, looked into it and created the world and all the creatures that He created in the world, and He included in it the upper ones and the lower ones without any separation whatsoever, and He included in it ten *Sfirot* and all the names and appellatives. And the Supreme Cause, who is Master of All and there is no God beside Him there is not to be found in upper and lower ones lesser than it (*Malkhut*), for it is the connection among all of them, the perfection of all of them, to establish in it: "And His kingdom rules over all" (Psalms 103:19); and there is no Cause of All to be found in even one of the upper and lower ones below it in which it (*Malkhut*) is not included. This is so and is called the faith of Israel. From the point of view of the Supreme Cause, it is said: "For you saw no manner of form" (Deuteronomy 4:15), but from the point of view according to which it (*Malkhut*) includes the other creatures, it is said: "And the similitude of the Lord does he behold" (Numbers 12:8).

503 The Holy Luminary came and the other companions and they prostrated themselves before him, saying: Certainly there is now none that can take from him, from man, his portion, for not one in the world gave him a part, except the Creator of the World, the First Cause alone, and on Him depends his (man's) punishment or reward and not on an angel nor a seraph nor any other creature that is in the world. Thus the sages of the Mishnah

taught: Anyone who combines (in worship) the Name of Heaven and something else is uprooted from the world, (cf. *Talmud Bavli, Sanhedrin* 63a) in the name of Rabbi Shimon bar Yoḥai). Immediately on his hearing what Rabbi Shimon, the Holy Luminary, said, the Faithful Shepherd rejoiced. And all the companions blessed him, the Faithful Shepherd, and said: O, Faithful Shepherd, if a man were to have come into the world just to hear this, it would suffice him.

504 Happy is he who makes an effort in the last exile to know the *Shekhinah,* to honor her with all the precepts and to suffer for her a number of exigencies, as they said: The merit of attending the *Kallah* (convention to expound and discuss the law) lies in the crush and trouble (*Talmud Bavli, Berakhot* 6a). That is to say: According to the suffering so is the reward (*Mishnah, Pirke Avot* 5, 23). "And he lay down in that place" (Genesis 28:11). The Hebrew word for `And he lay down' [*vayishkav*] can be read as two words: *vayesh kaf bet,* meaning: And there are twenty-two. That is: If the twenty-two letters of the Torah (i.e. all the letters of the Hebrew alphabet) exist, i.e. that he is perfect in Torah, then the *Shekhinah* lies with him.

505 What is the meaning of `*yesh*' (there is)? The answer is that it refers to *Ḥokhmah,* which is *ex nihilo* (literally: there is from nothing), that is to say that it is drawn down from *Keter,* which is called nothing. For in the place where the upper *Shekhinah,* which is *Binah,* there also is *Ḥokhmah,* for *Ḥokhmah* is revealed only in *Binah,* and for it is said: "That I may cause those that love me to inherit *yesh* (substance)" (Proverbs 8:21). For *Ḥokhmah* that is in *Binah* illuminates only in *Ḥesed,* and those that cleave to *Ḥesed* (loving kindness) are called `they who love the Lord' and it is only they who can inherit *yesh,* which is *Ḥokhmah,* because they have *Ḥesed,* and this is: "Showing mercy to the thousandth generation of those that love Me" (Exodus 20:6),

i.e. from the side of the love of *Ḥesed*, for 'the thousandth generation' is the secret of *Ḥokhmah*, and He shows mercy [*Ḥesed*] in attiring *Ḥokhmah* with *ḥasadim*. And this *yesh*, which is *Ḥokhmah*, is on the right, or it illuminates only when attired in *Ḥesed* of the right, as has been taught: He who wants to grow wise should turn to the south (cf. *Talmud Bavli, Baba Batra* 25b). [For a man at prayer facing east, to turn to the south would be to turn to the right. And that is why it is written: "That I may cause those that love me to inherit *yesh* (substance)" (Proverbs 8:21), since they have *Ḥesed*, which is the right.

506 Come and see into the implicit secrets, into the attributes of the Holy One, blessed be He, for about the same quality over which people make an effort, and which they mention, it is said: With the same measure that a man metes out, so is it measured to him (*Mishnah, Sotah* 1,7), for he is treated with the same attribute that he mentions. And there are seventy countenances to the Torah [that is, there are seventy ways of expounding the Torah] (*Midrash Numbers Rabba* 13, 16). In the secret of the 70 attributes, there are the seven: *Ḥesed, Gvurah, Tiferet, Netzaḥ, Hod, Yesod* and *Malkhut*, each of which is composed of ten *Sfirot*, making seventy, this being the secret of: There are seventy countenances to the Torah. Thus "In every place where I cause My name to be mentioned, I will come to you and bless you" (Exodus 20:21). Should Scripture not have said: In every place where you mention My name, I will come to you and bless you? No, for the meaning is: With the same attribute that I mentioned my name, with that very same attribute I will come to bless you. [Note: Our text validly reads the Biblical verse as: 'In every place where I mention My name...']

507 "According to the lot shall their inheritance be divided between the more and the fewer" (Numbers 26:56). Rabbi Yehuda began by quoting: "I know that, whatsoever God does, it shall be forever; nothing can be added to it, nor anything taken from it; and God has so made it, that men should fear before Him" (Ecclesiastes 3:14). This was said by King Solomon [traditionally the author of the Book of Ecclesiastes whose wisdom was greater than that of all other men.] I, Myself, did not know that whatsoever God does, it shall be forever, until he (King Solomon) said: "I know that..." For he (King Solomon) knew what no one else knows.

508 The explanation of this is that of course King Solomon's wisdom was greater than that of other men, and he knew what was not known to other people. Come and see: Any other craftsman in the world, when he has something to make, looks at it and considers it once and twice and then makes it. Subsequently, he adds to it or takes away from it. With the Holy One, blessed be He, it is not like that: He brings true craftsmanship out of chaos, that has no substance at all, and it is corrected properly and actually, and He does not need to add or take anything away from it. That is why it is written: "And God saw everything that He had made, and, behold, it was very good" (Genesis 1:31). And it was about this that Solomon said: "I know that, whatsoever God does, it shall be forever; nothing can be added to it, nor anything taken from it" (Ecclesiastes 3:14).

WHATSOEVER GOD DOES, IT SHALL BE FOREVER

509 "Whatsoever God does" (Ecclesiastes 3:14). A further explanation is that whatsoever He does to correct the world, it will surely be forever, but the demons and the evil forces will be nullified at the completion of the correction, and are not eternal. Rabbi Yitzḥak said: If that is so, what is the meaning of the last part of the verse: "And God has so made it that men should fear before Him" (Ecclesiastes 3:14)? For the meaning of this verse would appear to be that He caused the evil forces to cast fear on the world. It is not so, for we have learned, that the verse,

and this is a divine secret amongst the companions, should be read as follows: That whatsoever God does, it shall be forever. But what is meant by: "Whatsoever God does," for is it not written "That which is has been long ago, and that which is to be has already been" (ibid. v.15)? Yet you say: "Whatsoever God does" (ibid. v.14)?

510 The answer to this quandary is that we can understand the matter from another verse. It is written: "Neither has the eye seen a God beside You, Who works for Him that waits for Him" (Isaiah 64:3). It should have said 'worked' instead of 'works' and 'who waits for You' instead of 'who waits for Him.' But the answer is that it is an upper place that is drawn down and emerges and kindles all the lights, i.e. all the *Sfirot* of *Zeir Anpin* and *Malkhut*, in all directions, both to the right and to the left, and is called the next world, i.e. *Binah*. And from it emerges one tree, which is *Zeir Anpin*, to be watered and corrected. And this tree is higher and more precious than all other trees, and we have already learned about this. And that next world, which is *Binah*, which is drawn down and emerges, corrects this tree always, and waters it, i.e. it emanates intelligences to it, and corrects it in its work; i.e. *Binah* corrects the tools of *Zeir Anpin* with its tools so that it should be fitted to receive the intelligences from it (from *Binah*) (as above, *Bereshith Aleph*, page 7); and crowns him (*Zeir Anpin*) with diadems, which is the secret of the upper three *Sfirot*, and none of the fountains ceases to flow from him forever and ever.

511 On that tree, which is *Zeir Anpin*, hangs faith, which is *Malkhut* that is called faith (as above *Vayikra*, 273), which rests on it, of all the trees, in the secret of the verse: "As an apple-tree among the trees of the wood, so is my beloved among the sons" (Song of Songs, 2:3). The existence of everything is to be found in Him, inasmuch as he is the central column that gives everything its existence. And therefore it is

written: "Whatsoever God does, it shall be forever" (Ecclesiastes 3:14). Surely He was, He is, and He will be. "Nothing can be added to Him, nor anything taken from Him" (ibid.). And thus it is written in the Torah: "You shall not add thereto, nor diminish from it" (Deuteronomy 13:1). For this tree is the Torah, since *Zeir Anpin* is called Torah. And God, who is *Binah,* corrects this place always. And 'the God' [*ha-Elohim*], unless specified otherwise, is *Gvurah* from the Infinite and Unfathomable One, i.e. *Binah* that is called *Gvurah,* in the secret of the verse: "I am understanding [*Binah*]; power [*Gvurah*] is mine" (Proverbs 8:14). As it is written: "His discernment is unfathomable" (Isaiah 40:28), i.e. there is no fathoming his *Binah* (understanding). This is why *ha-Elohim* (the God) is written and not *Elohim* (God), for *Elohim* without the definite article refers to *Malkhut.* Thus 'does' means 'always,' as a spring whose waters will not cease for all generations.

512 For this reason is it written: "And God [*ha-Elohim*] has so made it, that men should fear before him" (Ecclesiastes 3:14). This means that He ordained for that tree, which is *Zeir Anpin,* a perfect correction, until it is held on all sides, the right and the left, above and below, i.e. by *Binah* and *Malkhut,* so "that they should fear before Him" and not replace him with any substitute for all generations.

513 Rabbi Abba said: What you have said is indeed nice, but one has to look into it ever further. At the beginning of the verse (ibid.) it says 'does,' and later 'God made' [the former in the present continuous, the latter in the past —tr.]. Why this difference? The answer to this is surely because He does correct this tree, *Zeir Anpin,* so that its waters should not cease for all generations, since the waters of *Binah* do not cease for all generations as they are drawn down from the upper Father and Mother, whose mating is forever connected. And then in the second part of the verse, it is writ-

ten 'made,' in the past tense. What did He make? God [*ha-Elohim*], which is *Binah*, made another tree, which is *Malkhut*, below it, but He does not make it like this one, like *Zeir Anpin*. That is to say: *Binah* will not emanate anything to it that is forever connected, as, for example, the *ḥasadim* from upper Father and Mother, as emanating to *Zeir Anpin*. Therefore it is written: "God made" and not "makes," for this lower tree, which is *Malkhut*, made it and corrected it in the aspect of the left, which is judgment so when one enters the upper tree, which is *Zeir Anpin*, one will so enter with the permission of the lower tree, which is *Malkhut*, and, on finding the lower tree, he will be afraid to enter the upper tree other than in a proper way.

514 Come and see that this one, the lower tree which is *Malkhut*, is the doorkeeper of *Zeir Anpin*, and *Malkhut* is therefore called "He who keeps Israel" (Psalms 121:4), for it keeps *Zeir Anpin*, who is called Israel. And it is this lower tree that God [*ha-Elohim*], which is *Binah*, made, that it should be watered and nourished from the upper tree, which is *Zeir Anpin*. And it is therefore not written 'makes' but 'made,' for He made him a keeper and so that he should be nourished from *Zeir Anpin*. What was the reason for His making him a keeper? It was so that men should be fearful of Him, and not draw close to Him, except for those who are fitted to come close, and not any others, and that men should keep the ways of the Torah and not deviate to the right nor the left, but should cleave to the central column.

ACCORDING TO THE LOT (NUMBERS 26:56)

515 Come and see: About this tree, *Malkhut*, on which rest all of the hosts of the worlds of *Briah*, *Yetzirah*, and *Assiah*, David said: "You maintain my lot" (Psalms 16:5). What is the meaning of 'my lot?' It is the lot to which David is attached, which is *Malkhut*, and it is therefore written: "According to the lot" (Numbers 26:56) [where

the Hebrew for 'according to' is, literally: 'On the mouth of']. This alludes to *Malkhut*, which is called 'mouth.' And the same expression is used in the verse: "So Moses the servant of the Lord died there in the land of Moab, according to the mouth of the Lord" (Deuteronomy 34:5), where 'mouth' is *Malkhut*. Consequently, a lot is written, with the definite article, to refer to *Malkhut*. Happy are the portions of those who engage in the study of Torah day and night and who know its ways, and they each day eat the divine food, of the emanation of *Ḥokhmah*, as it is written: "Wisdom [*Ḥokhmah*] preserves the life of him that has it" (Ecclesiastes 7:12), for the Torah on high, i.e. *Zeir Anpin*, is nourished from this place, from *Ḥokhmah*. And it is said about them: "Behold, My servants shall eat" (Isaiah 65:13).

516 Rabbi Abba started by quoting: "Then there was a voice above the firmament" (Ezekiel 1:25). About this voice (*Zeir Anpin*), which is attached to this firmament (*Yesod* of *Zeir Anpin*) and participates with him, it is said: "He has made a memorial for His wonderful works" (Psalms 111:4), which refers to the firmament which is *Yesod* that is called memorial. And this firmament stands over those beings, as it is said: "Then there was a voice above the firmament that was over their head" (Ezekiel 1:25). And this is the firmament that was created on the second day of the Works of Creation, about which it is said: "Let there be a firmament in the midst of the waters, and let it divide the waters from the waters" (Genesis 1:6). The reference here is to the upper waters and the lower waters.

Commentary:

The beings are in the world of *Briah*, while the firmament is the secret of *Yesod* of *Zeir Anpin*, which terminates the world of *Atziluth*. It is therefore over the heads of the beings and is the firmament that divides between the world of *Atziluth*, which is the upper waters, and the world of *Briah*, which is the lower waters. And *Malkhut* of the world of *Atziluth* stands on this firmament, which is *Yesod* of *Zeir Anpin*, which is the secret of the verse: "And above the firmament that was over their heads was the likeness of a throne" (Ezekiel 1:26). And the one who sits on the throne is *Zeir Anpin*, which is the inner meaning of the continuation of the verse: "And upon the likeness of the throne was a likeness as the appearance of a man upon it above" (ibid.). For the Tetragrammaton [*yud hei vav* and *hei*] which is *Zeir Anpin* with the letters spelled out and filled in the *aleph*s [*yud* = *yud vav dalet*, 10 + 6 + 4 = 20; *hei* = *hei aleph*, 5 + 1 = 6; *vav* = *vav aleph vav*, 6 + 1 + 6 = 13; *hei* = *hei aleph*, 5 + 1 = 6], has the numerical value of 45 (20 + 6 + 13 + 6 = 45), which is the same as the numerical value of man [*adam*: *aleph dalet mem*, 1 + 4 + 40 = 45].

517 It has been taught: There are seven firmaments on high (cf. *Talmud Bavli, Hagigah* 12b), paralleling *Ḥesed, Gvurah, Tiferet, Netzaḥ, Hod, Yesod* and *Malkhut*, that are in *Yesod*. Certainly Curtain (the lowest of the seven firmaments cf. *Hagigah* 12b), which is parallel to *Malkhut* that is in it, serves no purpose (cf. *Hagigah* 12b), for *Malkhut* has nothing of its own, apart from what *Zeir Anpin* gives it. And the poor [Hebrew root: *ayin nun yud*] take hold of it, this being the inner meaning of the verse: "In my straits [Hebrew root: *ayin nun yud*] I have prepared for the house of my Lord" (I Chronicles 22:14) inasmuch as David [the speaker in this verse was attached to *Malkhut*, which is poor, as above]. And this (the lowest) firmament, Curtain, which is *Malkhut*, introduces the morning and ushers out the evening (cf. *Talmud Bavli, Hagigah* 12b), for at night *Malkhut* brings out its hosts in all directions, to the right and to the left, and has control over these hosts and regiments, for

then is the rule of *Malkhut*. And in the morning, it collects together all its hosts, and brings them into their hole, that is to say to the aspect of the female [hole (nekev) originates from the Hebrew word *Nekevah* (female)], and they are not in control. For the morning includes them all, as it is written: "To declare Your loving kindness [*Ḥesed*] in the morning and Your faithfulness in the night" (Psalms 92:3). But this has already been taught.

Commentary:

Malkhut is constructed from the left column of *Binah*, which is the secret of *Ḥokhmah* that is on the left. And *Zeir Anpin* is the secret of the right of *Binah*, which is the secret of *ḥasadim*. There are, therefore, two dominions. For when the left is in control without the right, there is darkness, for *Ḥokhmah* is unable to illuminate without *ḥasadim* (as above, *Bereshith Aleph*, page 47). Thus the time of the rule of *Malkhut*, which is the secret of the dominion of the left, is darkness and is called night. Its dominion is then at maximum strength, in the secret to the verse: "She rises also while it is yet night" (Proverbs 31:15), and it has control over its hosts, i.e. over the stages that spread out from the left. Contrary to this, there is the dominion of the day, which is *Zeir Anpin*, which is the dominion of the light of *ḥasadim*. However *Zeir Anpin* is also inclusive of the illuminations of *Ḥokhmah* of *Malkhut*. And on the text: "And in the morning it brings them all in:" For then the power of the dominion of *Malkhut* and its illumination of *Ḥokhmah* wane away completely, and thus *Malkhut* "brings them into their hole, and they are not in control": That is to say, they return to the aspect of the female, for the illumination of *Ḥokhmah* departs from them. "For the morning includes them all." For the illumination of *Ḥokhmah* is then included in *Yesod* of *Zeir Anpin*, that is called morning, but then only *ḥasadim* have control.

518 And voice, which is *Zeir Anpin,* is over this firmament, for from it is this firmament nourished, since *Yesod* receives from *Zeir Anpin.* When this voice awakens, none of the hosts are in motion, and they have permission to do nothing but stand still where they are. And this is the secret of the verse: "Then there was a voice above the firmament that was over their heads, as they stood, and had let down their wings" (Ezekiel 1:25); i.e. when the voice stirs over their heads, then they stand still, and the hosts draw near and wait for that *Ḥesed* which is drawn down from the voice, which is *Zeir Anpin,* to that firmament, which is *Yesod,* and they are blessed because of it, i.e. that they receive from the firmament. And therefore, *Zeir Anpin* is above the firmament that is over their head, and they cannot receive other than from the firmament, which is *Yesod.*

519 Come and see: "And above the firmament that was over their heads was the likeness of a throne, as the appearance of a sapphire stone" (Ezekiel 1:26). "As the appearance of a sapphire stone" refers to the stone of Israel, which is *Malkhut.* And this is the inner meaning of what is written: "And they rolled the stone away" (Genesis 29:3). From on high descended one stone, which is *Malkhut,* when Israel wanted to inherit the Land of Israel, and about it is written: "Lot," i.e. "According to the lot" (Numbers 26:56) (as above, 515), and the lot would say: This part for so-and-so, this part for so-and-so [Context: The division of the land to the twelve tribes according to the lot —tr.]. And this stone descended from under the divine throne, i.e. *Malkhut,* which is the secret of the Throne of *Zeir Anpin.* Surely "From thence, from the Shepherd, the Stone of Israel" (Genesis 49:24) is written, for this is the stone of *Zeir Anpin* that is called Israel. And for this reason: "According to the lot (which is *Malkhut*) shall their inheritance (certainly) be divided" (Numbers 26:56).

520 Rabbi Yitsḥak and

Rabbi Yehuda were walking from Usha to Lod. Rabbi Elazar encountered them and they ran after him, saying: Shall we not run after the *Shekhinah*? When they caught up with him, they said: Let us now join you and hear a new matter.

521 He (Rabbi Elazar) began by quoting: "Hearken to Me, you that follow after righteousness, you that seek the Lord" (Isaiah 51:1). "Hearken to Me, you that follow after righteousness" refers to those who follow the faith, which is *Malkhut*, that is called righteousness, for those who follow righteousness are certainly the ones who "seek the Lord." If you want to know the faith and to take hold of this righteousness, then do not look at it on its own, without *Zeir Anpin*, as do other people who cleave to *Malkhut* without *Zeir Anpin*, this being the secret of left without right, and for this reason they bring death to themselves. But "Look to the rock whence you were hewn to the hole of the pit whence you were dug." (ibid.), i.e. to unite it [*Malkhut*] with *Zeir Anpin*, and Father and Mother.

THE SACRIFICES

522 "Command the Children of Israel, and say to them: My food which is presented to Me for offerings made by fire" (Numbers 28:2). It is written: "Has the Lord as great a delight in burnt-offerings and sacrifices, as in hearkening to the voice of the Lord?" (I Samuel 15:22). The Holy One, blessed be He, does not desire that a man sin and then offer a sacrifice because of his sin; but a sacrifice that is without any iniquity (as its reason) is the perfect sacrifice [*korban shalem*]. And it is called "peace-offerings" [*shelamim*]. The daily offering [*tamid*] is also a perfect sacrifice, for although the daily sacrifice atones for sins, it is nevertheless a perfect sacrifice.

523 Rabbi Abba began by quoting: "The sacrifices of God are a broken spirit; a broken and contrite heart, O God, You will not despise" (Psalms 51:19). This verse has been interpreted to mean that the Holy One, blessed be He,

does not want a man to bring a sacrifice for his sin, but, rather, He wants a broken spirit. Those that say this do not know what they are talking about! From the Holy Luminary I heard as follows: When a man becomes impure in his iniquities, he draws down onto himself a spirit from the side of uncleanliness, and the spirit is proud of that person and controls him at will. The uncleanliness, from which the spirit is drawn down, grows stronger with his strength and becomes more powerful and controls him to its heart's content. When a man comes and takes control over it, thus becoming pure, he is purified from above.

524 In the period when the Temple was still standing, the sinner would offer a sacrifice, his whole atonement being dependent on it, until he feels remorse and breaks the hold of that spirit from the side of uncleanliness that came to him with his sin, in his pride, and humiliates him. And it is this that is meant by the breaking of those stages of uncleanliness, from which the spirit is drawn down onto him, and when that spirit of uncleanliness is broken, and he offers his sacrifice, this is an acceptable, welcome and proper sacrifice.

525 But if that spirit of uncleanliness is not broken, then his sacrifice is worth nothing and is given to the dogs, for this is a sacrifice not for the Holy One, blessed be He, but for the dogs. And this is why Scripture says that the proper sacrifices of God are a broken spirit, for that spirit of uncleanliness has to be broken so that it will not be in control. Consequently, about the one who breaks it as it should be broken, it is written: "A wind that passes away and comes not again" (Ps. 78:39). And that person can be certain that it will not ever come to him again.

"A broken and contrite heart, O God, You will not despise" (Ps. 51:19). A broken and contrite heart refers to a man who is not proud and does not take pleasure in the delights of the world. And God will not despise him for he has a place of honor with Him.

526 "Command the Children of Israel" (Numbers 28:2). To what does `command' refer? It refers to idolatry, (cf. *Talmud Bavli, Sanhedrin* 56b on the verse: "And the Lord God commanded the man, saying..." [Genesis 2:16] That is, he should not bring himself in to become impure in the spirit of uncleanliness, for this would be real idolatry.

527 Rabbi Elazar began by quoting: "I have come into my garden, my sister, my bride" (Song of Songs 5:1). We have already learned this verse, but it contains secrets concerning the sacrifices. But then we have already learned it all. Rabbi Shimon said to him: It is good that you have started the discussion on these matters, but why have you concealed them? It is as though you have said something, but it has not been fully said. Tell us what you know about the sacrifices." Rabbi Elazar replied: It was because I saw something in the Book of Enoch and learned it that I said something as though it were not said." Rabbi Shimon said: "Tell us that matter that you have seen and heard."

528 He said: It is all really just one matter. The Holy One, blessed be He, said "I have come into my garden" (Song of Songs 5:1) because all the sacrifices that are made in the world, when they ascend to the Female Waters first enter into the Garden of Eden, which is the secret of *Knesset Yisrael* (The Congregation of Israel), which is *Malkhut*. But how is it at the beginning of the sacrifice? For I have said that they (the sacrifices) first come into the Garden of Eden. When a man confesses his sins over the sacrifice, at the time of the slaughtering and the scattering of the blood over the altar, the sacrifice ascends to the Female Waters, to the Garden of Eden. And then, says the Holy One, blessed be He, who is *Zeir Anpin*: "I have come into my garden" (ibid.) which is the Garden of Eden, *Malkhut*, for the Female Waters of the sacrifice awaken the mating.

529 Now one has to concentrate to understand how these holy spirits benefit from this, from the ascent of the Female Waters of the sacrifice. Also, what is the reason that the sacrifice has to be of an animal, when it is more important that a man should break that spirit that is drawn down by his sin, and return in repentance? What is the reason for the ritual slaughtering of the animal, and the burning of it by fire on the altar?

530 The answer is that it is a secret. There is an animal that lies on a thousand hills, which is the secret of *Malkhut*, which is the aspect of the Tetragrammaton [*yud hei vav* and *hei*], spelled out and filled in with *heis* [*yud* = *yud vav dalet*, 10 + 6 + 4 = 20; *hei* = *hei hei*, 5 + 5 = 10; *vav* = *vav vav*, 6 + 6 = 12; *hei* = *hei hei*, 5 + 5 = 10], whose numerical value (20 + 10 + 12 + 10) is 52, which is the same as that of animal [*behemah*: *bet hei mem hei*, 2 + 5 + 40 + 5 = 52], and this animal devours a thousand hills each day, all of which (all of the thousand hills) are the secret of the stages of *Ḥokhmah* that are drawn down from the left, for *Ḥokhmah* is termed a thousand [*elef*] in the secret of the verse: "I will teach [Hebrew root: *aleph lamed pei*] you wisdom [*Ḥokhmah*]" (Job 33:33), and they are called: "The animals upon a thousand hills" (Ps. 50:10). And we have already learned about this, that there is an animal that devours animals. And what do the animals consist of? They are of fire, and this animal, which is *Malkhut*, consumes all of them with one gobble, as it is written: "For the Lord your God is a devouring fire, a jealous God" (Deut. 4:24). And all the waters of the Jordan, which is *Yesod* of *Zeir Anpin*, that flow through it during six years (which it receives from *Ḥesed*, *Gvurah*, *Tiferet*, *Netzaḥ*, *Hod*, *Yesod*, of *Zeir Anpin*, that are called six years) are made into one gulp, i.e. one swallow, by it, *Malkhut*, as it is written: "He is confident, though the Jordan rush forth to his mouth" (Job 40:23).

531 And the secret of the

matter is that from the leftovers of those animals on a thousand hills, which is the secret of the illumination of *Ḥokhmah* that is on the left, is the principle and basis for those animals below, for the spirit spreads downwards from them, and this spirit is reflected in the animals below, that is to say, it becomes the spirit of the animal below. And when a sinner brings an animal for sacrifice, then that spirit of the animal ascends and returns to its place, to the upper animal, which is *Malkhut*, and this spirit spreads through all the animals that are on a thousand hills, as above. And all those that are of this sort, i.e., the evil forces that are drawn down from the left, come close and enjoy that fat and blood that are the raiment of this spirit (as was clarified above, par. 13, in the Commentary, which should be well studied). And this spirit is from their side, i.e. from the left side, and they all benefit and are nourished and become advocates of that person, for the prosecutor becomes defense counsel (as above, *Vayera*, 385), and the Female Waters of the sacrifice enter by way of the esophagus, as we have learned (see Commentator's Interpolation, par. 7), which is why the sacrifice is taken from an animal.

532 Said Rabbi Shimon: Blessed is my son (Rabbi Elazar) to the Holy One, blessed be He. About you it is said: "Let your father and your mother be glad, and let her that bore you rejoice" (Prov. 23:25). Let your father on high be glad, that is *Zeir Anpin*, and your mother, *Knesset Yisrael* (the Congregation of Israel), which is *Malkhut*. And let her that bore you rejoice i.e. the daughter of the pious Rabbi Pinḥas ben Ya'ir, the mother of Rabbi Elazar. Elazar, my son, what you have said is correct regarding the sacrifice of an animal, but tell us, what is the reason for the offering of fowls? For it is written: "And if his offering to the Lord be a burnt offering of fowls" (Leviticus 1:14). He said to him: "I have not seen, but I draw an analogy from what is said about animals to what is said about fowl."

Nevertheless, I have not seen it (written anywhere) nor, until now, have I heard it (from anyone).

533 Rabbi Shimon said: Elazar, what you have said is good, but there are many secrets among the secrets of the sacrifices, and they have not been handed down to be revealed, except to the truly righteous, from whom their master's secret is not lost. The secret of the sacrifices is the secret of the holy beasts, the four forms engraved on the Throne, this being the Throne of the Holy King, i.e. *Malkhut*, which is a throne for *Zeir Anpin*, and these four are: The face of an ox, the face of an eagle, the face of a lion, the face of a man (cf. Ezekiel ch. 1). The face of a man includes all of them, for lion, ox, and eagle are the secret of the three columns, and the face of a man is *Malkhut* that receives them and therefore includes all of them. And all four of the faces look at each other and are included in each other, and from them they spread out in many directions, and tens of thousands, above and below, without measure, number, or account.

534 From the face of an ox, which is the secret of the left, spreads a spirit to the animals in four species, that are included in each other, namely: cattle, sheep, rams and goats, and these serve for the sacrifices. And because the sacrifice is from them, these holy hosts spread out from the face of that ox, and draw close, by the act of sacrifice, to their basis, which is the face of an ox, and benefit from that basis and their apparel. And were it not that they contain the basis (*Yesod*) of this world, which is the sacrifice that ascends to them, they would not draw close there, to their basis (*Yesod*), which is the face of an ox.

535 And just as the Holy *Shekhinah* takes pleasure in the spirits of the righteous that ascend to it for the Female Waters, and it draws close to welcome the spirit of a righteous person, and enjoys it because that spirit is drawn from it so is it also

with those hosts that spread forth from the face of an ox. They benefit from the side of their *Yesod*, which is the face of an ox, and from that raiment that is offered to their *Yesod*, which is the sacrifice, for the spirit of the sacrifice is from the raiment of their spirit, and this is why they enjoy it.

536 From the face of an eagle spreads a spirit to the fowl, for the spirit that is in the fowl is drawn from the face of an eagle. And eagle is on two sides, on the right and on the left, for eagle is *Tiferet*, the central column that includes the right and the left. And this is the secret of "And let fowl fly" (Genesis 1:20) [where the same Hebrew root is repeated twice, once in the verb and once in the noun, and this teaches about two spirits]. For this reason, the sacrifice of fowl spreads out and descends from the right and from the left, while the sacrifice of cattle is only from the face of an ox, which is the left, as above, the sacrifice of fowl is from the face of an eagle that includes the two columns.

537 Of all the pure fowl, only a pigeon and turtle-doves are sacrificed (see Leviticus 1:14), because they are true to their partners more than all the other fowl. And they are preyed upon but do not prey; they are faithful to each other, the female to her partner, and therefore the sacrifice is of them. And those holy spirits descend and draw close and enjoy their basis (*Yesod*) and principle, as above.

538 And you might well ask: How can the little that ascends from the pigeon or from the turtle-dove spread out in the number of directions to the hosts on high who are without measure? And the same question can be asked about the single animal. The answer is as follows: Come and see, the whole world fills with light from one thin burning candle. Again: One thin piece of wood enkindles a large piece. And this matter has already been clarified how the ascent of the Female Waters of man nourishes all the upper worlds on high (In the Commentator's

Interpolation, par. 1, and in The Introduction to the Wisdom of the Kabbalah, 161).

539 So far the sacrifice has been clarified from two sides engraved on the Throne, i.e. from the face of an ox for cattle, and from the face of an eagle for fowl. Now the question has to be put: There are four shapes that are engraved on the Throne, so what is the reason for there being no sacrifice from the others? The answer is that there is certainly sacrifice from all of them. The lion that is engraved on the throne: When the sacrifice is perfect, the lion descends and enters the fire, eats and has enjoyment from there. And the man that is engraved on the throne: Behold man is the main one of all of them, and he sacrifices there to the face of a man, which is *Malkhut*, his spirit and his soul, and upper man benefits from lower man. And each species draws near to its own and benefits from it, from that which is really its own, and from its basis (*Yesod*).

540 You might well ask: But lion has no basis below in the sacrifice, while the face of an ox has a basis below, in the animals; the face of an eagle has a basis below, in the fouls; the face of a man has a basis below, in the spirit and soul of the man offering the sacrifice, but lion has no basis below at all. The answer to this is that lion is included in all of them, for it is on the right, which is *Ḥesed*, and *Ḥesed* includes all of them. For this reason, it eats from all of them that are below it, while the others, ox, eagle, and man, do not eat from his species, because it is to the right and higher than they. Behold, all four of the forms that are engraved on the throne come close to the sacrifice, which is why it is a perfect sacrifice. And when they enjoy their principle and basis, then a spirit descends to kindle the upper candles, i.e. the mating is made between *Zeir Anpin* and *Malkhut*.

541 Priests, Levites, and Israelites give a basis and principle to the upper stages from which they are drawn, and each stage gives to its basis on high. First, the four shapes of the throne, as we have said in the preceding paragraph, each specie like unto like, and they first draw near, like unto like. The face of an ox, all the faces, i.e. the hosts and camps, that spread out to those species, as we have noted all of them draw near to their principle and basis. With the face of an ox and the face of an eagle it is as we have noted. So, too, with the face of a lion as we have noted as well as the face of a man who offers a sacrifice, his spirit and soul being sacrificed to the upper man, which is *Malkhut*.

542 The priest who pronounces the unity of the Holy Name over the sacrifice is himself sacrificed to the upper priest, which is *Ḥesed* of *Zeir Anpin*, the same that enters the house of the holy of holies, which is *Yesod* of *Malkhut*, and the former draws close to the latter and kindles the candles of *Malkhut* by his correction with the illumination of the countenances, paralleling the priest below who offers the sacrifice. The Levites who play their instruments happily when the sacrifice is made their side, which is *Gvurah* of *Zeir Anpin*, rejoices and illuminates countenances. Israel, who bring the sacrifices, who begin to pray over the sacrifice, for prayer was ordained for all the sacrifices, towards them awakens Israel Grandfather, the Holy Indefinite, and illuminates countenances.

543 And each species is sacrificed, like unto like, and everything follows its basis on high, with the lower stages awakening the higher stages, and although all of them stir, and the stages that are engraved on the throne, which are the four beasts, awaken for the stages that are on earth, being their basis, i.e. the face of an ox for animals, the face of an eagle for fowl, as above, and also those upper hidden stages, they all stir and come close for the meal of the sacrifice and find pleasure. But none of them has permission to eat, not the higher stages nor the lower stages, and not to have benefit, nor to put out a hand to the sac-

rifice, until after the Supreme King, who is *Zeir Anpin,* has eaten and enjoyed it, and given them permission.

544 **After he gives them permission, each one of them enjoys it and eats, this being as it is written: "I have gathered my myrrh with my spice; I have eaten my honeycomb with my honey; I have drunk my wine with my milk" (Song of Songs 5:1) "I have gathered my myrrh with my spice" these are the upper stages of *Zeir Anpin;* my myrrh and my spice eat and enjoy as is fitting, and this is the unity of the right arm, which is *Ḥesed,* with the left thigh, which is *Hod.* "I have eaten my honeycomb with my honey". This is Jacob with Rachel, i.e. the unity of *Tiferet* with *Malkhut.* And this is proper eating, for only here is the word "eat" used. "I have drunk my wine with my milk". This is the unity of the left arm with the right thigh, i.e. *Gvurah* with *Netzaḥ.* And these are all the upper stages from which the Holy King has enjoyment at the beginning. And this is His eating and His pleasure. So far we have discussed first the food of the Supreme King.**

Commentary:

For there are three types of unity of *Ḥokhmah* and *ḥasadim*, according to Scripture, namely: The unity of smell, the unity of eating and the unity of drinking. And you already know the difference between head and body (as above, Commentator's Interpolation, par. 3). Now the unity of smell is in the head, in the nose, and is mainly *Ḥokhmah*, but since it is the illumination of *Ḥokhmah* of the left, it is accepted only upwards from below, which is the secret of *Netzaḥ, Hod, Yesod* of the head. And therefore, smell which is the secret of the left that is in it is the secret of *Hod* that is garmented in the light of *Ḥesed* of the body. And on the text: "My myrrh and my spice... is the unity of the right arm... with the left thigh," i.e. *Ḥesed* of the body with *Hod* of the head. And the unity of the eating is mainly *ḥasadim*, and is in the body. And this is the secret of the overall unity of *Zeir Anpin* and *Malkhut*. And on the text: "I have eaten my honeycomb with my honey." This is Jacob with Rachel, i.e. *Zeir Anpin* with *Malkhut*. "And this is proper eating." That is to say, this is the main mating of *Zeir Anpin* and *Malkhut*. And the unity of the drinking is also in the body as is that of the eating, but it is mainly *Ḥokhmah* of the left, and is specifically the drinking of wine, but the drinking of milk is *Ḥesed*, as is that of water. And on the text: "I have drunk my wine with my milk." This is the unity of the left arm with the right thigh, for wine is the left of the body, which is *Gvurah*, and milk is *Netzaḥ* of the body. And do not be astonished that ḥasadim are at a lower level than *Ḥokhmah*, for in smell *Ḥokhmah* is in the head and *ḥasadim* in *Ḥesed* of the body. And likewise with the drinking: *Ḥokhmah* is in *Gvurah* and *ḥasadim* in *Netzaḥ*. This is so because *Ḥokhmah* cannot be the main thing over *Ḥesed* that attires it, unless *Ḥesed* is at a lower level than it. Consequently, the unity is, *Ḥokhmah* of *Hod* of the head with *Ḥesed* of the body, and *Ḥokhmah* of *Gvurah* of the body with *Ḥesed* that is in *Netzaḥ* of the body. For the right which is *Ḥesed* that is at the same level as the left that is *Ḥokhmah* is always higher and more important than it. For *Ḥesed* is the secret of *Keter* and *Ḥokhmah* of the level, and *Ḥokhmah* is the secret of *Binah* and *Tiferet* and *Malkhut* that returned to that level (as above, *Vayakel*, 130, in the Commentary).

545 From this point on, the King, which is *Zeir Anpin*, gives permission to the four forms that are engraved on the throne, and to all those that spread out from them, to enjoy and eat. For the verse continues: "Eat, O friends; drink, yea, drink abundantly, O beloved" (Songs of Songs 5:1). Friends are four forms that we have mentioned: lion,

ox, eagle, man. Drink, yea, drink abundantly, O beloved all those who spread out from them, and they all eat and enjoy as is fitting, and their countenances shine. And all the worlds rejoice, and each one, whether at the upper levels or at the lower levels, draws closer to its basis, i.e. each one to its parallel aspect: *Ḥesed* to the face of a lion; *Gvurah* to the face of an ox, etc., and they enjoy. This is the secret and mystery of the sacrifices.

546 Rabbi Elazar and Rabbi Abba, together with the other companions, came and prostrated themselves before him, before Rabbi Shimon. Rabbi Abba said: Had the Torah not been given at Mount Sinai, but instead the Holy One, blessed be He, had said: Here is (Rabbi Shimon) ben Yoḥai to give you the Torah and My secrets, it would have sufficed for the world. Woe for when you depart from the world! Who will then kindle the lights from the Torah? Everything will be in darkness from that day! For until the arrival of the King Messiah there will be no generation such as this generation, in whose midst is Rabbi Shimon!

547 Concerning this secret (above 544), a man is forbidden to taste anything until the Supreme King has eaten (cf. *Talmud Bavli, Berakhot* 10b). And what is meant by His eating? This means prayer, which is in the stead of sacrifices. A man's prayer is similar in respect to what we said above about the sacrifices (433 ff.). First the four forms that are engraved on the throne are invited, that they should dwell over these creatures, over the fowl and the animals, for the spirits of the four beasts spread out over them so that they should be sacrifices, for they are creatures the basis of whose spirit in this world is of them, of the four beasts (as above, 534 and 539), and that is: "How manifold are Your works, O Lord!" (Psalms 104:24). For the creatures whose spirit is suitable for sacrifice over them spread out the four forms that are in the throne, which are invited over these sacrifices. And it is to this that we

refer when we say "*Ofanim* and holy beasts" [in the hymn "*El Adon,*" inserted into the first blessing before the morning *Shema Yisrael* on sabbaths and festivals —tr.] for this is the secret of the four beasts that are in the throne, and all those other hosts who spread out from them, to which are joined the spirit of animals and fowl that are fitted for offering as sacrifices.

548 And afterwards the high priest proclaims the unity of the Name (as above, with the sacrifices, 532), i.e. "With abounding love..." [the second blessing before the recital of the *Shema Yisrael* in the morning service where love is *Ḥesed,* the attribute of the priest. The unity that the priest proclaims is: "Hear, O Israel, the Lord our God, the Lord is One" (Deuteronomy 6: 4 the *Shema Yisrael*). And afterwards the Levites (as above, 532) arise to play, which is: "And it shall come to pass, if you hearken diligently to My commandments..." (Deuteronomy 11:13). "Take heed to yourselves lest your heart be deceived..." (ibid. 16-21) which section [which is the last of the *Shema Yisrael* parallels the left which is *Gvurah*. For this is the melody of the Levites, that is to say that the signing of the Levites is from the left, in order to awaken this side, the side of the left with this sacrifice namely, with the prayer that is in the stead of the sacrifice. And then come the Israelites (as above, 532) with: "True and firm, established and enduring..." [the paragraph immediately following the *Shema Yisrael* —tr.], which alludes to Israel Grandfather, who stands over the sacrifice, for He — the ten upper levels, the inner meaning to everything, i.e. the ten *Sfirot* — is at the table, while they are, true and firm and established and enduring.

549 But not one of them has permission to eat and to stretch a hand out to the sacrifice, i.e. the prayer, until the Supreme King, who is *Zeir Anpin,* has eaten, by which is meant the first three blessings and the last three blessings of the *Shemoneh Esreh,* which is where the

mating of *Zeir Anpin* and *Malkhut* takes place, and this is the secret of the King's eating. After He has eaten, He grants permission to the four forms, i.e. the four beasts of the throne, and to all those parties that spread out from them, to eat.

550 And then man, who is the form that includes all the other forms, demeans himself, and throws himself on his face and gives himself and his spirit to supernal man (as above, with the sacrifices, 539) who stands over these forms and who includes all the forms, that he should awaken towards Him as is fitting. And this is what is meant by: "To You, O Lord, do I lift up my soul" (Psalms 25:1), i.e. in order to awaken other forms and all those who spread out from them. And this is what is meant by saying in "Praise of David" (Psalms 145): "They shall utter the fame of Your great goodness, and shall sing of Your righteousness" (v.7); and "They shall speak of the glory of Your kingdom, and talk of Your might" (v.11) which is said of the forms that spread out from them. And they all eat and enjoy the prayer, each one as is fitting for him. [And see above in the Commentator's Interpolation, where the whole matter of the ascent of the prayer to the Female Waters and how it is accepted on high is dealt with at length, and there is no need to do so here.]

551 From here on a man may mention the troubles that are in his heart. (cf. *Shulḥan Arukh, Oraḥ Ḥayim,* 119), as it is written: "The Lord will answer you in the day of trouble" (Psalms 20:2), for example, a pregnant woman in labor, so that they should all become advocates for the person. Therefore, is it written: "Happy is the people that is in such a case" (Psalms 144:15).

552 Rabbi Shimon was on his way to Tiberias when Elijah met him and said: "Greetings, sir." Rabbi Shimon said to him: "With what is the Holy One, blessed be He, engaged in the firmament?" Elijah replied: "He is occupied with the sacrifices, and saying new things in your name. Happy are you! And

I came to welcome you with greetings, and there is one thing that I wanted to ask you to settle for me. A question has been asked in the heavenly academy: In the next world there is no eating and drinking (cf. *Talmud Bavli, Berakhot* 17a), yet it is written: "I am come into my garden, my sister, my bride; I have gathered my myrrh with my spice; I have eaten my honeycomb with my honey; I have drunk my wine with my milk" (Song of Songs 5:1). Would one for whom there is no eating nor drinking say: "I have eaten my honeycomb with my honey; I have drunk my wine with my milk?"

553 Said Rabbi Shimon: And what did the Holy One, blessed be He, reply to them? Elijah answered: The Holy One, blessed be He, said: There is (Rabbi Shimon) ben Yoḥai. Let him tell you! So I (Elijah) came to ask you. Said Rabbi Shimon: In what great affection did the Holy One, blessed be He, hold the Congregation of Israel, and out of the intense love with which He loved them, He altered his deeds from the way He had been doing, for, although He does not usually eat and drink, nevertheless, because of the love of Israel, he ate and drank. Since He had come to her, He did as she wanted. If a bride just entering the wedding canopy wants to eat, does it not follow that her bridegroom will eat with her, even if he is not used to doing so? This is what is written: "I have come into my garden, my sister, my bride." Since I have come to her, to go with her into the wedding canopy, "I have eaten my honeycomb with my honey; I have drunk my wine with my milk."

554 And we can learn this also from David, who invited the Holy One, blessed be He, and changed His actions from the way the Holy One, blessed be He, was accustomed, and the Holy One, blessed be He, accepted it and did as he wanted, for he (David) invited the King, together with the Queen, as it is written: "Arise, O Lord, to your resting-place, You and the ark of Your strength" (Psalms 132:8), i.e. the King together with

the Queen. And in order not to make any separation between them, he changed the vessels, and he altered the deeds of the King.

555 This is what is written: "Let Your priests be clothed with righteousness and let Your pious ones shout for joy. For Your servant David's sake, turn not away the face of Your anointed" (ibid. v.9). It should have said: Let Your Levites be clothed with righteousness, and not: Let Your priests be clothed with righteousness, since righteousness is from the side of the Levites; i.e. *Malkhut* from the aspect of the left is called righteousness, and the left is the aspect of the Levites. Similarly, it should have said: Let Your Levites shout for joy, and not: Let Your pious ones shout for joy, since joy and song are from the side of the Levites, i.e. from the left side. But he (David) changed things and said: Your priests and Your pious ones, who are from the right side.

556 The Holy One, blessed be He, said to him: David, this is not the way I do things. David replied: "For Your servant David's sake, turn not away the face of Your anointed" (Psalms 132:10). Do not alter the correction that I have instituted. Said to him the Holy One, blessed be He: David, since you have invited Me, I have to do what you want and not what I want. From this we learn that if one invites another, the guest has to do as the host wishes, even if that is not his way.

557 Thus: "And he took of the stones of the place" (Genesis 28:11). Since the bridegroom comes to the bride for Jacob is the secret of *Tiferet* and place is the secret of *Malkhut*, where *Tiferet* and *Malkhut* are the secret of the bridegroom and bride although it is not his custom to lie down without pillows and cushions, when she gave him stones to lie on, he accepts it all willingly, as it is written: "And he lay down in that place" (ibid.), on those stones, although that was not what he was used to.

558 This same applies in our case: "I have eaten my

honeycomb with my honey" (Song of Songs 5:1). Although this was not His way, he nevertheless did it because of love of the bride. And this only happens in the house of the bride and not anywhere else. In His own place He neither eats nor drinks, but in her place He both eats and drinks, as it is written: "I have come into my garden" (ibid.), i.e. the Garden of Eden, which is the place of *Malkhut*. Similarly, the angels whom the Holy One, blessed be He, sent to Abraham neither ate nor drank in their own place, but for the sake of Abraham they both ate and drank (see Genesis 18:1-8). Elijah said to him (to Rabbi Shimon): Master, upon your life! The Holy One, blessed be He, wanted to relate this matter, but in order not to pay Himself a compliment before the People of Israel, He raised it to you. Happy are you in this world, that your master on high is praised through you. About you is it written: "The righteous, even he that rules in the fear of God" (II Samuel 23:3).

Commentary:

Zeir Anpin always cleaves above to *Binah*, which is the secret of the world to come, where there is no eating nor drinking, for eating and drinking are the secret of intelligences of *Ḥokhmah* attired with *ḥasadim* (as above, 544), and it is known that *Ḥokhmah* is revealed only in *Malkhut*, and not in any other sfirah above it (as above, *Bereshith Aleph*, page 276 et al.). It follows that there is eating and drinking only in *Malkhut*. And on the text (553): "For, although he does not usually eat and drink," since not the intelligences of *Ḥokhmah*, but only *ḥasadim* are revealed in *Zeir Anpin*. "Since He had come to her, He did as she wanted." Since He had come and been united with *Malkhut*, *Zeir Anpin* is also included in the intelligences of eating and drinking as is *Malkhut*. And on the text (558): "And this only happens in the house of the bride and not anywhere else." For there is no revelation of *Ḥokhmah* in any other place but its own. And on the text: "In His own place, He neither eats nor drinks," for in the place of *Zeir Anpin* the intelligences of eating and drinking are not revealed.

559 **"My food which is presented to Me for offerings made by fire" (Numbers 28:2). Rabbi Yehuda said: In sacrifices there is smoke, there is smell, and there is aroma. Smoke is those with a temper, as it is written: "But then the anger of the Lord shall be kindled" (Deuteronomy 29:19). [The Hebrew idiom used here is: `The nose of the Lord will smoke'.] And those with a temper enjoy smoke, the meaning of which is anger in the nose (see above 203). Smell refers to those who are called apples. Said Rabbi Abba: Those who are like apples, as it is written: "And the smell of your nose like apples" (Song of Songs 7:9) (See *Idra Rabba*, 171).**

560 **"The one lamb you shall offer in the morning" (Numbers 28:4). What is meant by morning? This refers to the morning of Abraham, i.e. the light of *Ḥesed*, as it is written: "And Abraham rose early in the morning" (Genesis 22:3). How do we know that this morning is that of Abraham? Rabbi Elazar answered: From here, where it is written: "As soon as the morning was light" (Genesis 44:3). Not `morning' but `the morning' is written, with the definite article, for this was the first light that the Holy One, blessed be He, created in the Act of Creation. Thus is it written: "You shall offer in the morning" (Numbers 28:4), i.e. on the particular morning, for this sacrifice is offered against the morning of Abraham. The lamb that is offered as a sacrifice at dusk (see ibid.) is against Isaac, against the evening of Isaac, which is the light of *Gvurah*, which is Judgment. How do we know this? Because it is written: "And Isaac went out to meditate in the field at eventide" (Genesis 24:63), which is the evening of Isaac. And we have already learned this.**

THE FAITHFUL SHEPHERD

561 It is a positive precept to offer the afternoon sacrifice each day, and the additional sacrifice on the Sabbath. And subsequently, to arrange the showbread and the frankincense and the additional sacrifice on the first of the month. Holy Luminary, each day a gift has to be sent to the King, to *Zeir Anpin*, in the hands of the Queen. And if she is in her husband's domain, i.e. in the mating of greatness with *Zeir Anpin*, a supplement has to be given, i.e. the additional sacrifice of the Sabbath, the first of each month and of all the festivals.

562 For she, *Malkhut*, is his, *Zeir Anpin*'s private property, and the central column, *Zeir Anpin*, is the owner of this property. And the level of Jacob, who instituted the evening prayers (cf. *Talmud Bavli, Berakhot* 26b), is that of the central column, which is *Zeir Anpin*. For this reason, the sages of the Mishnah taught: The evening prayer is optional [*reshut*], (ibid. 27b), for the prayer, which is *Malkhut*, is in the domain [*reshut*] of her husband. For although being in exile, which is like the night-time, which is the time for the evening prayers, and where Samael and Serpent and all those appointed over his regiments have control, and although the *Shekhinah* goes into exile with Israel, nevertheless she is to be found in the domain of her husband, as it is written: "I am the Lord, that is My name, and My glory I will not give to another" (Isaiah 42:8).

563 Because of this it is written: "And he chanced upon the place" (Genesis 28:11), for chancing upon [Hebrew root: *pei gimel ayin*] is only conciliation and appeasement, as in: "Neither make intercession [Hebrew root: *pei gimel ayin*] to Me" (Jeremiah 7:16) (and cf. *Talmud Bavli, Berakhot* 26b). *Knesset Yisrael* (the Congregation of Israel) appeased *Zeir Anpin*, that he should not leave her, for the Holy One, blessed be He, *Zeir Anpin*, is the Place of the world. (cf. *Midrash Bereshith Rabba* 68, 9). What is meant by world? The *Shekhinah*. For the Hebrew word for world is *olam* [*ayin vav lamed mem*], of which the Aramaic equivalent is *alma* [*ayin lamed mem aleph*], which is like the Hebrew *almah* [*ayin lamed mem hei*], as in the verse: "...the maiden [*ha-almah*]..." (Genesis 24:43), i.e. *Malkhut* that is a maiden. And what is written about him [Jacob, *Zeir Anpin*]? "And he stayed there all night" (Genesis 28:11), that is *Zeir Anpin* made peace with her, to stay there in the exile with the *Shekhinah*. And should you suggest that the meaning of "And he chanced upon the place" (ibid.) is that Jacob appeased *Malkhut* (as above, 557), that is fine, but it can also be taken to mean that *Malkhut* appeased Jacob, who is *Zeir Anpin*, that he should not leave her in the exile, as above. And because every night, which is the aspect of exile, she is in the domain [*reshut*] of her husband, as above, the sages taught that the evening prayers are optional [*reshut*] (cf. *Talmud Bavli, Berakhot* 27b), for prayer is *Malkhut* and evening is exile, so that saying that the evening prayers are optional is the same as saying that *Malkhut* in exile is in the domain [*reshut*] of her husband. And the other, literal, explanation of the saying, i.e. that the evening prayers really are optional and not obligatory, is but straw for the fodder of material animals, by inference from minor to major it is easy for one who is just a physical presence to understand, but not for one of intelligence. The sages of the Mishnah came down to him, prostrated themselves before him, and were happy over this matter, and they bound him with a number of knots of mysterious secrets, i.e. they expounded that matter in a number of ways with Torah secrets. And they crowned him and raised him up to the other companions who had remained there.

564 The Faithful Shepherd said to Rabbi Shimon: Holy Luminary, this is why it is obligatory with the remaining prayers, imposed on them as a promissory note, to bring together

Malkhut and the Righteous One, the Life of all Worlds, which is *Yesod*. For in this connection the sages taught: One who joins *ge'ulah* [Redemption, the reference being to the conclusion of the *Emet ve'Yatsiv* prayer, which is one paragraph after the morning recital for the *Shema Yisrael*, namely the sentence: "Blessed are You, O Lord, who redeemed Israel" —tr.] to the *Tefilah* [literally: Prayer], i.e. prayer par excellence, that is the *Shemoneh Esreh* will meet with no mishap for the whole of the day (cf. *Talmud Bavli, Berakhot* 9b) where *ge'ulah* is *Yesod* and *tefilah* is *Malkhut*. And how is *Malkhut* joined to *Yesod*? By the right arm, which is *Ḥesed*, as it is written: "As the Lord lives; lie down until the morning" (Ruth 3:13), i.e. until *Ḥesed* that is called morning shall give light (as above, 560).

565 The time of the afternoon prayer [*minḥah*] is the secret of "In the evening she came" (Esther 2:14), i.e. the unity just before dusk, as it is written: "And the dove came unto him at eventime" (Genesis 8:11), for the dove is *Malkhut*, because of "It is a present [*minḥah*] sent to my lord (in the exile of) Esau" (Genesis 32:19), for evening is the secret of exile. "And, behold, he also is behind us" (ibid.), i.e. *Zeir Anpin* is coming after us to redeem us from the exile. Furthermore, 'to my lord' refers to the Lord of all the world, which is the Righteous One, i.e. *Yesod*. For from there, from the aspect of the mating, the *minḥah* (double entendre: afternoon prayer and present) that is at eventime, it is said about Joseph, the Righteous One: "His firstling bullock, majesty is his" (Deuteronomy 23:17). For the unity of the *minḥah* comes from the control of the left that is called evening, and since the *minḥah* is "sent to my lord" (Genesis 32:19), i.e. to *Yesod*, which is Joseph, therefore Joseph also becomes the aspect of "firstling bullock" (Deuteronomy 33:17), which is the left column. And in the future the Messiah the son of Ephraim will issue from the left column, for Messiah the son of David is the aspect of the right and Messiah the son of Ephraim is the aspect of the left. And for his sake, for the sake of Messiah the son of Ephraim, it is said: "And, lo, my sheaf [Hebrew root: *aleph lamed mem*] arose, and also stood upright, and behold, your sheaves came round about and bowed down to my sheaf" (Genesis 37:7), for Messiah the son of Ephraim is called mute [Hebrew root: *aleph lamed mem*] in the exile. And about the Righteous One it was said: Everyone who bows should do so at the word 'Blessed' (cf. *Talmud Bavli, Berakhot* 12a bot.). And it was therefore said for his part: "And bowed down to my sheaf" (Genesis 37:7), which is Messiah.

566 Said the Holy Luminary, that is Rabbi Shimon: Faithful Shepherd, it is said about you: "And Moses took the bones of Joseph" (Exodus 13:19). Since Moses is *Tiferet*, which is called body, and Joseph is *Yesod*, that is called covenant, and we consider body and covenant to be one, it is therefore said about you: "And, lo, my sheaf arose, and also stood upright" (Genesis 37:7), i.e. *Malkhut* that is called '*El*' (God) in exile, for so is the *tefilah* (prayer, *Shemoneh Esreh*) said while standing upright, where prayer is the secret of *Malkhut*. Likewise: Everyone who returns to an upright position, should do so at the mention of the Divine Name (*Talmud Bavli, Berakhot* 12a bot.), which is *Tiferet*, i.e. Moses, and therefore it is said about him: "My sheaf arose" (Genesis 37:7), and about the Righteous One: Everyone who bows, should do so at the word 'Blessed' (cf. *Talmud Bavli, Berakhot* 12a bot.) (as above, 306, q.v.); and thus it is said "and bowed down to my sheaf" (Genesis 37:7), for, from the point of view of *Tiferet*, the rising up is to *Malkhut*, while, from the point of view of *Yesod* the bowing down is to *Malkhut*. For you are attached to the right and to the left of the body and covenant, which are *Tiferet* and *Yesod*, and *Tiferet* inclines to the right, and *Yesod* inclines to the left.

Subsequently, you will ascend on them to *Binah*, to open there fifty gates of freedom for Israel, i.e. to draw down the great intelligences of freedom, to fulfill the verse: "As in the days of your coming forth out of the land of Egypt, will I show to him marvelous things" (Micah, 7:15). For this reason the morning prayer is obligatory and the evening prayer is optional.

Commentary:

It is as explained above (563) that the evening prayer is optional [*reshut*], meaning that the prayer, which is *Malkhut*, in the evening, which is the aspect of exile, is in the domain [*reshut*] of her husband, but there is no obligation to draw *ḥasadim* down for her, for in exile it is impossible to draw down *ḥasadim*, for the light of *ḥasadim* is drawn down only in the daytime, which is the aspect of redemption. But with the morning prayer, which is recited during the daylight hours, it is obligatory to draw *ḥasadim* down to her by *Yesod* (as above, 564), for then is the time of *ḥasadim*.

567 In the evening prayer, *Malkhut* is *Hashkivenu* ['Cause us to lie down' the second blessing after the recital of the *Shema Yisrael* at evening services], i.e. she lies between the arms of the King in exile, for she lies down and has no standing upright, since night-time is the aspect of exile. When the morning, which is the aspect of redemption, comes, the Festival of Passover, which is the secret of right, i.e. *Ḥesed* of *Zeir Anpin*, takes hold of her on the right, i.e. emanates *ḥasadim* to her. But it is said about the left arm of *Zeir Anpin*, that is called Isaac, which is the aspect of (the month of) *Tishrei* [the seventh month of the year on the Hebrew calendar, whereas Passover falls in the month of *Nissan* which is the first month]. "And it

came to pass, before he (Isaac) had done speaking, that, behold, Rebeccah came out" (Genesis 24:15) from the exile, for the Redemption comes from the correction of the left side, which is Isaac; and so that *Malkhut* should not emerge from the exile from the side of Judgment, for the left is Judgment, therefore, Jacob, who is *Zeir Anpin,* "guided his hands wittingly" (Genesis 48:14), and placed ox, which is left, on his right, which is *Ḥesed.* And lion, which is right, he placed on the left, which is Judgment, for which reason: "The Lord said to my master: Sit at My right hand", (Psalms 110:1). This is the Righteous One, which is *Yesod,* that parallels Messiah the son of Joseph, which is Judgment (as above, 565); and he said to him: "Sit at My right hand" (ibid.), which is the arm of Abraham, which is *Ḥesed* at the time of the exile of Ishmael (see Genesis, chapter 21). That is, because Jacob "guided his hands wittingly" (Genesis 48:14), he said to my master, which is the left of *Yesod,* which is the Messiah the son of Ephraim, which is Judgment, that he should sit at the right, which is *Ḥesed,* "Until I make your enemies your footstool" (Psalms 110:1).

AN EXTRA NEFESH (COGNITIVE SOUL), AN EXTRA RUAḤ (SPIRIT), AN EXTRA NESHAMAH (ETHICAL SOUL)

568 At that time an extra spirit will awaken, that is, an additional spirit, over Israel, as it is written: "I will pour out My spirit upon all flesh" (Joel 3:1), and Israel will have rest from the nations of the world, "rest from their enemies" (Esther 9:16). And it will be as on the Sabbath when an extra soul [*nefesh*] is added to a person (cf. *Talmud Bavli, Bestah* 16a), and he obtains rest therein. And if he has rest with an extra soul [*nefesh*] which is feminine, how much more will he have rest with the spirit which is masculine.

569 And *Tannaim* and *Amoraim* heard that the extra soul on the Sabbath is, for the whole of Israel together, just one, which is the secret of *Keter,* but for each person it is allocated according to his deeds, i.e. for each one according to his level. And this we have learned from repentance by inference from minor to major. For all of Israel together, on making repentance, are all found acceptable, as it is written: "As the Lord our God whensoever we call upon Him" (Deuteronomy 4:7), this being the reason for it (the extra soul) being for all Israel together. They are crowned with the Name of Names (the Tetragrammaton), with his crown, which is Upper *Keter* (crown). And this letter (upper *Keter*) is an additional soul [neshamah] for all Israel together on Sabbaths and festival days. For this reason it was decreed that each of the blessings in the daily prayer (the *Shemoneh Esreh*) be concluded with the name of the Tetragrammaton, which indeed "seals" each blessing of the prayers, but no additional service is said without the illumination of *Keter*, for *Keter* of the Tetragrammaton does not illuminate every day, and the blessings are therefore concluded with the Tetragrammaton, which is *Zeir Anpin*, while no additional service, which is the crown [*Keter*] of *Zeir Anpin*, is recited on weekdays. But on the Sabbath, it was decreed that "A crown will be given to You, O Lord our God" [in the reader's repetition of the *Shemoneh Esreh*, the opening line of the third blessing, the *Kedushah*, in the Sephardi version only be said]. Because on the Sabbath the *Keter* of *Zeir Anpin* illuminates, and the additional service is therefore recited. And this *Keter* of *Zeir Anpin* is the secret of the additional soul [*neshamah*] that gives light for the whole of Israel together, as above.

570 For each individual of Israel, the additional soul [nefesh] descends to him according to his level. If he is pious [*ḥasid*], he is given an additional soul [*nefesh*] from the attribute of *Ḥesed*, according to his level. If he is a mighty man [gibor], fearful of sin, he is given an additional soul [*nefesh*] from the attribute of might [*Gvurah*]. If he is an honest man [*tam*: *tav mem*], he is given an additional soul [*nefesh*] from the attribute of truth [*emet*: *aleph mem tav*]. For the additional soul [*nefesh*] is *Malkhut*, and is made up of the ten *Sfirot*, and therefore a person receives from a *sfirah* of *Malkhut* according to his character. That is: If he is a chief (court president/president) in Israel, or a scholar or one who understands wisdom or Torah about which is said: "To understand a proverb and a figure" (Proverbs 1:6) or the Prophets or the Hagiographa, so is he given an additional soul [*nefesh*], which is called *Keter* (the crown of) *Malkhut*, if he is a chief of Israel.

571 Continuing the explanation of "If he is a scholar, as we have learned:" Who is a scholar? He who stimulates others' minds (cf. *Talmud Bavli, Hagigah* 14a), as it is written: "In wisdom (same root as the word for scholar) have You made them all" (Psalms 104:24). He is given an extra soul [*nefesh*] from there, i.e. from *Ḥokhmah* (Wisdom). And if he [*mevin*] understands one matter from another (i.e. deduces) in the Torah, he is given an extra soul [*nefesh*] from *Binah* (understanding). And if he is a scholar in the Prophets and Hagiographa, he is given an extra soul [*nefesh*] from *Netzaḥ* and *Hod*. And if he is completely righteous, keeping the sign of the covenant, the sign of the Sabbath, the sign of the festivals, and the sign of the phylacteries, he is given an extra soul [*nefesh*] from the Righteous One, which is *Yesod*. And in every case, the extra soul that the individual receives is from *Malkhut*. And if it has been said that it is *Yesod*, for example, then this means the *sfirah Yesod* of *Malkhut*, and so with the other *Sfirot*.

572 And if he is a person who has all the above-mentioned qualities, then he is comparable and similar to the whole of Israel together (569) and is given *Keter* in the name of the Tetragrammaton. And this is in the secret of the verses: "As the Lord our God whensoever we call upon Him" (Deuteronomy

4:7) and "There is none holy as the Lord" (I Samuel 2:2) [In both these cases the word `as' is a prefixed letter *kaf*, such that `as the Lord' is, in Hebrew, just one word — tr.]. The *kaf* that is prefixed to `the Lord' is the secret of *Keter* [*kaf tav resh*] of *Zeir Anpin*. And this is an extra soul [*neshamah*] from the world of the Male, which is *Tiferet*, and is not as the extra soul [*nefesh*] of an individual, which is only from the *Sfirot* of *Malkhut*. For it is a king crowned with an upper *Keter* (crown) from *Binah*, in which He rules with His *Shekhinah*, which is extra soul [*nefesh*]. And *Keter* is extra soul [*neshamah*] that is received from the Tetragrammaton, which is spirit [*ruaḥ*], about which it is said: "I will pour out My spirit upon all flesh" (Joel 3:1). And this spirit, which is the Tetragrammaton [*yud hei vav* and *hei*] is composed of the ten *Sfirot*, downwards from above, as follows: *Yud* is *Ḥokhmah*, *hei* is *Binah*, *vav* [whose numerical value is six — tr.] incorporates the six *Sfirot*, from *Ḥesed* to *Yesod*, and the last *hei* is *Malkhut*. And the *kaf*, meaning `as' in `As the Lord our God' is the *Keter* (crown) on the head of the holy Name (Tetragrammaton). And this is the soul [*neshamah*] that is added on the Sabbath either to all of Israel together or to an individual who has all ten of the qualities that are in *Malkhut*.

573 And because the Prime Cause is superior and covered with this crown, and on the Sabbath days and festivals the crown [*Keter*] spreads with the Tetragrammaton, there is, therefore, no rule for Samael and Serpent and all his officials, nor does Gehenna (Hell), which is the wicked Female of Samael, have any rule, nor his camps, for all of them take cover before the camps of the King, just as the idolatrous nations of the world will hide when the Messiah is revealed, as it is written: "And the men shall go into the caves of the rocks" (Isaiah 2:19); "And in the holes of the rocks" (ibid. 7:19).

574 The *Tannaim* and the

Amoraim **arose and said: Faithful Shepherd, you are the one who is equivalent to all of Israel, filled with all good qualities (as above, 572), and certainly in you rests He about whom it is said: "There is none holy as the Lord" (Samuel I 2:2), i.e. the *kaf* that is prefixed to the Tetragrammaton which alludes to *Keter* (the crown of) the Tetragrammaton (as above, 572). You are a crown [*keter*] on each and every one of Israel, for there is no man who can be a crown over you, not a chief, nor scholar, nor one who understands, not a pious man, a mighty one, nor an honest man, not a prophet, a righteous person, nor a king, for these are the ten *Sfirot* of *Malkhut*, from which each individual one of Israel takes (as above, 571). But you are in the form of the Holy One, blessed be He, i.e. *Zeir Anpin*, which is the secret of the world of the Male, as above, the son being in the form of his father, for Moses is the son of *Zeir Anpin*, just as is Israel as a whole, about whom it is written: "You are the children of the Lord your God" (Deuteronomy 14:1). Do the precept of your master perfectly, for there is no precept of those that you perform with which the Holy One, blessed be He, and His *Shekhinah* will not be adorned above and below, with upper *Keter* in every attribute.**

575 The Faithful Shepherd opened and said: *Tannaim* and *Amoraim*, listen, and the Zohar explains that every time that the Faithful Shepherd called the companions, with Rabbi Shimon among them, by the title '*Tannaim* and *Amoraim*,' he said to them: I praise you according to your munificence, for you are the sons of princes, namely: Abraham, Isaac, and Jacob. No one but the Master of the Universe can praise you, for even the whole of the Torah *ad infinitum* is dependent on you [where Torah is to be understood in its widest sense of the total body of revealed teachings and not just the Pentateuch]. As it is said in the Torah: "Its measure is longer than the earth and broader than the sea" (Job 11:9) so is your praise. But may what was

fulfilled in me be fulfilled in you also, for I rejoiced in the honor of Aharon, my brother, as we have learned about Aharon: The heart that rejoiced at the greatness of his brother shall put on the *Urim* and *Thumim* (in the breast-plate of the high priests) (cf. *Talmud Bavli, Shabbat,* 139a).

576 And listen, *Tannaim* and *Amoraim,* all the additional prayers of sabbaths and festivals, every additional service in which *Keter* is mentioned [e.g. 'A crown will be given to You, O Lord our God' see above, 569 —tr.] they are known from here, i.e. *Keter* of *Zeir Anpin,* about which is said: "There is none holy as the Lord" (Samuel I 2:2) (as above, 572). And the smell of all the prayers of Israel is as the smell of myrrh and frankincense and all scented powder. This is the case of weekdays, but on Sabbaths and festivals, when the *Keter* of *Zeir Anpin* illuminates, as above, the prayer is much more important for the Holy One, blessed be He, than all sorts of spices.

Commentary:

All sorts of spices and smell are the secret of the illumination of *Ḥokhmah* of the left, while *Keter*, which illuminates on Sabbaths and festivals, is the secret of the light of *ḥasadim*, but it is much more important than the spices that illuminate on other days, for they are the illumination of *Ḥokhmah*.

577 On festival days the prayers are more sublime and important than all scented powder [Hebrew root: *aleph bet kuf*], about which it is said: "And there wrestled [Hebrew root: *aleph bet kuf*] a man with him" (Genesis 32:25), for Samael wrestles with faulty prayer, using it to fight and accuse, using that fault of a transgression in the prayer; i.e. with that dust [Hebrew root: *aleph bet kuf*] of the prayer, he ascends and accuses, and this rises up to the heavens.

EVENING PRAYERS

578 And there are two sorts of dust, for the dust of Jacob, i.e. his war, comes to teach merit about prayers, in a number of groups of merits that are regiments and camps that gather with him to teach merit about prayer. And the dust from the level of Samael ascends in a number of camps of liability, teaching a liability about prayer. And this prayer that is recited in the evening is called Jacob's Ladder, concerning which it is written: "And behold the angels of God ascending and descending on it" (Genesis 28:12). These are the prayers that ascend when they are liabilities, and merits descend in their place. For the camps of the teachers of merit (defense) of Jacob overcame the camps of the teachers of liability (prosecution) of Samael. And there are those that ascend as merits and liabilities descend in their stead. In this case, the camps of the teachers of liability (prosecution) of Samael have overcome the others, for these camps are humiliated in a number of wars.

579 For they, the ones that teach merit, are the defenders in the war of the Torah, until the war becomes audible to the large mountains, that is to Abraham, Isaac, and Jacob, as it is written: "Hear, O mountains, the Lord's controversy" (Micah 6:2). This is the controversy of prayer, the controversy of Torah, i.e. the controversy of those who teach merit and of those who teach liability over man's Torah and prayer. And this war of the evening prayer continues until sunrise, for Rabban Gambiel determined it (the time until which the evening recital of the *Shema Yisrael* is still permitted) as until the rise of dawn (*Mishnah, Berakhot* 1,1), for the evening prayer may be said at any time during the night, but the sages made a fence around it and determined it as until midnight (*Mishnah, Berakhot* 1,1).

580 And because the duty of reciting the evening prayer is until the rise of the dawn, it is said: "And

there wrestled a man with him until the breaking of the day" (Genesis 32:24). What is meant by the dawn? It refers to the evening prayer, i.e. the Shekhinah, whose limit is until the morning of Abraham, for its time is until the fourth hour (*Berakhot* 26a). "And Abraham rose early in the morning" (Genesis 22:3), i.e. at the beginning of the first hour at the end of the dawn, which is *Netzaḥ* of Jacob, for there "For the leader, upon the morning star" (Psalms 22:1), to wreak vengeance on Samael for having touched Jacob's left thigh, which is *Hod*, of which it is said: "He has made me desolate and faint [*davah: dalet vav hei*] all the day" (Lamentations 1:13), where the letters of the word *davah*, re-arranged, spell *Hod* [*hei vav dalet*]. From the side of *Hod*, which is the fifth thousand [years since the Creation, according to the traditional calculation] the Temple remained destroyed and barren.

Commentary:

Malkhut attires *Zeir Anpin* from the chest downwards and occupies the four *Sfirot Netzaḥ*, *Hod*, *Yesod*, and *Malkhut* of *Zeir Anpin*, since the right column of *Malkhut*, which is *Ḥokhmah*, *Ḥesed*, and *Netzaḥ*, is made from *Netzaḥ* of *Zeir Anpin*; and its left column, which is *Binah*, *Gvurah*, and *Hod*, is made of *Hod* of *Zeir Anpin*. The central column of *Malkhut*, *Da'at*, *Tiferet*, and *Yesod* is made from *Yesod* and *Malkhut* of *Zeir Anpin*. And on the text: "What is meant by the dawn?" It refers to the evening prayer, i.e. *Malkhut*, which is called evening prayer and also called dawn, and this teaches about the judgments that come from the color black. "Whose limit is until the morning of Abraham, for its time is until the fourth hour." For the limit of *Malkhut* in receiving *ḥasadim* of *Zeir Anpin*, called Abraham, is the four *Sfirot* of *Zeir Anpin*, *Netzaḥ*, *Hod*, *Yesod*, and *Malkhut*, from where it receives the emanation of *Zeir*

Anpin. "And Abraham rose early in the morning" (Genesis 22:3), i.e. at the beginning of the first hour at the end of the dawn, which is *Netzaḥ* of Jacob. For the four hours of the morning are *Netzaḥ*, *Hod*, *Yesod* and *Malkhut*, so that the first hour is *Netzaḥ* of *Zeir Anpin*, who is called Jacob. And it must be understood that Samael's main hold is on *Hod*, for that is his place in *Malkhut*, since *Ḥesed*, *Gvurah*, *Tiferet*, *Netzaḥ* and *Hod* are parallel to *Keter*, *Ḥokhmah*, *Binah*, *Tiferet*, and *Malkhut*, and it therefore follows that *Malkhut* is *Hod*. However, in *Netzaḥ*, which is *Zeir Anpin*, it has no hold whatsoever, except in the secret of "with the shrub the cabbage is smitten (the good suffer with the bad.)." For with the ascent of *Malkhut* in *Binah*, the hold of Samael is also raised to *Netzaḥ*. But Samael's ascent to grasp *Netzaḥ* also is not to its benefit. On the contrary, its whole downfall stems from this, for at the time of greatness, when *Malkhut* returns, descending from *Binah*, the upper three *Sfirot* emerge and humiliate all the evil forces, making them surrender (as above, Vaera, 109 in the Commentary). And on the text: "Which is *Netzaḥ* of Jacob, for there `For the Leader, upon the morning star' (Psalms 22:1), to wreak vengeance on Samael, for having touched Jacob's left thigh which is *Hod*." For *Netzaḥ* of *Zeir Anpin* is the place of victory over evil forces, after they ascend and take hold there, as above, but on the left thigh, which is *Hod* and where Samael touched, etc. There he has a real hold. And on the text: About which it is said: "He has made me desolate and faint all the day" (Lamentations 1:13), where faint [*davah*] refers "to *Hod*: For there, in *Hod*, is the power of *Malkhut*, whose correction will come in the seventh thousand. Therefore, destruction occupies the period from the end of the fourth thousand, which is *Netzaḥ*, and just into the sixth thousand, which is *Yesod*. Unlike the fourth and sixth thousand, the fifth thousand, which is *Hod*, that is "faint all the day," for from its beginning until its end it is destruction and desolation. And on the text: "From the side of *Hod*, which is the fifth thousand." For there is absolutely no correction from the side of *Hod* until completion of the correction. This is not the case with *Netzaḥ* and *Yesod*, where there is some correction, as above.

MOSES AND TWO MESSIAHS AND THE RAINBOW AND MALKHUT

581 Rabbi Shimon said: Faithful Shepherd, this is your honor [*Hod*], in which your prophecy is dried up on the left, and because you "cause to go at the right hand of Moses" (Isaiah 63:12), which is *Netzaḥ*, which is the head of the dawns, for *Netzaḥ* and *Hod* are called two dawns, since the evil forces hold on to both of them, as above in the preceding paragraph; and *Netzaḥ* is the head of the dawns, and from its point of view, *Malkhut* is called "a lovely hind" (Proverbs 5:19) [*hind* = *ayalah*]. Therefore David stated: "For the Leader, upon the morning star [*ayeleth hashahar*]" (Psalms 22:1), for the victors (= leaders) in the wars will come at *Netzaḥ*. For it is only possible to win [Hebrew root: *nun tzadi ḥet*] a war with the evil forces in the *sfirah Netzaḥ* [Hebrew root: *nun tzadi ḥet*], as above in the preceding paragraph. And since *Netzaḥ* and *Hod* are two dawns, it was taught in the Mishnah: From what time may one recite the *Shema* in the mornings? [The Mishnah as quoted in *Talmud Bavli, Berakhot* 9b has "in the morning," but the variant text "in the mornings" appears in *Talmud Yerushalmi*]. It does not say, in the morning, but in the mornings, in the plural, the reference being to *Netzaḥ* and *Hod*, which illuminate towards the Female during the first two hours of the morning, as above in the preceding paragraph, and they are called 'mornings.'

582 And two Messiahs, coming from two *Malkhuts* (kingdoms) awaken for them, for *Netzaḥ* and *Hod*. Messiah son of David parallels *Netzaḥ* and is connected with the morning of Abraham, which is *Ḥesed*, since *Ḥesed* is

drawn down to *Malkhut* from *Netzaḥ* of *Zeir Anpin* (as in 504), which is as is written: "Bliss in Your right hand for evermore [*Netzaḥ*]" (Psalms 16:11). *Hod* is connected to *Gvurah*, since to it, to *Hod*, is attached Messiah the son of Ephraim, for *Gvurah* is drawn down to *Malkhut* from *Hod* of *Zeir Anpin*, as above. You, Moses, the Faithful Shepherd, are in the center, for your level is *Tiferet*, for the central column, which is *Tiferet*, is connected with you, and also *Yesod*, the Life of the Worlds, is your level. Therefore Moses is the central column, between the two Messiahs that parallel *Netzaḥ* and *Hod*, for *Yesod* is the central column of *Netzaḥ* and *Hod*. And *Ḥokhmah* (wisdom) is on the right; he who wants to be wise turns to face the south (to the right) in his prayer (cf. *Talmud Bavli, Baba Batra*, 25b). And *Binah* is on the left; he who wants to be rich turns to the north (to the left) in his prayer (ibid.). And it follows that *Ḥokhmah*, *Ḥesed*, and *Netzaḥ*, which are on the right, receive the Messiah son of David from *Netzaḥ* of *Zeir Anpin*, while *Binah*, *Gvurah*, and *Hod* receive Messiah son of Ephraim from *Hod* of *Ze'ir Anpin*. And Moses is in between them and illuminates *Da'at*, *Tiferet*, and *Yesod* to them, uniting the two Messiahs with each other (as above, 580).

583 It, *Malkhut*, is a rainbow with you, for *Malkhut* receives from him the three colors of the rainbow, which are the secret of the three columns. And the rainbow is the apparel of the *Shekhinah* and the apparel of the Righteous One, which is *Yesod*, that is called the covenant of the rainbow (cf. Genesis 9:8-17). And it is the sign of the Sabbath and the sign of a festival, and the sign of phylacteries, and the sign of the covenant of circumcision. And the Holy One, blessed be He, said: One who is not marked with the sign shall not enter into this vision, this room, which is *Malkhut*. And *Malkhut* is a bed, for the central column, which is *Zeir Anpin*, inclines on it towards *Ḥesed* (loving kindness), which is the secret of the right column,

for the completely righteous, to accord them merits with the 18 blessings of the prayer (the *Shemoneh Esreh*), and inclines towards liability, which is the secret of the left column, for the wicked, to judge them the Judgment in *Gvurah* according to their deeds. And in the central column it is lenient to those who are mediocre, being neither righteous nor yet wicked. And this is the form of the letter *shin*, that has three heads, paralleling these three columns.

584 The three colors of the rainbow, white, red, and green, which are the secret of the three columns, are a sign of the covenant, i.e. of *Yesod*. The rainbow itself is an only daughter, the Sabbath Queen, which is *Malkhut* that receives the three colors of the rainbow from *Yesod*, and it, *Malkhut*, has six stages *Ḥesed*, *Gvurah*, *Tiferet*, *Netzaḥ*, *Hod* and *Yesod* of Metatron under its control, for they are the six days of Creation that are included in Metatron, about which it is said: "Six days shall you do all your work" (Exodus 23:12), but the only daughter, *Malkhut* of *Zeir Anpin*, is a Sabbath to the Lord: "Whoever does any work therein shall be put to death" (Exodus 35:2).

585 The Tetragrammaton is called by the letter *hei*, that is to say the letter *hei* completes the name: *yud hei vav* and *hei* (the Tetragrammaton). For *Zeir Anpin* is the *yud hei vav*, and the final *hei* is *Malkhut*. And from this side to the right, *yud hei vav*, where the *hei* is its completion. And so it is with each of the six intermediate *Sfirot* of *Zeir Anpin*, the *hei* is the completion. For there are six combinations of the letters *yud*, *hei*, *vav* in the six intermediate *Sfirot* of *Zeir Anpin*, namely: *yud hei vav*; *hei vav yud*; *vav yud hei*; *yud vav hei*; *hei yud vav*; and *vav hei yud*. This comes to a total of 18 letters that are included in the Righteous One, Life [*ḥai*: *ḥet yud*, 8 + 10 = 18] of the Worlds, which is *Yesod*. *Malkhut* is the fourth part of the *hin* [a unit of liquid measure on each side]. That is to say *Malkhut* is the fourth letter, that is the final *hei*

that complements each of the above six combinations. Thus it is called the fourth part of the *hin* because it is the fourth letter and therefore the fourth part, and of the *hin* because it is the letter *hei*.

586 And it, *Malkhut*, is *hei* filled in with *aleph*, i.e. spelled *hei aleph*, from the point of view of the Name of Names (the Tetragrammaton), the first three letters of which [*yud hei vav*], when spelled out and filled in with *alephs*, are: *yud vav dalet hei aleph vav aleph vav*. *Yud vav dalet* is in *Ḥesed*; *hei aleph* is in *Gvurah*; *vav aleph vav* is in *Tiferet*, while the final *hei* [*hei aleph*] is in *Malkhut*. And the numerical value of the sum of these three letters [*yud vav dalet*, 10 + 6 + 4 = 20; *hei aleph*, 5 + 1 = 6; *vav aleph vav*, 6 + 1 + 6 = 13; and 20 + 6 + 13 = 39] is thirty-nine. And when these 39 are in control, the sages prohibited forty save one types of work (*Mishnah, Shabbat* 7, 2) that are called the main classes (literally: the fathers) of work, because they are parallel to the patriarchs who control them, i.e. the *Sfirot Ḥesed, Gvurah*, and *Tiferet* that are called patriarchs. For *yud* [*yud vav dalet*] *hei* [*hey aleph*] and *vav* [*vav aleph vav*] are the three *Sfirot Ḥesed, Gvurah*, and *Tiferet*, as above, and their numerical sum is 39, i.e. forty save one.

587 And with these forty save one types of work that are permitted on weekdays, lashes were administered, ten to Adam, ten to Eve, ten to the serpent, and nine to the land (*Midrash Tadshe*, ch. 18 and see *Pirkei d'Rabbi Eliezer*, ch. 14), making a total of 39 curses. And because these 39 rules, namely (the numerical sum of) *yud vav dalet*, *hei aleph*, and *vav aleph vav*, on the Sabbath, which is *hei* [*hey aleph*] no lashes are administered. (See Maimonides, *Mishneh Torah, Hilkhot Shabbat*, XXIV, 7: Punishment is not administered on the Sabbath, for although it is a positive precept it does not take precedence over the Sabbath; cf. also *Talmud Bavli, Sanhedrin* 35b). And these 39 are not the same as the 39 types

of work permitted on a weekday, for the former are from the side of the servant Metatron, while the forty save one types of work are sowing, ploughing, etc. [For full list, see *Mishnah, Shabbat* 7, 2].

588 The Faithful Shepherd said to Rabbi Shimon: Old man, old man, the *Shekhinah* is called earth of the Holy One, blessed be He, as it is said: "And the earth is My footstool" (Isaiah 66:1). From the point of view of *Ḥesed*, the *Shekhinah* is called water, and from the point of view of *Gvurah*, it is called fire. While from the point of view of the central column, which is *Tiferet*, it is called air. But in itself, the *Shekhinah* is called earth, for, all of them, it is earth, i.e. it accepts all of them.

589 And the extra soul [*neshamah*] spreads in the *Shekhinah*, which is the Sabbath Queen, about which is said: "And His kingdom [*Malkhut*] rules over all" (Psalms 103:19). It is *Malkhut* whose rule is over the earth and over the trees and the seeds; and the Tree of Life, which is *Zeir Anpin*, it is the extra soul [*neshamah*] that comes on the Sabbath (as above, 572). In it are all her offspring, and the earth, which is the *Shekhinah*, has rest.

Commentary:

Since on the Sabbath, *Malkhut* mates with the Tree of Life, which is *Zeir Anpin*, she therefore has rest, for all the shells surrender before the illumination of this mating, and there is no rule in any of the worlds apart from her rule.

590 And the upper *Shekhinah*, which is *Binah*, spreads in the land, which is *Malkhut*, and about it, about *Malkhut*, it is said: "a red heifer, faultless, wherein is no blemish, and upon which never came yoke" (Numbers 19:2). It is forbidden to plough with an ox on the Sabbath, as it is written: "The ploughmen ploughed on my back" (Psalms 129:3), i.e. the

judgments of the left, for it is therefore said about *Malkhut* "upon which never yoke came." And the lower *Shekhinah*, which is *Malkhut*, is a red heifer from the point of view of *Gvurah*, faultless from the point of view of *Ḥesed*, which is the level of Abraham, about whom it is said: "Walk before Me and be faultless" (Genesis 17:1). "Wherein is no blemish" is from the side of the central column, which is *Tiferet*. "Upon which never yoke came" is from the side of the upper *Shekhinah*, which is *Binah*, which is freedom, for it is in control, "and the stranger that draws close shall be put to death" (Numbers 1:51), since permission to control is not granted to the evil forces, not to Satan nor to Destruction nor to the Angel of Death, for they are from the side of Gehenna (Hell).

591 For this reason, on weekdays Israel says: "But He, being full of compassion, forgives iniquity and destroys not; many a time does He turn His anger away and does not stir up all His wrath" (Psalms 78:38). On weekdays the lower *Shekhinah* puts on these shells of death and judgment, but on the Sabbath she sheds them, because the Tree of Life, which is *Ben Yah* [the son of *Yah*, *yud hei*], has the intelligences of *Yah*, which are *Ḥokhmah* and *Binah*, being *yud hei vav*, where *Zeir Anpin* is *vav* and has the intelligences of *Yah* [*yud hei*]. And on the Sabbath, it joins up with *hei* (the fourth and final letter of the holy Name, Tetragrammaton), which is *Malkhut*. At the time there is rest for the hei and everything that is under it, which is why it is not necessary, on the Sabbath, to say: "But He, being full of compassion..." (ibid.). And who are they who are under it? This refers to Israel and wherever Israel is to be found, observance and rest are to be found.

592 And this is why it is forbidden to plough the land or to make ditches in it, for the land alludes to *Malkhut*, and it is like one who makes a defect in the holy land, which is the *Shekhinah*. And it is forbidden to use the tools of the land, even to move a

stone, or any tool, so that they should have rest in the merit of the *Shekhinah* that is called stone, about which is written, "And this stone which I have set up for a pillar" (Genesis 28:22), in the prayers. And it is called a pillar because it stands up for Israel, and for its sake Israel exists in the world. And it is said about it: "From thence, from the Shepherd, the Stone of Israel" (Genesis 49:25); and "Upon one stone are seven eyes" (Zekhariah 3:9); and "The stone which the builders rejected" (Psalms 118:22).

593 And the sayings are for this reason: "Wherefore the Children of Israel shall keep the Sabbath, to observe the Sabbath throughout their generations [*ledorotam*: *lamed dalet resh tav mem*, i.e. the abbreviated spelling] for a perpetual covenant" (Exodus 31:16), which they have to keep in their homes [*bediratam*: *bet dalet resh tav mem*, where *dorotam* (their generations) and *diratam* (their homes) are, in unpointed Hebrew, spelled the same]. That is, they must not leave the private domain for the public domain, and this is what the Sages of the Mishnah taught: There are two [which are, indeed, four] kinds of 'going out' on the Sabbath, i.e. transfer from one domain on to another and also bringing in is considered going out (*Mishnah, Shabbat* 1,1). And as for Samael and Serpent, Israel has to guard against their entering the dwelling of the *Shekhinah*, which is the private domain. What is the public domain? It is: A bondwoman, a prostitute, a menstruating woman, a gentile woman, who are in the domain of Samael and Serpent and the 70 appointees over the peoples.

I HAVE GATHERED MY MYRRH DRINK, YEA, DRINK ABUNDANTLY, O BELOVED

594 He began by quoting: "I am come into my garden, my sister, my bride; I have gathered my myrrh with my spice; I have eaten my honeycomb with my honey; I have drunk my wine with my milk. Eat, O friends; Drink, yea, drink abundantly, O beloved" (Song of Songs 5:1). "I

have gathered my myrrh with my spice" refers to the right arm on the left thigh. "I have eaten my honeycomb with my honey" refers to Jacob with Rachel. "I have drunk my wine with my milk" refers to the left arm on the right thigh. The explanation of this is: The right arm on the left thigh are *Ḥesed* with *Hod*. Jacob with Rachel are the central column, which is *Tiferet*, along with *Malkhut*. Left arm with right thigh is *Gvurah* with *Netzaḥ*. (An explanation of these matters is to be found above, 544, in the Commentary.)

595 The question is put: Why did He so change His attributes? The answer is that the secret that is here stated is because David said here: "Let Your priests be clothed with righteousness, and let Your saints shout for joy" (Psalms 132:9). And we learned there that He should have said Your Levites (above, 555). Said the Holy One, blessed be He: It is not My way to change My attributes, but since you have invited Me, I have to do your will. And we further learned that even when a householder invites the king, the latter has to do the will of the former. It was thus taught: Whatever the host tells you to do, do, except when he says leave (cf. *Talmud Bavli, Pesaḥim* 86b, where Rashi notes the source as the Mishnaic tractate *Derekh Eretz Rabba*, ch.5). Nevertheless, for all that this secret is beautiful, it is still written: "For I, the Tetragrammaton, change not" (Malakhi 3:6), and indeed in respect of all the sacrifices, it is written "For, the Tetragrammaton only, for there is no change in Him," and how could it indeed be that He would change the levels of His name with the sacrifices?

596 What about "I have gathered my myrrh with my spice" (Song of Songs 5:1)? The answer is that "I have gathered my myrrh" refers to the `*Yotzer Or*' prayer [the first benediction before the recital of the *Shema Yisrael* in the morning and "with my spice" refers to the `*Ahavat Olam*' prayer [the second blessing before the recital of the *Shema*

Yisrael in the morning. "I have eaten my honeycomb" is the _Shema Yisrael_ itself, and "with my honey" is (the silent response) 'Blessed be His name, whose glorious kingdom is forever and ever.' "I have drunk my wine" refers to the next section of the recital of the _Shema Yisrael_ (Deuteronomy 11:13-21), and "with my milk" refers to the final section (Numbers 15:37-41) up to 'True.' "Eat, O friends" refers to the first three blessings and the last three blessings of the _Shemoneh Esreh_, while "Drink, yea, drink abundantly, O beloved" refers to all the remaining blessings of the prayer.

597 And in the first part, he said: The secret of the sacrifices is that cattle and sheep and rams and goats are the four countenances of the face of an ox, the face of an eagle, etc., and these are two turtle-doves or two young pigeons (533-4), but this matter is in need of further clarification. Lion, which is _Ḥesed_, descends to ox, which is left, which is _Gvurah_, in order to link _Ḥesed_ with _Gvurah_, i.e. that they should be incorporated within each other. Man, which is _Malkhut_, descends to eagle, which is _Tiferet_, which is the level of Jacob, so that _Tiferet_ and _Malkhut_ will mate with each other. This is why the sages of the Mishnah taught: Jacob's beauty was that of Adam (first man) (cf. _Talmud Bavli, Babba Matsi'a_, 84a). And who caused his ascendancy so that he should be called Israel? None other than the Holy One, blessed be He, as it is written: "Your name shall be called no more Jacob, but Israel" (Genesis 32:29) the meaning of which is that Israel should mainly spread among them.

Commentary:

For *Zeir Anpin* is mainly *ḥasadim* and *Malkhut* is mainly *Ḥokhmah*, and when *Zeir Anpin* mates with *Malkhut*, *Ḥokhmah* is also included in *Zeir Anpin*. And the illumination of

Ḥokhmah is called beauty. And on the text: "Jacob's beauty was that of Adam (first man)." For the *Ḥokhmah* of Jacob, that is *Zeir Anpin*, comes from *Malkhut*, which is the secret of Adam (first man), and this is the secret of "the face of a man" (Ezekiel 1:10). However, when the mating is in the aspect of the large Male and Female, then *Zeir Anpin* is called Israel, and there is then no revelation for the *Ḥokhmah* of *Malkhut*, but the *ḥasadim* of *Zeir Anpin* have control over both of them, both *Zeir Anpin* and *Malkhut*. And on the text: "Your name shall be... Israel" (Genesis 32:29), the meaning is that Israel should mainly spread among them. For in the mating of Israel with *Malkhut*, which is the secret of the large *Zeir Anpin*, then Israel, which is *ḥasadim*, has the main control to spread among them, and *Ḥokhmah* of *Malkhut* is not revealed.

598 (Referring to the discussion above, 247 ff.) Why "the tenth part of an *efah* [a Biblical unit of dry measure of fine flour"] (Numbers 28:5)? The answer is that the tenth part of an *efah* parallels *Knesset Yisrael* (the Congregation of Israel), which is the tenth stage, i.e. *Malkhut*, and it has to be placed between the two arms, which are *Ḥesed* and *Gvurah* of *Zeir Anpin*, so that it should be made up of *Ḥokhmah* of the left and *ḥasadim* of the right. And then it is fine flour for the baking of bread, and it is bread. And because *Malkhut* is the secret of bread, no official in the world is appointed over bread made of the five kinds of grain, that are wheat, barley, rye, oats, and spelt, and no one is appointed over them, excepting the Holy One, blessed be He, alone.

599 And therefore anyone who squanders bread and throws it on the ground, poverty follows him. And an angel is appointed over this matter and follows after him to assure him poverty. And he will not depart from this world until he has been in need

of assistance from others. And it is written about such a one: "He wanders abroad for bread: 'Where is it?'" (Job 15:23), the meaning of which is that he shall wander abroad, going from pillar to post, moving from place to place, in his search for bread: 'Where is it?' And no one will have any regard for him, as it is written: "Where is it?" (ibid.) Where is the one who will have mercy on him? For such a one will not be found.

THE FAITHFUL SHEPHERD

600 And in the first part, the Faithful Shepherd said: Whoever squanders crumbs of bread and throws them where they should not be, and even more so one who squanders pieces of marrow, that are drops of seed, and throws them on the ground it being said about them: "For all flesh had corrupted their way on earth" (Genesis 6:12) who throws them to a menstruating woman, or the daughter of an idolater, or a bondwoman or a prostitute, and much more so one who disdains the crumbs of the bread of the Torah, which are the secrets that are in the tips and crowns of the letters, about which it is said: He that makes worldly use of the crown shall perish (*Mishnah, Pirke Avot* 1, 13).

601 And how much more so whoever transmits secrets of the Torah and the secrets of the Kabbalah and the secrets of the Works of Creation or secrets of the letters of the Name of Names (The Tetragrammaton) to people who are not suitable, who are in the control of the evil inclination, a harlot, about whom it is written: "For on account of a harlot a man is brought to a loaf of bread" (Proverbs 6:26). And whenever bread is mentioned the meaning is the twenty-two letters (of the Hebrew alphabet) with which is written the Torah, and whenever loaf is mentioned the meaning is even a single *halakhah*, legal ruling.

602 And in the first part, he did not reveal the secret of these crumbs, but interpreted the texts according to the straightforward meaning, nor did

he determine the amounts. But the sages of the Mishnah taught: The amount of the crumbs is not less than the size of an olive (cf. *Talmud Bavli, Berakhot* 52b). And how much more so if they are of a quantity the size of an egg, for the sages of the Mishnah were stringent about them: How much should one eat to have to say the Grace after Meals? An olive's bulk, (but Rabbi Judah says) an egg's bulk (*Mishnah, Berakhot* 7, 2).

AN OLIVE'S BULK AND AN EGG'S BULK

603 And by the secret method: The letters *aleph ḥet* [whose numerical value is 1 + 8 = 9] of the word 'one' [*Eḥad*: *aleph ḥet dalet*] make nine crumbs, three in each direction. And with three of the four of the *dalet* [whose numerical value is 4 of the word *Eḥad*], we have, together with the nine, a total of twelve crumbs. Again, the nine crumbs, together with the remaining one of the four of the *dalet*, after the three have been taken away, gives us ten. And this completes the *dalet*, which is the four letters of the Tetragrammaton [*yud hei vav* and *hei*]. What is the ten? They are the ten letters formed by filling in the letters of the Tetragrammaton with *alephs*, e.g. *yud vav dalet* (3), *hei aleph* (2), *vav aleph vav* (3), *hei aleph* (2). Now the tip of the letter *dalet* from the word one [*Eḥad*: *aleph ḥet dalet*] is the size of an olive's bulk. The *yud* of the Tetragrammaton [*yud hei vav* and *hei*] is the size of an egg's bulk. (And see the explanation, below, 611.).

C o m m e n t a r y :

It is clarified here that there is no perfection without *Malkhut*, and everything is considered as crumbs without it. And it is known that *Malkhut* itself does not receive its correction until after the completion of the correction, and for over six thousand years *Malkhut* itself is not revealed at all. For this is the secret of the number twelve wherever it is mentioned, for it teaches about the three columns and *Malkhut* that accepts them, and when they are included in each other, it follows that each one of these four is composed of three columns, and they come to the number twelve. And in truth they should have been four times four, but since *Malkhut* itself, which receives the three columns, is hidden away, only the three columns that it receives are taken into account and not *Malkhut* itself. The result is that these four, namely the three columns and *Malkhut*, are not to be found in each of them, and the aspect of *Malkhut* is missing in each of them, and is not revealed even in *Malkhut* itself. Therefore they are twelve (3 x 4) and not sixteen (4 x 4). However, there is here an overall illumination from the aspect of *Malkhut*, mitigated by *Binah*, which is called the Key, and this illumination supplements them, until such time as *Malkhut* itself is corrected. But the complete perfection of *Malkhut* will be revealed only on completion of the correction. And on the text: "The letters *aleph ḥet*...of the word `one' [*Eḥad*: *aleph ḥet dalet*] make nine crumbs, three in each direction." For the numerical value of the letters of the word `one' [*Eḥad*: *aleph ḥet dalet*, 1 + 8 + 4] is thirteen, and they parallel the above-mentioned thirteen. And the *aleph ḥet* of *Eḥad*, which teach of *Ḥesed*, *Gvurah*, and *Tiferet* of *Zeir Anpin* when they are composed of each other, then each one has three columns, thus making nine columns. And they are comparable to the crumbs, for there is no perfection other than by their joining with *Malkhut*. Now the *aleph ḥet* (1 + 8 = 9) are nine crumbs, three for each column. "And with three of the four of the dalet... of the word *Eḥad*, we have, together with the nine, a total of twelve crumbs." For *Malkhut*, too, which is the *dalet* of *Eḥad*, is also part of the same three columns, and, as above, it follows that they come to twelve. "For this is the secret of the number twelve wherever it is mentioned." And on the text: "Again, the nine crumbs, together with the remaining one of the four of the *dalet*, after the three have been taken away, gives us ten." For the fourth *sfirah* of the *Eḥad* is *Malkhut* itself, of which nothing is revealed before the completion of the correction except the general illumination that is called the Key, and it is this that completes the nine crumbs that are in the secret of the *aleph ḥet* of *Eḥad* [*aleph ḥet dalet*], making them complete. And on the text: "And this completes the *dalet*, which is the four letters of the Tetragrammaton [*yud hei vav* and *hei*]: for it completes the four-letter Name, which is *Zeir Anpin*. "What is the ten?" They are the ten letters formed by filling in the letters of the Tetragrammaton with *aleph*s, and this alludes to the ten complete *Sfirot*, completed with *Malkhut*, as above, the secret of the nine crumbs being without *Malkhut*. (And the secret of an olive's bulk and an egg's bulk will be explained below, 611.)

604 This was the dalet that is the secret of "the face of a man" (Ezekiel 1:10), which is the completion of the Chariot of Man, which is *Zeir Anpin*, that is called man, in the secret of the Tetragrammaton [*yud hei vav* and *hei*], with the letters written out and filled in with *alephs* [*yud* = *yud vav dalet*, 10 + 6 + 4 = 20; *hei* = *hei aleph*, 5 + 1 = 6; *vav* = *vav aleph vav*, 6 + 1 + 6 = 13; *hei* = *hei aleph*, 5 + 1 = 6], whose numerical sum (20 + 6 + 13 + 6 = 45) is the same as that of man [*adam*: *aleph dalet mem*, 1 + 4 + 40 = 45]. And it is also the four faces that are in the face of a man, for the face of a man is *Malkhut*, which itself has four faces: lion, ox, eagle, and man, and is the fourth face which is the secret of *Malkhut* that is in *Malkhut*. For this reason, it is written: "The Lord lift up His countenance upon you" (Numbers 6:26). And the sages of the Mishnah taught: Is it not written (about God): "Who regards not persons" [literally: "Who does not lift up countenance"] (Deuteronomy 10:17)? (And is there not a contradiction here, between the two verses?) But the Holy One, blessed be He, said: Did I not command them: "And you shall eat and be satisfied and bless the Lord your God"

(Deuteronomy 8:10)? And they are very particular about saying the grace after meals even if the quantity is but that of an olive's bulk or an egg's bulk [which is hardly satisfying]. How then should I (God) not then lift up My countenance for them? (cf. *Talmud Bavli, Berakhot* 20a). And not only that but because the sages of the Mishnah and the *Amoraim* arranged their whole study according to the secrets of the Torah.

605 The Faithful Shepherd rose, spread out his hands before the Holy One, blessed be He and His Divine Presence, and spoke thus: O Holy One, blessed be You, may it be Your will to give us perfect food for correction to You and to the heavenly Queen, that is the world to come, i.e. *Binah,* about which it is said: "For the kingdom is the Lord's, and He is the ruler over the nations" (Psalms 22:29), and regarding the second Queen, which is *Malkhut,* it is said a second time: "And the kingdom shall be the Lord's" (Obadiah 1:21), and a whole table is corrected with all delicacies and dishes.

606 And I invite Your people, all the sages of the Mishnah, the scholars of the Bible and the sages of the Talmud, and especially the masters of the secrets of Your Torah, and Your bride, who is Your Holy Queen, both the upper one, which is *Binah,* and the lower one, which is *Malkhut,* everything being with the permission of the Cause who is above all heavenly beings, the Lord of all lords, King over all the kings who are above or who are below, for He is unique and unequalled, and there is no letter nor vowel sign that will join with Him, and no variations as is customary with man, for He is the Master of all the keys to all the secrets of Tetragrammaton and names and appellatives and all the hidden secrets of *Ḥokhmah,* for You open them all for us, for the sake of Your glory, O Cause over all causes. I beseech You to open for us Your glory, for Your glory is of Father and Mother of the Heavens, i.e.

Ḥokhmah and Binah, which are Father and Mother of *Zeir Anpin,* who is called Heavens. And the Father of all of Israel is *Zeir Anpin,* and their Mother is *Malkhut,* about which it is said: "Forsake not the teaching of your mother" (Proverbs 1:8), and Your people have no connection with any other mother in the world.

607 He rose a second time and said: O sages of the Mishnah, your souls [*neshamah*] and spirits and souls [*nefesh*] have now stirred in all of you, and removed sleep from you, for this certainly changes the straightforward explanations of this world, but I stirred you only with heavenly secrets of the world to come, for you are involved with them, and in this respect it is said: "Behold, He neither slumbers nor sleeps" (Psalms 121:4).

Commentary:

Sleep comes from the left column of *Binah*, which illuminates without *ḥasadim* (as above, *Vaera*, 74), but there, in *Binah*, sleep achieves nothing at all and changes nothing, unless the illumination of this left column is drawn down to *Malkhut*, where sleep is active and changes everything, which is to say that the illumination of the intelligences departs. And on the text: "For this certainly changes the straightforward explanations of this world." For the sleep that is drawn from the left column to this world, which is *Malkhut* (that is called this world), changes the simple meaning; that is to say, it conceals the illumination of the intelligences; "but I stirred you only with heavenly secrets of the world to come, for you are involved with them." For the Faithful Shepherd stirred them that they should bring themselves up to the next world by means of the secrets of the Torah that he enunciated, and there, in the next world, which is *Binah*, it is said: "Behold, He neither slumbers nor sleeps" (Psalms 121:4), for there no one sleeps, as above.

608 **He began by saying: The sages of the Mishnah taught: The host breaks bread (i.e. says the grace before the meal) and the guest says grace (after the meal) [cf. *Talmud Bavli, Berakhot* 46a]. And they also taught: (In the grace before meals, namely: Blessed are You, Lord our God, King of the Universe, Who brings forth bread from the earth), one must pronounce clearly the letter *hei* [cf. *Talmud Yerushalmi, Berakhot* 6, 1]. And the two heis of the Tetragrammaton [*yud hei vav* and *hei*] which are *Binah* and *Malkhut,* stand for the two loaves of bread, the two *ḥallot* of the Sabbath. (cf. *Talmud Bavli, Berakhot* 39b.) The *yud* of the Tetragrammaton [*yud hei vav* and *hei*] is a slice of bread equal in size to the bulk of an egg that is given to each one. And what is 'The host breaks bread' (see above)? This is the *vav* of the Tetragrammaton [*yud hei vav* and *hei*], and so all the four letters of the Tetragrammaton are here alluded to.**

609 **While they were still discoursing, behold, Great- grandfather, which is upper *Ḥokhmah,* descended to him and said: Faithful Shepherd, take back what you have just said, for bread is the *vav.* His two loaves of bread are, as you have said, the two *heis* of the Tetragrammaton [*yud hei vav* and *hei*], but *vav* is surely parallel to Jacob, who is *Zeir Anpin,* while the two *heis* parallel Leah and Rachel [the wives of Jacob]. And therefore bread is in general the secret of *vav,* which is *Zeir Anpin,* that has two matings. One mating is with Leah, who is his female from the chest and up, while the second mating is with Rachel, who is his female from the chest and down, and this is why the bread is divided into two loaves. The *yud* of the Tetragrammaton [*yud hei vav* and *hei*] is the slice that is given to each one, and each one receives the bulk of an egg, for egg is the secret of *yud* of the Tetragrammaton, which is *Ḥokhmah,* which is the emanation that is drawn down by the *vav* and the two *heis* of the Tetragrammaton [*yud hei***

vav **and** ***hei*****].**

610 The Faithful Shepherd said to him: Grandfather, grandfather, in how many places is it taught that Jacob is the host, which is *Zeir Anpin*, and Joseph is a guest whose level is *Yesod*, Life [*ḥai*: *ḥet yud*, 8 + 10 = 18] of the Worlds, which incorporates the 18 blessings of the *Shemoneh Esreh* prayer, for which reason it was taught about it: "Blessings are upon the head of the righteous" (Proverbs, 10:6). Therefore they said that the host, who is *Zeir Anpin*, breaks the bread, while the guest, which is *Yesod*, pronounces the grace after meals, but now you say that *Zeir Anpin* is the secret, not of the host, but of the bread. The Grandfather replied to him: That is how it is, and everything is true. Each secret has its rightful place, both what I said and what you said. And now, according to my opinion that *Zeir Anpin* is the bread, who is the one who breaks the bread and distributes it?

611 The Faithful Shepherd said to him: Grandfather, it is you; i.e. the Grandfather himself, which is the secret of *Ḥokhmah*, is the form of the host who breaks the bread, which is *yud hei vav* and *hei* (the Tetragrammaton), spelled out and filled in with *alephs* [*yud* = *yud vav dalet*, 10 + 6 + 4 = 20; *hei* = *hei aleph*, 5 + 1 = 6; *vav* = *vav aleph vav*, 6 + 1 + 6 = 13; and, *hei* = *hei aleph*, 5 + 1 = 6], whose numerical sum (20 + 6 + 13 + 6) is 45, which is the secret of *Ḥokhmah* [*ḥet kaf mem hei*], whose letters spell out, *koaḥ Mah* [*kaf ḥet, mem hei*], meaning the Power of *Mah* [*mem hei*, 40 + 5 = 45] which is man [*adam*: *aleph dalet mem*, 1 + 4 + 40 = 45]. And *Mah* is of the upper Chariot, the inner side of which, i.e. *Ḥokhmah*, is the Tetragrammaton written out and filled in with *alephs*, the numerical value of which is, as above, *Mah*, 45. And for this reason, *vav* is bread, there being two loaves, the two *heis*, and the amount of the emanation, as taught, is the bulk of an olive and the bulk of an egg. And we have already learned in which name it is

measured as an olive, i.e. in the *yud*, but the sages have taught: One does not make precepts into bundles (cf. *Talmud Bavli, Berakhot* 49a), but each precept must stand on its own. Here also, we do not give two quantities in the one letter *yud*, that both an olive's bulk and an egg's bulk should be *yud*, but there are two alphabets, where the large alphabet is in *Binah* and the small alphabet is in *Malkhut*. Therefore, there is an upper *yud* and a smaller *yud*. The *yud* which is the *yud* of the Tetragrammaton [*yud hei vav* and *hei*] is the upper *yud* which is the secret of upper *Ḥokhmah*, while the *yud* of the 'The Lord' [*aleph dalet nun yud*] is a small *yud*, which is the secret of *Ḥokhmah* of the left. And these two *yuds*, one is an olive's bulk, i.e. the small *yud* of 'The Lord' [*aleph dalet nun yud*], and the other is an egg's bulk, i.e. the upper *yud* of the Tetragrammaton [*yud hei vav* and *hei*]. And they are in the secret of *yud aleph hei dalet vav nun hei yud*, i.e. the combination of the Tetragrammaton [*yud hei vav* and *hei*] and 'The Lord' [*aleph dalet nun yud*], where the initial *yud* is the secret of an egg's bulk, and the final *yud* is the secret of an olive's bulk. The Grandfather came and kissed him.

Commentary:

In every stage *Keter*, *Ḥokhmah*, *Binah*, *Tiferet*, and *Malkhut* can be discerned, and also in *Zeir Anpin*, *Keter*, *Ḥokhmah*, *Binah*, *Tiferet*, and *Malkhut* discerned, where the secret of the simple four-letter Tetragrammaton [*yud hei vav* and *hei*] is *Keter*, and the secret of the Tetragrammaton filled in with *aleph*s [*yud* = *yud vav dalet*, *hei* = *hei aleph*, *vav* = *vav aleph vav*, *hei* = *hei aleph*] is *Ḥokhmah* and the Tetragrammaton in the filling of the filling with *aleph*s is *Binah*, and the Tetragrammaton filled in with *aleph*s is *Tiferet*, since *Ḥokhmah* and *Tiferet* are both equal, and the sum of the

Tetragrammaton filled in with *alephs* is the secret of *Malkhut* (see *Panim Masbirot*, page 299).

612 While they were still considering this, the Holy Luminary, that is Rabbi Shimon, arose, and opened by saying: "What [*Mah*: *mem hei*] is his name and what [*Mah*: *mem hei*] is his son's name" (Proverbs 30:4) they come together, for *Ḥokhmah* is the secret of the Tetragrammaton [*yud hei vav hei*] filled in with *alephs* [*yud* = *yud vav dalet*, 10 + 6 + 4 = 20; *hei* = *hei aleph*, 5 + 1 = 6; *vav* = *vav aleph vav*, 6 + 1 + 6 = 13; *hei* = *hei aleph*, 5 + 1 = 6] whose numerical value is (20 + 6 + 13 + 6 =45), which is the same as *Mah* [*mem hei*, 40 + 5 = 45]; and the son of *Ḥokhmah*, which is *Tiferet*, is also the Tetragrammaton filled in with *alephs*, i.e. *Mah*, 45, as above, in the preceding paragraph. And it follows that *Mah* is the name of *Ḥokhmah* and *Mah* is the name of his son, which is *Tiferet*. And the Grandfather, who is *Ḥokhmah*, joined with the Faithful Shepherd, who is *Tiferet*. The companions rejoiced and said: Happy is the one who was privileged to eat of this bread, which is the *vav* of the Tetragrammaton [*yud hei vav* and *hei*], about which it is said: "Come, eat (from the same Hebrew root as the word for bread) of my bread" (Proverbs 9:5). And happy is the soul [*nefesh*] of whom it is said: "She may eat of her father's bread" (Leviticus 22:13) "And no stranger shall eat of it" (ibid.), for about the Holy One, blessed be He, it is said: "Have we not all one father?" (Malakhi 2:10), and the soul that occupied herself with the Torah shall eat of her father's bread."

613 And who is the cause for her soul [*nefesh*] to eat of her father's bread? This is because she returned in repentance and united with the Holy One, blessed be He, as in her youth, as it is written: "She returns to her father's house as in her youth" (Leviticus 22:13). And the meaning of this is the same as: "He shall return to the days of his youth" (Job 33:25),

just like a tree that has been cut down and has grown again from its roots. And this is a secret for one who dies childless, that by levirate marriage he transmigrates and is renewed.

614 And there is a further secret, for the person who dies childless will later come back in a transmigration and be renewed as formerly, as it is written: "...be a widow or divorced, and have no seed, she returns to her father's house as in her youth" (Leviticus 22:13). Divorced [Hebrew root: *gimel resh shin*] here refers to the soul being driven out of the Garden of Eden as in: "So he drove out the man..." (*Bereshith* 3:24). And what was the reason for this? It was because she had no seed, for he died childless. And she returns to her father's house, that is returns to this world, and transmigrates to the son of the levirate marriage [e.g. between the widow and the deceased's brother, her brother-in-law]. This is the meaning of "And she returns to her father's house as in her youth" (ibid.). And after she has been privileged to have offspring, "she may eat of her father's bread, but no stranger shall eat of it" (ibid.). This is what is written: "The wife of the dead man (who was childless) shall not be married abroad (to one not of the family)" (Deuteronomy 25:5), i.e. shall not be married to a stranger. For if she does not marry a kinsman, she will fall into the hands of a stranger, i.e. the evil forces.

615 The Faithful Shepherd said: Hillel and Shammai: That is, you two — one of whom is of the side of Mercy, i.e. Hillel, while the other is of the side of Judgment, i.e. Shammai — are *Ḥesed* and *Gvurah*, the levels of Abraham and Isaac, and you are of their stock: gather round here, you and the eighty pupils that Hillel had, as well as the pupils of the House of Shammai, gather around for the banquet of the King.

616 You have taught, you and those with you who give instructions, you have taught: He who breaks bread may not eat until

the diners have answered '*amen*,' (cf. *Talmud Bavli, Berakhot* 47a) and: The guests may not eat anything until the one who breaks the bread has eaten (ibid.). Obviously, when the host breaks the bread and gives it to the guests, he does not measure out the same amount for each person, for those who break bread do not usually break it into equal parts, and he could give to one an egg's bulk and to another an olive's bulk. And when they respond '*amen*' over this breaking of the bread, before the host eats, they join together the two quantities, the egg-size and the olive-size, where the egg-size quantity is drawn down from the *yud* of the Tetragrammaton [*yud hei vav* and *hei*] and the olive-size quantity is from the *yud* of 'The Lord' [*aleph dalet nun yud*], as above, and thus the joining of the egg's bulk and the olive's bulk is the secret of the combination of the Tetragrammaton and 'The Lord': *yud aleph hei dalet vav nun hei yud* (10 + 1 + 5 + 4 + 6 + 50 + 5 + 10 = 91), which is the secret of *amen* [*aleph mem nun*, 1 + 40 + 50 = 91], and this unification is not over the eating but over the breaking of the bread. And therefore, after these quantities, the egg-sized and the olive-sized, have joined together in the unification *yud aleph hei dalet vav nun hei yud*, in the saying of '*amen*,' then the host may eat. And this is: "I have gathered my myrrh with my spice; I have eaten my honeycomb with my honey; I have drunk my wine with my milk," after which comes: "Eat, O friends; Drink, yea, drink abundantly, O beloved" (Song of Songs 5:1). "Eat, O friends" refers to the guests, so that the sons, who are the guests, should be as their father, who is the host who breaks the bread, which is the secret of upper *Ḥokhmah*, that is called Father (as above, 611).

617 And here we have bread in two loaves, where bread is *vav*, and each of the loaves is *hei*, and the amount of the eating is an olive's bulk and an egg's bulk, which is the secret of the unification *yud aleph hei dalet vav nun hei yud*, as above. The question is

asked: What is the showbread that is on the King's table, i.e. the twelve *ḥallot* that were arranged on the Temple table? The answer to this is: Have we not already learned that the bread, which is *Zeir Anpin*, has twelve countenances? And what are they? They are the four faces of an ox, the four faces of a lion, the four faces of an eagle, for the lion, ox, and eagle are the secret of the three columns, in each one of which are *Ḥesed, Gvurah, Tiferet*, and *Malkhut*, and four times three comes to twelve, and they are the secret of the three Tetragrammaton [in the priestly benediction], namely: "The Tetragrammaton will bless you... The Tetragrammaton will cause to shine... The Tetragrammaton will lift up..." (Numbers 6:24-26), where each Tetragrammaton has four letters, and three times four makes twelve letters.

THE TWELVE ḤALLOT

618 And how do we know that the showbread comes from the King's table? Because of what is written: "And he said to me: This is the table that is before the Lord" (Ezekiel 41:22), and the numerical value of 'this' [*zeh*: *zayin hei*, 7 + 5 = 12] refers to the twelve countenances.

619 And you might wish to suggest that from the Torah we learn about six, not twelve, *ḥallot*, as two loaves were required for each of the three meals, making a total of six only. The answer to this is that we cannot mention *vav* (whose numerical value is six), without also mentioning its companion *vav* i.e. *vav vav*, the two *vav* sounds in the name of the letter *vav*, and this points to the six *Sfirot Ḥesed, Gvurah, Tiferet, Netzaḥ, Hod*, and *Yesod*, of the direct light from above downwards, and the six *Sfirot* of *Ḥesed, Gvurah, Tiferet, Netzaḥ, Hod*, and *Yesod*, of reflected light from below upwards. And they parallel the six stages that are in the upper throne, from the chest and upwards of *Zeir Anpin*, namely *Ḥesed, Gvurah, Tiferet, Netzaḥ, Hod* and *Yesod* that are included in *Ḥesed, Gvurah* and *Tiferet*; and the six

stages of the lower throne, from the chest downwards of *Zeir Anpin*, namely *Ḥesed*, *Gvurah*, *Tiferet*, *Netzaḥ*, *Hod*, and *Yesod* that are included in *Netzaḥ*, *Hod*, and *Yesod*. The six of the upper throne are concealed, for *Ḥokhmah* has no revelation from the chest and upwards, while the six from the chest downwards are in the open, for *Ḥokhmah* does have revelation from the chest and downwards. And this is the secret of the verse: "The secret things belong to the Lord our God, but the things that are revealed belong to us and to our children forever" (Deuteronomy 29:28), where from the chest and upwards of *Zeir Anpin* are the hidden things, and from the chest and downwards are the things that are revealed.

TEN THINGS THAT A MAN MUST OBSERVE AT THE SABBATH TABLE

620 The breads of thanksgiving are forty *ḥallot* (cf. *Talmud Bavli*, *Menaḥot* 77b), ten wafers, ten mixed with hot water and oil, ten of leavened bread, ten of unleavened bread, making a total of forty, paralleling the four *yuds* [the numerical value of *yud* being ten that are in the four Tetragrammaton that are in the four faces, i.e. paralleling the yud of the Tetragrammaton [*yud hei vav* and *hei*] of the four faces of a man, and paralleling the *yud* of the Tetragrammaton of the four faces of a lion, and paralleling the *yud* of the Tetragrammaton of the four faces of an ox, and paralleling the *yud* of the Tetragrammaton of the four faces of an eagle. And this is the first correction of the King's table, for there are ten things that a person must observe at the Sabbath table.

621 The first correction that is in the Sabbath table is to correct the table, as for one who eats in the presence of a King, as it is written: "This is the table that is before the Lord" (Ezekiel 41:22). The second correction is to wash the hands to the extent that the sages decreed, namely five knots, that is the five fingers of the right hand, which contain 14 joints,

for each finger has three joints, and the thumb only two, totalling 14 joints. And just as there are fourteen joints in the right hand, so are there fourteen in the left, making a total of 28, and against these 28 joints is the secret of "the power of the Lord" [where the word for `power' is *koaḥ*: *kaf ḥet,* 20 + 8 = 28], and these are the 28 letters of the first verse in the Creation Story: "In the beginning [*bereshith*]: *bet resh aleph shin yud tav,* 6] God created [*bara elohim*: *bet resh aleph aleph lamed hei yud mem,* 8] the heaven [*et hashamayin*: *aleph tav hei shin mem yud mem,* 7] and the earth [*v'et haaretz*: *vav aleph tav hei aleph resh tzadi,* 7]" [6 + 8 + 7 + 7 = 28] (Genesis 1:1). There are 28 letters in the verse, and about them it is written: "And now, I pray You, let the power [*koaḥ*: *kaf ḥet,* 20 + 8 = 28] of the Lord be great" (Numbers 14:17).

622 The ten fingers correspond to the ten "sayings" (of which God made use) at the creation of the world:

1) Let there be light;

2) Let there be a firmament in the midst of the waters;

3) Let the waters be gathered together;

4) Let the earth bring forth grass;

5) Let there be lights in the firmament of the heaven;

6) Let the waters bring forth abundantly the living creature;

7) Let the earth bring forth the living creature after his kind;

8) Let us make man in our image;

9) Behold, I have given you every herb-bearing seed;

10) It is not good for man to be alone. (See Genesis chapter 1, and cf. *Midrash Pesikta Rabbati, Pesikt* 21, 108a.)

For this reason, the sages of the Mishnah taught: Whoever is careless over the washing of the hands is uprooted from the world (cf. *Talmud Bavli, Sotah* 4b). Why is this? It is because the ten fingers of the hands and the 28 joints of the fingers contain the secret of the ten sayings and the 28 letters with which the world was created.

623 The third correction is the cup of benediction, for which ten things were ordained: It requires washing, rinsing, crowning, wrapping, and must be undiluted, full, taken up with both hands, and placed in the right hand; he who says the blessing must look at it, it must be raised a handbreadth from the ground, and he must send it around to those members of his household who are present (cf. *Talmud Bavli, Berakhot* 51a). [Note: There are here not ten but eleven things. In the text in *Berakhot*, the first ten are given, and the eleventh is preceded by 'Some also say...']

624 And the secret of the cup is "and full with the blessing of the Lord" (Deuteronomy 33:23), for the numerical value of the word cup [*kos*: *kaf vav samekh*, 20 + 6 + 60 = 86] is the same as 'God' [*Elohim*: *aleph lamed hei yud mem*, 1 + 30 + 5 + 10 + 40 = 86], which is *Binah*, i.e. *Malkhut* enclothing in *Binah* (as below, 632). And from there comes the soul [*neshamah*] that is named after it, cup, as it is written: "I will lift up the cup of salvation" (Psalms 116:13). What is the meaning of 'salvation?' It is the five fingers that hold the cup and which correspond to the five *Sfirot*: *Ḥesed, Gvurah, Tiferet, Netzaḥ, Hod,* and *Yesod*, that are with the cup, which is the living God which is *Binah*, (*245b) that spreads with the five *Sfirot* to fifty gates, fifty being five times ten. That is, the letter *yud* (whose numerical value is ten) stands for the ten things that the sages ordained for the cup, which is the living God, and the five [*hei*] letters of the word 'God' [*Elohim*: *aleph lamed hei yud mem*], and five times ten comes to the fifty gates (cf. *Talmud Bavli, Rosh haShanah* 31b: Fifty gates of *Binah* were created in the world).

625 And they taught about the cup that it needs washing and rinsing, where washing refers to the outside, rinsing to the inside (cf. *Talmud Bavli, Berakhot* 51a). And the secret of the matter is that the inside and the outside of the cup should be the same, for whoever has been privileged to receive a soul [*neshamah*] from this cup, which is *Binah*, such a soul [*neshamah*] must be pure both within and without. And the secret of the matter is: "And he shall cleanse it and hallow it" (Leviticus 16:19) with purification on the inside and sanctification on the outside (and see above, *Tazria*, page 45, for an explanation of the terms 'purification' and 'sanctification'). And just as the cup, whose purification and sanctification both inside and outside is only with water, so the purification and sanctification of the soul, both inside and outside, is only with the Torah. And this is why Rabban Gamliel said: No one whose character does not correspond to his exterior may enter the school house (cf. *Talmud Bavli, Berakhot* 28a). This is because such a person is not from the Tree of Life, but from the Tree of Knowledge of Good and Evil (see Genesis 2:17), for whoever is lacking holiness on the outside or purity on the inside is a mixture of good and evil.

626 Regarding the crowning that is stated in respect of the cup, they taught: He crowns it with pupils (*Talmud Bavli, Berakhot* 51a) (i.e. makes them sit around it). And the secret is that *hei* is the cup, i.e. *Binah*, and it is crowned with pupils, with the letter *yud*, which is a diadem on the *hei* (See *Ekev*, 59), for the pupils multiply and draw down *Ḥokhmah*. The wrapping that is mentioned in respect to the cup refers to the need to wrap the head, i.e. to cover it, because the *Shekhinah* is over his head. For this is what the sages of the Mishnah taught: A person is forbidden to walk four cubits with his head uncovered because "The whole earth is full of His glory" (Isaiah 6:3) (cf. *Talmud Bavli, Kiddushin* 31a). And even more so is it forbidden to go with uncovered head during a blessing or the mention of the Holy Name!

627 And the reason for the prohibition of going with uncovered head is that the letter *yud* of the Tetragrammaton [*yud hei vav* and *hei*], which is *Ḥokhmah*, is enwrapped in

light [*or*: *aleph vav resh*] and becomes air [*avir*: *aleph vav yud resh*], since the letter *yud*, which is *Ḥokhmah*, is in the ether. And this is the light with which He enwrapped himself when He created the world, as it is written: "Who covers Himself with light as with a garment" (Psalms 104:2). Thus "Let there be light" (Genesis 1:3) is "Let there be ether." And the sages of the secrets of the Torah taught: Before anything else was formed, the heavenly essences were formed. Thus: "Let there be Light, and there was Light" (ibid.) refers to Light that had existed previously.

Commentary:

The *yud* of the Tetragrammaton [*yud hei vav* and *hei*] is the secret of *Ḥokhmah* and the secret of the upper Father and Mother. The *hei* of the Tetragrammaton [*yud hei vav* and *hei*] is the secret of *Binah* and of *Yisrael* Grandfather and Understanding. And it is known that before any other correction, the correction of the mitigation of *Malkhut* in *Binah* was made, this being the secret of the point of the *ḥolam*, and thereby *Binah* withdrew from the Light of its upper three *Sfirot* and became the six intermediate *Sfirot*. And this is the secret of the *yud* that entered the Light [*or*: *aleph vav resh*] and became air [*avir*: *aleph vav yud resh*]. (As above, *Bereshith Aleph*, page 44, q.v.). And later, at the time of greatness, the *yud* descends again from the air [*avir*: *aleph vav yud resh*], i.e. *Malkhut* descends from *Binah*, and the Light [*or*: *aleph vav resh*] returns to its place. (As above, *Bereshith Aleph*, page 45, q.v.). And this is only with regard to the *hei* of the Tetragrammaton [*yud hei vav* and *hei*], which is *Yisrael* Grandfather and Understanding, but with the *yud* of the Tetragrammaton [*yud hei vav* and *hei*], which is upper Father and Mother, the *yud* never leaves air [*avir*: *aleph vav yud resh*].

(As above, *Bereshith Aleph*, page 251.) And on the text: "The letter *yud* of the Tetragrammaton [*yud hei vav* and *hei*]... is enwrapped in Light [*or*: *aleph vav resh*] and becomes air [*avir*: *aleph vav yud resh*]" since the *yud* is from the Tetragrammaton, which is upper Father and Mother, to whose *Binah Malkhut* ascended. And this is the secret of the ascent of *yud* in Light [*or*: *aleph vav resh*] and becoming air [*avir*: *aleph vav yud resh*], which is the six intermediate *Sfirot* that are called air and wind. And this is understood to be as though the Light of the upper three *Sfirot* of Father and Mother were enwrapped, i.e. covered and hidden. And on the text: As it is written: "Who covers Himself with Light as with a garment" (Psalms 104:2) just as though the Light were covered with a garment. And on the text: Thus "Let there be Light" (Genesis 1:3) is "Let there be air," for this correction of the ascent of the *yud* to the Light is the correction of Male and Female and the worlds of *Briah*, *Yetzirah*, and *Assiah*, that they should be fitting to receive Light. For were *Malkhut* not to have been mitigated with *Binah*, the worlds would not have been fitted to receive any Light at all (as above, *Bereshith Aleph*, page 7). And therefore the first correction, when "Let there be Light" (Genesis 1:3) was said, is `Let there be air,' i.e. that the *yud* should enter the Light and become air, for had this not been so it would have been impossible for there to have been any Light in the worlds. And on the text: "Before anything else was formed, the Tetragrammaton was formed." For this is the secret of the *yud* of the Tetragrammaton [*yud hei vav* and *hei*], where this correction of the ascent of the *yud* into air has remained. And on the text: Thus "`Let there be Light and there was Light' (ibid.) refers to the Light that had existed previously." That is to say, subsequently, in the greatness, when it is said "And there was Light," there is no new Light, but only the same Light that had previously contracted to be air, for afterwards, the *yud* descends from the ether, and the Light thereby returns and is revealed as it was previously. (All this can be studied in *Bereshith Aleph*, 33.)

628 And regarding the 'undiluted' in respect to the cup of blessing, they taught: Undiluted from the barrel (cf. Tosaphists, *Berakhot* 50b), which means that it should not be mixed with any water there. And the secret is: The upper *Shekhinah*, which is *Binah*, is the eighth *sfirah* of the ten *Sfirot*, when one starts to count from the bottom up, and is for that reason called *ḥet* (whose numerical value is 8). And this is alluded to in the verse: "Through wisdom is a house built" (Proverbs 24:3). And barrel [*ḥavit*: *ḥet bet yud tav*] is the letters *ḥet bait* [*bet yud tav*, house]. For this shows that the wine, which is the secret of *Gvurah* of *Zeir Anpin*, is to be drawn down from *Binah*, that is called barrel, i.e. *ḥet bait*. And because *Binah* is life, as it is written. "It is a tree of life to those who take hold of it" (Proverbs 3:18) therefore, the wine that is drawn down from there, from *Binah*, is undiluted [the Hebrew for which is *ḥai*, 'alive']. And this is the wine of the Torah, for whoever engages in it is called alive. And furthermore, the Righteous One, which is *Yesod*, is called alive and is undiluted from the barrel, i.e. alive from *Binah*, because its lights are drawn from *Binah*, that is called barrel, as above.

629 Wine comes in two colors, white and red. The numerical value of wine [*yayin*: *yud yud nun*, 10 + 10 + 50] is seventy, which is seventy facets, and together with the two colors, this makes 72, and this alludes to the fact that the lights of the 72-letter Name illuminate in wine. And corresponding to the two colors of the wine are 'Remember' (Exodus 20:6) and 'Keep' (Deuteronomy 5:12), referring to the Sabbath [i.e. in the two versions of the Decalogue], and these, together with the 70 words of Sabbath Eve *Kiddush* [sanctification over the wine] [Sephardi version only the Ashkenazi text has a greater number of words!], make 72.

630 And the cup of benediction must be full (as above, 623), as it is written: A cup "and full with the blessing of the Lord" (Deuteronomy 33:23); and

also he who says the blessing has to be full of the wine of the Torah, and so must a person be perfect, as it is written: "A whole man" (Genesis 25:27). [The word here translated `whole man,' can also mean `perfect,' `whole']. The meaning of this is `a perfect man,' as in the verse: "And Jacob came in peace (i.e. complete, whole) to the city of Shekhem" (Genesis 33:18), i.e. Jacob is here called complete or perfect. So also must the soul [*neshamah*] be perfect, without any fault being in it, because "Whatsoever man he be that has a blemish, he shall not approach" (Leviticus 21:18). So also here, the letters of `God' [*Elohim*: *aleph lamed hei yud mem*] can be re-written as two words: *Ilem*: [*aleph lamed mem*] and *Yah* [*yud hei*]. And the numerical value of these two words [*Ilem*: *aleph lamed mem*, 1 + 30 + 40 = 71, and *Yah*: *yud hei*, 10 + 5 = 15] is (71 + 15) 86, which is the same as cup [*kos*: *kaf vav samekh*, 20 + 6 + 60 = 86]. And the word *ilem*: [*aleph lamed mem*] written in reverse order is `full' [*male*: *mem lamed aleph*], and thus the cup has to be full, for the numerical value of the letters of the word cup [*kos*: *kaf vav samekh*, 20 + 6 + 60 = 86] is the same as `full of *Yah*' [*male'yah*: *mem lamed aleph yud hei*, 40 + 30 + 1 + 10 + 5 = 86]. For when is it full? When there is *Yah* there. And that is: "The hand upon the throne [*kas*: *kaf samekh*] of the Lord [*Yah*]" (Exodus 17:16), where the name is not complete, but lacks the *vav hei*. The numerical value of `The Lord' [*aleph dalet nun yud*], treating all tens as units, is 1 + 4 + 5 + 1 = 11, which is the same as the missing *vav hei* (6 + 5 = 11). The central column is full from both of them, from the *yud hei* and from the *vav hei*, and therefore it is called man [*adam*: *aleph dalet mem*, 1 + 4 + 40 = 45], which has the same numerical value as the Name of Names (the Tetragrammaton, *yud hei vav* and *hei*, i.e. *yud vav dalet*, 10 + 6 + 4 = 20; *hei*, *hei aleph*, 5 + 1 = 6; *vav*, *vav aleph vav*, 6 + 1 + 6 = 13; *hei hei aleph*, 5 + 1 = 6, and 20 + 6 + 13 + 6 = 45).

631 (Regarding the instruction that the cup of benediction) must be taken up with both hands (see above, 623), corresponding to the Torah which was written on two tablets of stone (cf. Exodus 34:4): And there were five commandments on the one tablet, corresponding to the five fingers of the right hand, and there were five commandments on the second tablet, corresponding to the left hand, that were given with the right, that is, the right hand, that is to say that the five of the left were included in the five of the right. And for this reason it is written: "And he took in his hand the two tablets of stone" (Exodus 34:4). It is written "in his hand," and not 'in his hands,' i.e. in only one hand, which was the right, and this is as Scripture testifies: "And from His right hand went a fiery law unto them" (Deuteronomy 33:2).

632 (And regarding the instruction that) he who says the blessing just looks at the cup of benediction (See above, 623), this is because this cup corresponds to the Land of Israel, which is *Malkhut* enclothing with *Binah*, about which it is said: "The eyes of the Lord your God are always upon it" (Deuteronomy 11:12); and the eyes of heaven are the seventy [numerical value of the letter, *ayin*, which, as a word, means eye] members of the Sanhedrin [the supreme court and legislature], with Moses and Aharon over them, they being the two upper eyes, namely, *Ḥokhmah* and *Binah*, being one right eye and one left eye, coming to the same numerical value as the expression 'with wine' [*b'yayin*: *bet yud yud nun*, 2 + 10 + 10 + 50 = 72]. For the seventy (members) of the Sanhedrin correspond to the seven *Sfirot*: *Ḥesed*, *Gvurah*, *Tiferet*, *Netzaḥ*, *Hod*, *Yesod*, and *Malkhut*, each one being composed of ten. And over them are *Ḥokhmah* and *Binah*, which are Moses and Aharon, and this is the secret of his looking at it, to draw down *Ḥokhmah* and *Binah* to the cup, which is *Malkhut*, and this is the secret of why he who says the blessing must look at the cup.

633 (And the cup of benediction) must be raised a handbreadth from the ground. (See above, 623). Since the letter *hei* of the Tetragrammaton [*yud hei vav* and *hei*] is a cup, it has to be raised up to the letter *yud* of the Tetragrammaton [*yud hei vav* and *hei*], which is called a handbreadth, for the *hei* is opened up in it with the five (numerical value of the letter *hei*) fingers, which is the secret of the fifty gates of *Binah* (see above, 624). And he must send it round to members of his household as present (see above, 623), i.e. in order that his wife should be blessed, for she is the secret of the soul [*nefesh*], about which it is said: "But now our soul is dried away; there is nothing at all" (Numbers 11:60), and she is blessed and prepares fruits, as it is written: "Let the earth put forth grass" (Genesis 1:11).

634 And the fourth correction (see above, 620) at the table is that matters of Torah should be discussed over the table so that the verse "For all tables are full of filthy vomit" (Isaiah 28:8) should not be fulfilled in him as it is with the ignorant. But it was taught in the secrets of the Torah: He who wants to grow rich turns to the north (cf. *Talmud Bavli, Babba Batra* 25b); i.e. he should place the table on the north side, for the table is left, which is Judgment. He has, therefore, to connect it to the right, which is the Torah that was given out of loving kindness [*Ḥesed*], which is Mercy, which is the right hand of the Lord.

635 And the fifth correction in the table was taught by the sages of the Mishnah: The meal must be drawn out for the sake of the poor, who might come and he will be able to give him something to eat (cf. *Talmud Bavli, Berakhot* 55a). And the secret of the matter is that charity should lengthen his days, that he should not die young, just as does the Torah which is longevity for the soul [*neshamah*] is two worlds: This world and the world to come. Charity, likewise, is longevity for the body in two worlds, as it is written: "For it is your life and

the length of your days" (Deuteronomy 30:20), which is interpreted to mean: `Your life' in this world, and `the length of your days' in the world to come (cf. *Talmud Bavli, Kiddushin* 39b); and the meaning of the world to come for the body is the resurrection of the dead, that after he rises at the resurrection of the dead, he will not die. And just as he will be in the world to come so will he be in this world.

A REVIEW OF BOOKS PUBLISHED

THE ZOHAR
BY RABBI SHIMON BAR YOḤAI

The Mantuan edition of the Zohar consists of three volumes written by Rabbi Shimon bar Yoḥai. The Zohar published by the Research Centre of Kabbalah includes the explanations and commentary of Rabbi Yehuda Ashlag and consists of 24 volumes. The writings of Rabbi Shimon bar Yoḥai are written on such a high spiritual level that it is difficult, if not impossible, to grasp the meaning on the ordinary level of consciousness. Rabbi Ashlag, with the assistance of the works of Rabbi Isaac Luria, brings with his commentary explanations in a concise manner permitting those fluent in Hebrew and Aramaic to comprehend the Zohar. For those not fluent in Hebrew these volumes shine with the light of the Hebrew letters and the spiritual consciousness of the writers, with the result that wherever they are placed an influence of "good" prevails and the reading or scanning results in restoring one's state of imbalance to that of balance. The explanations and discussions you will find in the books of this Review stem for the most part from these 24 volumes.

AN ENTRANCE TO THE ZOHAR
BY RABBI YEHUDA ASHLAG

Rabbi Yehuda Ashlag (1886-1955) was an accomplished mystic and Kabbalist and is known as the pioneer of modern Kabbalism. He translated the entire Zohar into modern Hebrew with a commentary on difficult passages. In addition where the Zohar consisted of one continuous paragraph he divided it into separate paragraphs and sections indicating the topical discussions.

In this book *An Entrance to the Zohar* Rabbi Ashlag simplifies it further by dividing the subject matter into two parts: Part One, a preface to the Zohar, and Part Two, an introduction to the Zohar. Part One consists of nineteen chapters, each discussing a particular subject of interest. Part Two consists of eight chapters containing a subject of special interest to the average reader. This material will answer the questions often raised regarding Kabbalah and also will provide the information helpful to understanding the discussions contained in other books on Kabbalah.

An Entrance to the Tree of Life
by Rabbi Yehuda Ashlag

Here Rabbi Ashlag continues his explanations of the Zohar focusing on the role of mankind in the creation and the ten sfirot. To appreciate the past history of Kabbalah he introduces us to "the Ari" (Rabbi Isaac Luria), and the Baal Shem Tov. His writings not only furnish us with additional knowledge but inspire us with his spirituality and love.

Ten Luminous Emanations, Vol. I
by Rabbi Yehuda Ashlag

Here, in the first volume of a series, Rabbi Ashlag takes the writings of "the Ari", Rabbi Isaac Luria, and explains the difficult words and concepts enabling the reader to appreciate the Ari's disclosures. The Ari is writing about the period before *Bereshith* when the "Upper Light" filled all existence and there was no "empty space whatsoever." He discloses that the cause of creation was the Desire of the Endless; that the Endless Light is called "He"; that the Endless World is called "His Name;" and that He and His Name are one. From that point on the Ari describes the process of creation occurring before *Bereshith*. A general commentary by Rabbi Ashlag is also included, called "Inner Reflection."

Kabbalah for the Layman, Vol. I
by Rabbi P. Berg

Here is an opportunity to become familiar with some of the Kabbalah terminology you will be hearing over and over again as you delve into Kabbalistic Teaching. Words such as *En Sof*, *Yesh m'Ayin*, Bread of Shame, *Tzimtzum*, *Tikune*, and the names and functions of the ten *Sfirot* will become part of your language as you delve into the mysteries of creation. You will even have a peek at the life of Rabbi Shimon bar Yoḥai, the writer of the Zohar, leaving you eager to learn the reality of existence which has been withheld from the world until now.

KABBALAH FOR THE LAYMAN, VOLUMES II AND III
BY RABBI P. BERG

The subtitle of this series is "A Guide to Expanded Consciousness". These books will familiarize us with many Kabbalistic concepts which we will find referred to in our further readings of Kabbalistic writings. In Volume II these concepts and terms include *Adam Kadmon*, Circles and Straightness, Bonding by Striking, *Partzuf*, etc. In Volume III we have the Thought of Creation, the Light and Vessels, the "circular" condition.

In the Chapter on "Energy-Intelligence" you will be surprised to learn that a rock is a living thing. Everything in existence has a Desire to Receive but on different levels of degree.

In the Chapter on "Primordial Man" we become acquainted with the Central Column, an important aspect in Kabbalah.

Thus Volume II swings through the various aspects of creation from the metaphysical plane to physical existence bringing us to Volume III which is found in our present condition and is divided into four parts: The New Age of Reality, The Creative Process, Expanding Consciousness, and the Art of Living.

TIME ZONES: CREATING ORDER FROM CHAOS
BY RABBI P. BERG

The subtitle of this book is "creating order from chaos". Rabbi Berg brings to us the teachings of Rabbi Isaac Luria who points out that all of existence is divided into two aspects, that of circles and that of straightness. The reality of circles, unlike the reality of straightness, suffers no fragmentation. Only the realm of straightness must endure the pains and pitfalls of chaos and disorder. The important distinction between the two is that the realm of straightness is an illusion. Throughout this book our attention is drawn to the benefit and the methods of harmonizing the parallel universes so that the circular aspect is expressed and in control. As an example one chapter of the book explains the effect on the cosmos of human thought and action. In another chapter we learn that somehow our destiny and happiness are bound up with and connected to the stars. Rabbi Berg goes on to say that we must be aware of the profound connection between crisis, good fortune, and the cosmos.

The Star Connection: the Science of Judaic Astrology, by Rabbi P. Berg

The subtitle of this book is "the Science of Judaic Astrology". It may come as a surprise that Jewish teaching includes astrology, but as Rabbi Berg points out "there is more to it than what the conventional astrology books provide."

The Introduction raises the question "What is the purpose of the celestial bodies, and how and why did they begin?" The book proceeds to answer these questions. In addition the many relationships between the Bible's recorded events and the higher forms of extraterrestrial intelligence is described. Jewish holidays and festivals occur on days mandated by the Bible according to the lunar month but this must be reconciled with the solar system to prevent holidays from wandering through the solar period. If you have been wondering how this was done you will be pleased to learn that it is all explained in the Chapter on "the Calendar".

Reincarnation: Wheels of a Soul
by Rabbi P. Berg

Rabbi Berg describes reincarnation as a wheel "with souls studding its rim like stars on the edge of a galaxy" — a vivid description of a difficult subject. Many of us even have difficulty in remembering that we are a soul.

Very little has been written about the Jewish knowledge of reincarnation. Rabbi Berg corrects this paucity of information by referring to the Zohar and Rabbi Isaac Luria's *Gates of Reincarnation*. One of the surprises brought out is that a soul can return to a lower level. If the weight of *tikune* is sufficiently heavy, a human soul may find itself reincarnated into the body of an animal, a plant, or even a stone. Is there an end to the cycle of reincarnation? Rabbi Berg discusses this as well as the purpose of reincarnation.

The nature and origin of the soul and its soulmate is another aspect found in this book which will add to our clear understanding of the soul's existence on Earth.

The Power of the Aleph Beth, two volumes
by Rabbi P. Berg

The Introduction to this book relates that the Hebrew letters are animated with a spiritual force that is more immense than the invisible vitality of atomic energy and these letters have intelligence at the profoundest levels. "Thus the *Aleph Beth* provides direct experience of all phenomena...".

We find in this book the origin and history of the *Aleph Beth*, its relationship to numerology, and its relationship to the constellations. Then follows a chapter for each letter starting from the last letter "*Tav*" and going forward to "*Aleph*". Each letter has its own stories to tell and its own powers to reveal, improving our understanding of creation. One of the stories is that of each letter placing their request before the Creator to be the first letter of the Torah. As you know the Creator chose letter *Beth* which stated that " I represent the energy-intelligent force of *Berakhot* blessings" and the Creator's response was "Assuredly, through your channel I will create the world. Your energy-intelligence shall be at the starting point to the creative process."

Many such details help to bring the letters closer to us and to appreciate their lively characteristics.

Miracles, Mysteries, and Prayer
by Rabbi P. Berg

Printed as a set of two volumes this book covers questions that have occurred to us more than once but answers were not forthcoming. Rabbi Berg raises these questions and provides the answers.

For example, there is the question of prayer, its meaning and purpose. Rabbi Berg points out that "prayer is anything but a matter of obedience, a form of request for assistance or an expression of thanksgiving" Prayer properly understood and practiced may result in "restoring the Desire to Receive to one of also sharing." This is called *Tshuvah*. The Zohar states "that if the leaders of one synagogue return with *Tshuvah* in one synagogue, then the exiles of all the peoples will be brought to an end."

An interesting aspect of miracles is brought out. The Hebrew word for miracles is *Nes*. When the Egyptians gave chase and approached the

Israelites at the Red Sea, the chariots became bogged down. The Egyptians cried out "Let us flee (*Anusa*) from Israel" Here the word *Nes* means "to flee". Yet this Hebrew word also means miracle. Many miracles are recorded in the Bible. In each case Rabbi Berg points out that the miracle results from "fleeing the realm of the Tree of Knowledge of Good and Evil where chaos and disorder reign supreme".

To the Power of One
BY RABBI P. BERG

This book was published in 1991 and rounds out all previous books of the Rav by focusing on mankind.

Chapter One discusses the interplay between body consciousness and the celestial and terrestrial bodies. Sometimes this interplay appears as an attack. The Zohar points out that this predicament should convince us of the need to take control. To attain control we need to know the reality of who we are, what is the nature of this creation, and what is our role. This is the subject matter of the book.

The nature of the mind and body, its qualities and characteristics are reviewed to help us to understand what we are dealing with in the process of attaining control and balance. We are reminded of the basic law of cause and effect — every thought and action has its consequence. The Rav points out that to make certain that every action is right "the conscious mind must be subject to the authority of soul consciousness." In a chapter on the Mind-Body connection the matter of "soul consciousness" is explained.

This book also covers the subject of health and stress, including the remedies for a better state of health furnished by the study of Kabbalah.